Love + *Marriage* = *Death*

And Other Essays on Representing Difference

Stanford Studies in Jewish History and Culture
Edited by Aron Rodrigue and Steven J. Zipperstein

Love + Marriage = Death

And Other Essays on Representing Difference

Sander L. Gilman

Stanford University Press
Stanford, California 1998

Stanford University Press
Stanford, California
© 1998 by the Board of Trustees
of the Leland Stanford Junior University

Printed in the United States of America

CIP data appear at the end of the book

Preface

These essays examine the world of the constructed imaginary. And these fantasies represent categories of difference. Each category of difference constructs a world in which other categories are elided and effaced. All these essays deal with categories of difference as represented in texts—in high literature, in medical literature, in art—from the last fin-de-siècle to our own fin-de-siècle. The essays focus on a number of creative voices, ranging from Sigmund Freud to R. B. Kitaj to Martin Amis. The cultures represented are "European" in scope, including the cultures of North America.

These essays deal with the world of the text and categories of difference. Most deal with representations and self-representations of Jews in the past one hundred years. They focus in general on the question of the constructions of the Jew's body in art and literature. Yet they also deal with my understanding of boundaries and borders—boundaries between my teaching and research, borders between national literature and cultures.

All offer readings, tentative and hesitant, which, however, are also platforms for action—for we read in order to understand the present, not to have the present understand the past. I do not see the present as constructing the past for the past's sake, as Sir Herbert Butterfield claimed in his classic *The Whig Interpretation of History* (1931). All these texts are radically whiggish: they depart from my construction of my world and from my attempts to reconstruct the antecedents to this world. We all write autobiography (or we write to repress our autobiographies). I know this is a crude claim, but all other claims put our vision beyond our desires, our scholarship beyond our passions. This I address in the first chapter.

This volume was completed while I was a fellow at the Center for Advanced Study in the Behavioral Sciences in Stanford, California. I am grateful for financial support provided by the Andrew W. Mellon Foundation.

Some of these chapters have appeared in earlier versions in other forums: Chapter 1, in a much shortened version as the introduction to the special "ethnicity" issue of the *PMLA* (January 1998): 19–27; Chapter 2, in Thomas Foster, Carol Siegel, and Ellen E. Berry, eds., *Sex Positives? The Cultural Politics of Dissident Sexualities* (New York and London: New York University Press, 1997), pp. 197–224; Chapter 3, in Linda Nochlin and Tamar Garb, eds., *The Jew in The Text: Modernity and the Construction of Identity* (London: Thames and Hudson, 1995), pp. 97–121; Chapter 4, in *Southern Humanities Review* 27 (1993): 1–25 (awarded the Theodore Christian Hoepfner Award for the Best Essay in the *Southern Humanities Review* for 1993); Chapter 5, in Nancy Harrowitz and Barbara Hyams, eds., *Jews and Gender: Responses to Otto Weininger* (Philadelphia: Temple University Press, 1995), pp. 103–21; Chapter 6, in *Modern Austrian Studies* 26 (1993): 1–34; Chapter 8, in a much shortened version, in *New Art Examiner* 24 (1997): 12–21. I am grateful to the editors for their input and forbearance.

Contents

Love + Marriage = Death

And Other Essays on Representing Difference

CHAPTER ONE

Ethnicities

Why I Write What I Write

During 1996–97 I was in residence at the Center for Advanced Study in the Behavioral Sciences at Stanford University. One day, drawn by the topic, I wandered down the hill onto the Stanford campus and listened to a lecture on ethnicity and literature by Vincent Cheng. A senior member of the "Joyce industry," he had revolutionized it with his work on Joyce and race, and he was now running the Asian-American program at the University of Southern California. His talk was serious and solid—an attempt to unravel the various strands of ethnicity. And then in passing he commented on the talks at the 1995 president's forum of the Modern Language Association's meeting in Chicago (which I, as the outgoing president, had organized), dismissing them as "ethnicity lite." What he meant by this was clear in his representation of the papers: two, according to him, were by white women, one by a Jew, and one by—Homi Bhabha. They were indeed ethnicity "light." Too white, too European, and therefore not quite "ethnic" enough.

Here is one of the central questions posed by this volume. What is ethnicity? Or rather—to talk the talk—how does ethnicity figure in our professional world? How does it figure in my world and in my work? Everybody today seems to be fascinated by ethnicity, but what is it and why has it become a political force in our ways of talking about (and diss-ing) the study of literature and culture? How does it function when one publicly identifies oneself as an "ethnic," and what impact does it have on one's writing and on one's selection of objects of study? All these essays reflect questions that revolve around the construction of categories of difference. Ethnicity is just one of those constructed categories.

Let me start by noting that ethnicity, as it is used in the humanities in North America, is a sociological concept. Defined against the categories of "race" and "class" in sociological discussion, it seems to have a life of its own. It seems to, at least, until you read how the sociologists actually use it. For example, M. Bulmer, in a widely cited essay, provides a standard sociological definition of ethnicity as "a collectivity within a larger society having real or putative common ancestry, memories of a shared past, and cultural focus on one or more symbolic elements which define the group's identity, such as kinship, religion, language, shared territory, nationality or physical appearance."[1] Such a view comes very close to definitions of race in both sociology and physical anthropology, resting one of its variables on the physical appearance of the members of the group. And certainly the question of class, the most fluid of all of these categories, both in terms of social mobility and in terms of self-representation, cuts across each of these variables. The fascination with ethnicity as a category in the humanities that bounds and overlaps the settings of other social boundaries comes out of the debates in the 1960s in the United States (and less so in Canada) about the advantages and disadvantages of particularism versus universalism in the acts of reading, writing, and teaching. (The Canadian debates focused more on "national" questions at that time, defining the "Canadian" as that which was not "American." In Bulmer's terms they, too, could have been defined as "ethnic," at least from south of the border.)

The debates about ethnicity were not only about the "melting pot," a concept that sociologists took over from the title of the 1909 play by (the Jewish but also very British writer) Israel Zangwill, but also about the role that literature plays in providing a medium for the expression and analysis of specific types of particularism. The melting pot discussion in literature gave way to discussions of (the German-Jewish sociologist) Georg Simmel's "sojourners," individuals who articulate their transitory presence in a society. Or the debates focused on the category of the "pariah" (coined by the German Protestant Max Weber), examining the creativity of those groups in perpetual imposed or self-imposed isolation from the collectivity. Or the discussion employed (the Norwegian-American) Thorstein Veblen's rethinking of the immigrant/emigrant dichotomy. Or . . . Each model for ethnicity demanded new ways of thinking; each model provided new and complex entries into the question of ethnicity and its literatures.

I note that ethnicity today is an American concept only because much of its complexity evolved out of specific debates about the value of particularism as opposed to universalism in the civil rights discussion. Thus, it was the specific setting of African-American culture and politics that defined ethnicity, a setting that by itself is not necessarily understood as "ethnic." And these discussions were clearly based on simultaneous discussions of class (the "underclass") and of race ("Blackness"). And yet the discussion of ethnicity today is, of course, not limited to the United States. Recently in the United Kingdom the B.B.C. Scotland initiative Migrations was created, aimed at fostering the talent of "Scottish writers of colour." This was understood by the South Asian writer Hardeep Kohli in *The Herald* (Glasgow, December 17, 1996) as "fostering the writing talents of ethnic minorities." Ethnicity, with all of its contradictions and conflicts, has become as much a British as an American concept.

One must understand that each culture adapts its own sense of what ethnicity is. But what about the expansion of the coverage of the ethnic? I have just co-edited with Jack Zipes *The Yale Companion to Jewish Writing and Thought in German Culture, 1096–1996.*[2] One of the goals of the volume is to pose the question of the relationship of Jews and "Jewish" writing in German, Hebrew, and Yiddish to German (as a language), the "Germans," and writing in Germany. I never thought of this as an "ethnic" project because the concept of ethnicity, if appropriate to this question of German or Jewish, only arises under the influence of "Jewish-American writing" on Jewish writing in German over the past decade. And yet the catalogers at the Library of Congress, who clearly need to create usable classifications, list the subject categories for this volume as follows:

Jews—Germany—History.
Judaism—Germany—History.
Jews—Germany—Intellectual life.
Germany—Intellectual life.
Germany—Ethnic relations.

All of these categories make sense from the American perspective on the "German" or "Jewish" or even from the "German-Jewish" perspective. But ethnicity is rarely a category used internally to discuss the cultural presence of Jews (however defined) in Germany (however defined). The American image easily conflates the roles of "ethnic" and "religious" groups in a majority culture, and sees them as equivalent to "class." (The "ethnic" Italians in the United States are seen as Catholic and "more heavily represented in the working class," according to one sociology textbook.)[3] And yet, saying the Jews in Germany are part of "ethnic relations" is both true and false.

What is ethnic writing, and, to use the old litmus test that every stage Jew in the borscht belt always applied to everything: Is it a "good" thing or a "bad" thing for the _____ (and now you fill in the blank)? Ethnicity is real, and yet, as Werner Sollors brilliantly reminds us, it is also highly constructed, and constructed under very specific conditions. Ethnic identity in the United States, at least in its "good" form, became accessible as a sign of acculturation.[4] After the stigma of ethnic identity (however defined) was removed from a group, that group could begin to think of itself as ethnically distinct—but, of course, not too distinct. This is the problem of "ethnic" writing: it becomes ethnic only when it is permitted to become ethnic. Thus it is assumed that "British" writing is not ethnic, even though the British very carefully constructed themselves with the Act of Union and the integration of Anglophone Scots, Welsh, and Irish into "English" writing to create the "universal," non-particularistic world of the British canon. When ethnic (read: nationalistic) writers such as Lady Gregory and the young William Butler Yeats rebelled against this claim of universalism, they created an "ethnic" Irish writing (in English) that answered the canonical demands of the universal—and that was answered, according to Vincent Cheng in *Joyce, Race, and Empire* (1995), by James Joyce in his antinational, multicultural, multilingual, high modernist, and *still* ethnic novels *Ulysses* and *Finnegans Wake*.[5]

This is not a question only of the United Kingdom. "German" literature is a literature, as I have noted, supposedly without ethnicities. And yet, as Peter Hohendahl has elegantly shown, the creation of "German" literature was the task of the academics of the nineteenth century.[6] These academics built a fantasy of a unified German culture that Gotthold Lessing and the Enlighteners never quite achieved. They took the regional literature of the nineteenth century—including that of the Swiss Germans, the Bavarians, and those who had worked in the transregional model, such as Lessing himself—and made a "German" literature beginning with Wolfram von Eschenbach and concluding with—themselves, of course. Certain "regionalisms" seemed to be "naturally" excluded, and they became definitions of difference. Thus acculturated Jews, beginning with Moses Mendelssohn, agreed with their Christian contemporaries and rejected the Western Yiddish tradition as part of a German tradition. It is clear in retrospect that such Yiddish writing was just as much part of a German culture of the Middle Ages and early modern period as the other Middle High German dialect writings.

And this view continues. When at a conference to honor the retirement of one of America's most notable survivor-authors, Ruth Klüger, at the University of California, Irvine, during the fall of 1996, I questioned why eighteenth-century Hebrew-language texts had been excluded from the canon of the German Enlightenment, given the fact that the authors were living in Germany, responding to the German literary Enlightenment, but choosing to write in a secular literary Hebrew rather than in the new literary German. My comments were dismissed by a distinguished German feminist scholar, who said, "Well, we are not dealing with texts from Africa!" During the nineteenth century, in the creation of the canon of "German" texts, Low German literature was grudgingly admitted, often only for comic relief (for example, *Reynard the Fox*), and then only because it was hard to include the North German regionalists such as Theodor Storm if their Low German writing cousins (like Klaus Groth) were dismissed from the canon.

The end result in both cases was that a universal canon was constructed out of particularistic moments taken together with writers who had begun to think of themselves as transcendental-universal in their language and in their audience. Regionalism became nationalism and nationalism became—the universal canon. Thus Elvis, who began as a regional "white ethnic," has become an icon of American universalism (for good or for ill). "[Elvis] is a global icon. Around the world, he represents a part of America. [It is] the Historical Elvis, [rather than] the Southernness of Elvis, that is not generally communicated to the world," said Vernon D. Chadwick, who is an assistant professor of English at the University of Mississippi and is also on the staff of the Center for Southern Culture, at the 1996 Elvis Festival.[7]

Today we reverse this a bit. Ethnicity figures in the North American multiculturalism debates in more complex ways. The claims of universalism have given way to the demands of the particular—but which particulars will be permitted? Are writers ethnic only if they are not in the canon of universal writing? What about "real ethnics," such as the Asian-American author of romances Tess Gerritsen, who clearly sees herself as nonethnic, writing against the type of "ethnic" writing represented by Amy Tan? "I'm an Asian author who's writing nonethnic stuff, so I'm really excited about it," she has said. "It's kind of a breakthrough."[8] Such writers seem "ethnic" only in that they represent groups that have rarely presented themselves within the world of literature (usually defined as "high culture"). The designation is less significant in the arena of mass or popular culture. Being "ethnic" seems fine (if not the norm) for such audiences.

Is the label "ethnic" a commodity? In the past decades there have been fascinating scandals in Germany, the United States, Great Britain, and Australia, where "ethnic" writers were revealed to be just plain old white folks writing under ethnic pseudonyms. There is Toby Forward, an Anglican vicar who managed to persuade the British feminist Virago Press that he was, in fact, a South Asian woman named Rahila Khan.[9] What about the late, blacklisted white Anglo-Saxon Protestant writer Daniel Lewis James, who wrote under the Hispanic pseudonym Danny Santiago? His *Famous All Over Town*, published in 1983, won the 1984 Rosenthal Award for literary achievement as an ethnic novel.[10] John Nichols's novel *The Milagro Beanfield War* was in recent years the most widely read work of fiction about Latinos.[11] The assumption was that Nichols was Latino, even if he himself never made that claim. What about Jakob Arjouni, often compared in Germany to Raymond Chandler, whose creation of the Frankfurt detective Kemal Kayankaya persuaded readers that this

Hessian writer was giving them "authentic insight" into Turkish life in Germany?[12] What about Helen Demidenko and her intensely anti-semitic novel *The Hand That Signed the Paper,* published in 1994?[13] Her work persuaded Australian critics to give her the Miles Franklin Award for the best novel of the year. She turned out to be the very English Australian Helen Darville, writing under an Eastern European pseudonym. Was she praised by the "politically correct" critics because of her ethnic insight? And just how "p.c." were they, given the antisemitic content of the work? Australian culture has recently discovered that a number of "aboriginal" writers and artists were anything but aboriginal. The widely shown aboriginal artist named "Eddie Burrup" was revealed to be the distinguished 81-year-old Australian painter Elizabeth Durack. Leon Carmen, a 47-year-old taxi driver from Sydney, won a prize for a first publication by a female author with his *My Own Sweet Time,* written under the name of Wanda Koolmatrie. Koolmatrie was, according to the fictitious biography, an aborigine kidnapped by whites as a child. An Australian academic named Colin Johnson suddenly transformed himself into the aboriginal critic Mudrooroo. The construction of fictional ethnic identity has now become a cultural commodity in a society searching for authenticity and meaning.

Here the questions of gender and ethnicity must also be raised. Is it better to be a woman ethnic? Is this "more ethnic" than being a male writer in a patriarchal ethnic society? Do such definitions of ethnic merely mirror a culture of victims? Is being ethnic the same as being oppressed? Or can successful "ethnics" still be ethnic? Saul Bellow went from trying to be Ernest Hemingway (in *Henderson the Rain King*) to being very Jewish (in *Herzog* and *Mr. Sammler's Planet*). And yet today he is the epitome of the American novelist (sans hyphen). "Jewish-American" has become "American."

Can such ethnic transformations be seen as another form of ethnicity, or are the ethnics who claim they have transcended their ethnicity in very different ways (V. S. Naipaul, Richard Rodriguez, or Anatole Broyard) simply trying to pass? And in all these cases, is race the same thing as ethnicity? Certainly historically it would not have been difficult to define the Jew, the Hispanic, and the Black racially. Can you be of a race and not ethnic; can you be ethnic as a member of a race—defined by you or for you?

These are the questions of the commodification of ethnicity, and they raise questions about who buys books and for what reason. Jewish writers in today's post-Wall Germany are often self-identified or defined as "Jewish" by their publishers. This often has nothing to do with religion. Indeed, one of the leading "Jewish" writers in Germany today is an American woman novelist by the name of Irene Dische, raised a Roman Catholic and writing in English. Is this a "good" thing or a "bad" thing for the ethnics? It is certainly a sign of the marketability of certain forms of ethnicity. And yet, on the other hand, self-labeled ethnic writers complain either that they do not have a broader audience or that they have too broad an audience. Who is ethnic, the writer or the reader—or both or neither?

Is "ethnic" the same as "authentic"? As Lionel Trilling noted, we need authenticity most in a world devoid of powerful beliefs, especially in ourselves.[14] Or is being a pseudoethnic sufficient in our day? Hypocrisy, as Nietzsche noted in the *Twilight of the Idols*, "has its place in the ages of strong belief: in which even when one is compelled to exhibit a different belief one does not abandon the belief one already has. Today one does abandon it; now, which is even more common, one acquires a second belief—one remains honest in any event. . . . That is the origin of self-tolerance."[15] Is the second belief the possibility that everyone is basically an ethnic?

What language does the "ethnic" writer write in? Is there an ethnic-specific language? Does the African-American writer need to write in "ebonics" or the Hispanic writer in Spanish? Are these two "languages" equivalent? Or does our search for the "right" language of the ethnic mean that some languages are more ethnic than others? Is Lakota an ethnic language? Or does a Native American have to write in English to become an ethnic? Are dialect and accent enough? Or are they too much? Certainly Joel Chandler Harris's *Uncle Remus: His Songs and His Sayings* (1893), Finley Peter Dunne's *Mr. Dooley says . . .* (1910), and Joe Hyman's sound recordings of "Cohen on the Telephone" (1913) were parodies of ethnic accents. But what about Zora Neale Hurston's *Their Eyes Were Watching God* or Leo Rosten's *The Education of H*Y*M*A*N K*A*P*L*A*N* (both published in 1937)? Is it less parodic when the "ethnics" themselves write the texts? Can the particularism of regional dialect in various languages be a sign of the ethnic? Or is it merely a parodying of the ethnic through the pens of everyone who uses such language, ethnic or not?

Does writing in literary German or Hindi or Japanese—which in Germany or India or Japan marks one as sharing in a universal, non-particularistic culture—become a sign of the ethnic when done in Australia or Brazil or South Africa? Does the process of acculturation become a sign of the ethnic? As ethnic writers and their descendants move ever farther away in time from sharing their common (universal) culture of origin and they experience culture turned into ethnic coloration and note the alteration of the language itself, does not this experience define the ethnic? At the end is the ethnic left with only— food? Whether it is the "southern" restaurants in Chicago still sought after by the fourth generation of the northern migration or the now nonethnic ubiquitous presence of pizza or bagels or tacos: Is this the last bastion of ethnic culture?

Octavio Paz, in his comments on American society (which are actually also comments on Western society), stressed that "the function of the patterns of normality in the domain of eroticism is no different from the role of 'healthy' cooking in relation to gastronomy. Both mean the removal or separation of that which is foreign, different, ambiguous, and impure."[16] Here the notion of food becomes another way of measuring the "ins" against the "outs," especially when one morphs into the other—a Hawaiian pizza with pineapple, or ham on a bagel with mayo, anyone? Thus "ethnic culture" becomes "world culture." (Woody Allen, where are you when we really need you?)

Is the ethnic only to be found in the Diaspora? Or can regionalism be ethnic? Certainly the flourishing of "Diaspora studies" has meant a focus on cultures in context and cultures in transition. But have "ethnics" only displaced "nationals"? Do they have to be "subalterns," or can they be good bourgeois, whether German academics fleeing the political repression of the nineteenth and twentieth centuries or African and European academics drawn to new lands and countries by economic opportunity in the past few decades? But does the movement of cultures only create "marginal" groups? And are these the essence of the ethnic? Well, then the "in" groups are denied and deny themselves ethnic status. Thus, are the English in Canada not ethnic while the Mennonites are? Certainly these traditions were weighted differently in the schools and in the process of canon formation. But do we want to differentiate between these traditions? The "ethnics" do.

Is ethnic writing necessarily "good" writing? Or rather, is it "better" writing because it is "ethnic"? Certainly ethnic writing has long been understood as belonging to the canon of high art. In my generation we read the English translation of O. E. Rolvaag's *I de dage* (*Giants in the Earth*) (1927) as a set part of the curriculum in high school. But would I want to think that it was "good" writing for that reason? Perhaps the criteria of readability and excellence are not unimportant. These are often the criteria demanded of us by those who dismiss ethnicity as "special pleading." Is it true that books get published and read that no one would actually want to publish or read just because they are "ethnic"? Or is not ethnicity often evoked by publishers who see too limited an audience for their books? Does the ongoing creation and re-creation of literary canons mean quite often "build it and they will come" or "no room, no room, move down, move down"? We need canons for historical and cultural reasons—and "ethnic" texts (whether "good" or "bad," "authentic" or "inauthentic") usually belong in whatever canon we create. But they can also be excluded from said canon on the grounds that only "universal" texts are canonical. And when we examine the list of the canonical texts, such as those used in the schools during the "golden age" when all was right and we all read Shakespeare, ethnic texts read as "ethnic," including Rolvaag, are canonical. Is the presence of "ethnic texts" in the schools today much different?

Let us not praise the complexities of ethnicity too much without acknowledging its downside. Fascism loves ethnicity. And this is as true of the fascism of the White Aryan Nation today (which may not define its texts as "white" ethnic—but that they are) as it was of the Nazis. The Nazis not only wrote in praise of an Aryan culture but also of seeing German regional writing, whether in German on the borders (in the Sudetenland) or abroad (among the Germans in North America), as the truest "German" writing. For the Nazis this was writing closest to the "soil" and therefore closest to the "soul." One can cite case upon case in which national and regional writing has been labeled as true and pure, as opposed to the claims of "civilization" and its universalizing tendencies. And after 1933 these claims were officially defined as "Jewish." But do we then capitulate and turn over the ethnic to the befouling hand of the racists? Is not the study of even such ethnic literature a task for all literary scholars who are interested in how literature serves as the battleground that defines the sphere of the literary?

Here the question of a "German" ethnicity in the American academy after the Shoah becomes a complex site of confrontation and understanding. The history of the Germans as the "best American ethnics" (so labeled since they disappeared so completely into the "melting pot") is a complex one. The existence of a complex German culture in the nineteenth century, the demonization of this culture during World War I, the humiliation connected with being German following the Shoah—all of these leave traces in my own work, which I write as an American Jew examining the "German" in the context of a culture in which German ethnicity has been virtually invisible.

Ethnicity figures in a number of critical discussions today. It is part of the debates for and against what is now referred to as multiculturalism. Whose culture gets included in the rainbow? Those stringently opposed to any discussion of ethnicity and its role in the study and teaching of literature—and I have heard from them frequently—believe that special pleading on the part of ethnics demeans the study of "real" literature. Where, they always ask, is Shakespeare? Thus Richard Lessner wrote in that ultimate conservative newspaper *The Union Leader* (Manchester, N.H., March 29, 1996): "The trend in recent years has been to drop required core courses and allow students—whee!—to make up their own curricula as they go. In these schemes students are able to load up on trendy courses in women's studies, gay studies, black studies, multiculturalism and sludge of various other politically correct fevers, while avoiding exposure to Shakespeare, Milton, Newton, Western Civilization, American history or rudimentary geography." This is the litany that sees the ethnic as part of the multicultural destruction of values. You, they say, waving their forefinger accusingly at me, want to place "ideology" and "politics" above aesthetics. You want us to focus on the ethnic and leave the values of Western civilization behind.

Ethnicity is certainly one lens through which we can read literature. Yes, even Shakespeare's sense of Englishness (not Britishness) is not missing, as the history plays well document. As James Shapiro has recently shown, Shakespeare used the Jews to represent that which was not "English."[17] For the role of ethnicity in early modern England is quite different from its role today, if one looks at the representation of such difference in the literary world of that time. The lens used then was usually religious, whether in constructing the Spaniard or the Jew.

"Ethnicity" could be used in as complex a series of definitions as any other critical term could. It could be applied to the Middle Ages in Spain and to the musicals on Broadway today. It is a term of clear definition and ambiguous application, of clear application and ambiguous definition. In other words, it is like all the critical apparatuses in literary studies. It is a concept (or set of contradictory and interlocking concepts) that enables us to tell a story about the stories that we tell. This is not a minor achievement. Any model that enables intelligent people to reflect on the way they and their culture tell stories is valuable.

Having spent a year among the social scientists, I find the stories that we as humanists tell more compelling and more interesting than most that they tell. We struggle with concepts such as "ethnicity," and we struggle with them on all sides with great affect. This is a good thing. If there is anything that differentiates the humanities, especially the study of literature and culture, from other endeavors in the academy, it is that we cannot expel our emotions from our work. And these emotions, for good or for ill, provide the power behind such concepts as the ethnic.

Where should ethnicity be placed in any professional discussion of literature? What makes a writer "ethnic"? Is it the writer's identity as given by circumstances or by labeling? Or is it the writer's self-identification? Then why not study the claims of ethnicity through the pseudonymous works that represent the ethnic writer as part of their fictions, especially when these claims resonate with the stereotypical perceptions of at least part of the audience? Is ethnicity therefore primarily a quality of the reader, actual or implied? Or is ethnicity a quality of marketing or of the mode of production? All of these questions postulate the importance of the "author" or "reader" as a social phenomenon in the definition of literature. But what does one do "after the death of the author"? Do such approaches mirror a vulgar materialism that has little or nothing to do with the truths espoused in the literary text? And what impact does this have on the professional reader, the critic? Is the critic's ethnicity a factor in the production of academic critics? Here my own persona must come into question. I write as an American Jewish academic, whose interests span everything from the history of medicine to the sociology of popular culture. My political and academic consciousness in the 1990s is rooted in my political education in the 1960s. Back then "Jewishness" as an ethnicity not only didn't exist but also was quite unacceptable. The American response to the Shoah had limited Jewish identity to religious identity. It was fine to be a "religious" Jew, but a secular "ethnic"—no, that was not possible. My work in this volume, including the title essay, exemplifies the power of ethnicity as an analytic category for both the professional reader and the author. And my interest in "health" and "disease" as categories of the cultural imaginary comes out of my fascination with stigma and its power. We stigmatize that which we fear and against which we need to define ourselves; this is a universal gesture. Ethnicity here is a factor because of the unique insight that shared experience of stigmatization (and stigmatizing) offers. It clearly does not block the ability to see the work in other, more universal contexts. Such critical approaches are central, and all of them resonate when one examines the problems attendant to the study of ethnicity.

CHAPTER TWO

Love + Marriage = Death

STDs and AIDS in the Modern World

The Problem: The Eighteenth Century

At least in a lesser-known variation of Jonathan Swift's oft-quoted poem, Strephon loves Chloe to no little degree because:

> Her graceful mien, her shape and face,
> Confessed her of no mortal race:
> And then, so nice, and so genteel;
> Such cleanliness from head to heel:
> No humours gross, or frowzy steams,
> No noisome whiffs, or sweaty streams,
> Before, behind, above, below,
> Could from her taintless body flow.[1]

Pure Chloe, "a goddess dyed in grain / Was unsusceptible of stain" (457). Until, of course the wedding night, when Chloe, having drunk "twelve cups of tea," needed "to leak" (459). Strephon hears his pure beloved "as from a mossy cliff distil" and "cried out, 'Ye gods, what sound is this? / Can Chloe, heavenly Chloe piss?'" (459).

Strephon seems to understand the actual physicality of his object of desire when the smell of Chloe's urine "struck his nose: He found her, while the scent increased / As mortal as *himself* at least" (459). For Strephon, all's well that end's well, for his realization of Chloe's physicality enables the marriage to be consummated.[2] And yet the happy end in which Strephon seems to have overcome his idealization of Chloe's body disguises a repressed moment.

What is missing in Strephon's realization that Chloe is a physical human being is the possibility of disease. Chloe, as the object of desire, may be "human" to the degree that she micturates, but the border of that "humanity" lies at the impossible notion that she could have a sexually transmitted disease. Once this repressed fear is articulated, the reader can understand what has been left unstated in Jonathan Swift's often-cited discussion of Strephon and Chloe. For Swift, the idea of Chloe's infection is impossible to both the writer and his creation, the lover. Yet Swift wrote about a different union in another satiric poem that, like the poem about Strephon and Chloe, stresses the physical, but without that pair's happy ending. Indeed, it is a poem in which the idea of infection is necessary to this vision of the marriage bed. It is not a pseudo-Arcadian marriage, but a May/December marriage of a fifty-two-year-old minister and "a handsome young imperious girl" (243). The minister desires the younger woman as proof of the power of his old age; she desires her marriage to provide her with social status. The result is quite different from Strephon and Chloe's marriage. Here the new wife cuckolds the minister over and over again after the wedding night, using the same artifice of beauty employed by Chloe ("She at the glass consults her looks" [243]), but to a much different end.

> But now, though scarce a twelve month married,
> His lady has twelve times miscarried,
> The cause, alas, is quickly guessed,
> The town has whispered round the jest." (245)

His sweet wife has gonorrhea and infects him, which shortens his life. He has been constantly cuckolded, and her lovers' having given her "a plenteous draught / Then fled, and left his horn behind" (245). The cuckold's horn is associated with the sexual transmission of disease in the marriage bed.

Thus the minister "Gets not an heir, but gets a fever; / A victim to the last essays / Of vigour in declining days. He dies . . . " (246). And the young widow immediately turns to the rake with whom she has been cavorting and whom she marries "for his face":

> And only coat of tarnished lace;
> To turn her naked out of doors,
> And spend her jointure on his whore;
> But for a parting present leave her
> A rooted pox to last forever. (247)

Her attraction for the physical aspect of her lover kills her just as certainly as the minister's attraction for her beauty has killed him. Strephon will not die of love, but the minister certainly has. Chloe's physicality is represented by her micturation, the widow's immorality by a case of syphilis. Death enters the frame only in the latter case.

The underlying difference between these two readings of the flesh's frailty and its relationship to the madness of love has to do with the absolute location of danger in the form of sexually transmitted disease. Swift has split the idealized, "good" love object from the dangerous, "bad" love object. Each is idealized for different reasons, and yet this division assures that the "good" love object can never be infectious. The passion that true love generates is the guarantee that this is the case. The "bad" object will always be the source of illness. The calculation that leads to such a choice of sexual object may blind the lover to this fact, as in the case of the minister, but it is not true passion. In this arbitrary dichotomy, passion protects. In a recent book, Otto Kernberg notes that:

Sexual passion reactivates and contains the entire sequence of emotional states that assure the individual of his own, his parents', the entire world of objects' "goodness" and the hope of the fulfillment of love despite frustration, hostility, and ambivalence. Sexual passion assumes the capacity for continued empathy with—but not merger into—a primitive state of symbiotic fusion (Freud's "oceanic feeling"), the excited reunion of closeness with mother at a stage of self-object differentiation, and the gratification of oedipal longings in the context of overcoming feelings of inferiority, fear, and guilt regarding sexual functioning. Sexual passion is the facilitating core of a sense of oneness with a loved person as part of adolescent romanticism and, later, mature commitments to the beloved partner in the face of the realistic limitations of human life, the unavoidability of illness, decay, deterioration, and death.[3]

Kernberg's comment on the nature of sexual passion as that which provides access to the complexity of the object of desire's reality implies the splitting of the "good" object of desire from the "bad" and dangerous one. Yet Kernberg, too, separates the anxiety about venereal disease from his analysis of sexual passion. Why is such a split necessary? Strephon's passion constructs Chloe as the idealized object of desire, and his realization of her physicality enables him to evolve into an awareness of her humanity (and of her mortality). But his very creation of her as the "good" object blinds him to the object of desire's potential for disease and betrayal. The death that Kernberg evokes is a "natural" death, that of an old age spent with the beloved, not of the horrors of sexually transmitted disease passed from the beloved. The "bad" object brings death into the immediate present in the act of betraying the marriage bed. Both types of death are rooted in the love madness that shapes the idealized object of desire. This is as true of the minister, who married a beautiful young girl as a sign of his station. He is blind to her own potential for destruction because he wishes to hold onto his own image of his object of desire. Swift is careful to show that his love madness has corrupt, material origins (in contrast to Strephon's) and that this makes it impossible for him to recognize his betrayal. Strephon's love madness allows him to acknowledge Chloe's physicality, and yet that move from unquestioned idealization to the "good" love object keeps him blind to her potential for disease and betrayal.

Swift splits the idealization of the love object ("love madness") into a "positive" world in which nonmaterial desire, with its blindness, gives way to insight and reproductive sexuality, and a "negative" world in which desire for status, with its stress of the material, leads to blindness and death. Swift, in most things more satirical than his contemporaries (and we), is unable, even ironically, to imagine Chloe as even potentially the source of illness and death. The pure beloved can be a human being, even with all those physical needs that we deem unspeakable because they seem to violate the imagined purity of the beloved. The (male) lover, as Swift shows in the tale of Strephon and Chloe, cannot hold two antagonistic thoughts about his beloved—the first, a total idealization of the object of desire, and the second, the notion that the idealized individual possesses all the mundane realities of human physicality, including the potential for disease. There are limits in Western culture to the internal image of imagined purity. Our culture shapes us, as human beings, to understand urine and excrement as disgusting, but with this understanding, we also come to see excrement as separate from us. We enter into human society through the labeling of inherent aspects of our own body as repellent and different from us.

Quite distinct is our anxiety about disease and its location. If excrement is always separate from us, then disease always seeks to enter us; it lurks within us, it penetrates us from the outside, like the "bad" lover. She (and in Swift's world the object of desire is always gendered feminine) represents the anxiety about castration, translated into a form of syphilophobia. In locating the source of disgust beyond ourselves, we seem to free the object of desire not only from the physical aspects of the body but also from being the source of any illness. How can the one I love hurt me, especially through the very act of love? And being outside of our imagined selves, the "good" and the "bad" objects are clearly separated in our fantasy. Only a "bad" object will want to, and is able to, hurt me.

The division of "good" and "bad" objects of desire may be necessary psychologically, because it is impossible in reality. There is no way to separate out the potential for infection and the potential or actual violation of the marriage bed from the idealized object of desire. We cannot, as Swift does, locate danger only in the materiality of the "bad" woman as the source of illness. Only in sexual passion, the domination of the lover by his or her fantasy of the object of desire as love madness, is it possible to construct an object of desire that refuses to link the physicality of the lover as approachable, as real, as tangible, with the potential for disease, infection, and death. Love madness, or sexual passion, may thus be a necessary quality of our construction of the object of desire. For the idealized object of desire must essentially be without stain. When we imagine the object we love, we suspend all images of disgust. And yet it is the repression of our own potential for infection and death that colors the object of desire.

Sex, with its implied risk for the male and its focus on the corrosive nature of female genitalia, is as marked in early modern culture by disgust as excretion is—if not more. In his account of Strephon's sexual passion, Swift sees this learning process about the idealized other as the true good, for the "Beauty [that] must beget Desire" (460) must give way to the sense of the object of desire as human. This inner fascination can both cause sexual excitement and block its consummation.[4] Judith Butler notes that "'sex' is an ideal construct which is forcibly materialized through time."[5] Such constructions are a "process of materialization that stabilizes over time to produce the effect of boundary fixity and surface we call matter" (9). Such boundaries are those between fear or disgust and pleasure, but also those potentially between excretion and disease.

Early in his work, Freud restates the tension between the physicality of the object of desire and its idealized manifestation. And Freud's restatement of this moment is much less ironic than Swift's. He notes that

> it is only in the rarest instances that the psychical valuation that is set on the sexual object, as being the goal of the sexual instinct, stops short of its genitals. The appreciation extends to the whole body of the sexual object and tends to involve every sensation derived from it. The same overvaluation spreads into the psychological sphere: the subject becomes, as it were, intellectually infatuated (that is, his powers of judgment are weakened) by the mental achievements and perfection of the sexual object and he submits to the latter's judgments with credulity. Thus the credulity of love becomes an important, if not the most fundamental, source of authority.[6]

"The credulity of love" or "love madness" weakens rationality and suspends judgment. The love object is perfect, and such perfection excludes any notion of disease. Indeed, the idealized "genitals" that are the focus of such passion are the imagined genitalia, that is, genitalia that only give pleasure and cannot be diseased. It is the "overvaluation" of the body of the object of desire that clouds the lover's judgment and makes the object of desire into the perfect being without those aspects that lead to disgust. Perfection here is a culturally constructed category that excludes everything that could evoke disgust.

Such an overvaluation places the body of the desired object as beyond the limits of the censuring mechanisms of society that make us read our bodily functions as corrupting and corrupt. It is the basis for the construction of the role of both the masochist, whose pathological state confuses the "real" object of desire with the object of desire who punishes desire, and the idealized object of desire, who is beyond physicality. It is difficult enough for Western society to keep in mind the double function of the genitalia—reproductive and excretory (except in St. Augustine's Pauline view of the body as inherently corrupt, or, pathologically, as an aspect of the act of sexual fetishization). It seems almost impossible to add the idea that the genitalia can also be the source of disease, and yet this idea comes to play a major role in the representation of female genitalia as the source of danger for the male in the fantasy of the eighteenth century.

In the eighteenth century, Johann Wolfgang von Goethe had his fictional protagonist Wilhelm Meister "bound by invisible bonds" to his Marianne after he observed her urinating. William Wordsworth's response to this scene in the novel was to be "struck with such disgust that he flung the book out of his hand, would never look at it again, and declared that surely no English lady would ever read such work" and/or so expose herself.[7] Even imagining a fictional character seeing his beloved urinating evokes Wordsworth's disgust. What is unstated is the danger that is evoked here by the genitalia, for the disgust associated with observing the beloved's micturation reveals the fantasy about the dangerous genitalia of the woman. For the male they are symbolically dangerous because they evoke castration anxiety, but this generalized anxiety in the eighteenth century takes the concrete form of anxiety about sexually transmitted disease and its effect on the male. Thus, that these texts, written by males, stress or repress the potential for infection is a sign of the anxiety generated by the physicality of the woman's body.

In Swift's world the minister's infection is the result of his own desire to possess that which transgresses the norms of his own culture. Here the disgust represented is aimed not only at the infected and infecting woman, but also at the violation of the marriage bed by the materiality of both parties, a violation certainly evoked by the literary trope (reaching back to Chaucer) of disgust at the May/December relationship. The male lover becomes the masochist who has created his own masochistic scenario. He has created an object of desire, who, however, punishes him through her sexuality, the same quality that he found most attractive about her youthfulness.

Such disgust is seen, of course, only from Swift's male perspective. Roy Porter and Lesley Hall point out that married women tolerated, or at least were forced to tolerate, their husbands' violation of the marriage bed. They quote from a report by James Boswell in which

he states that one of his woman friends would rather have her husband take "a transient fancy for a girl, or [be] led by one's companions after drinking to an improper place" than have him keep "a particular woman."[8] Here the anxiety about losing status as the object of
desire seems to have outweighed the anxiety about sexually transmitted disease. Given the ease with which men could remove themselves
from the obligations of the family, the mistress's threat to the wife's
status seemed greater than the risk to her person. Thus, women, too,
could repress the anxiety about sexually transmitted diseases that per-
meated their society.

The woman as sexual object in the first poem by Swift that we discussed, the tale of Chloe and Strephon, may be imagined as pissing,
but not as infected. And yet certainly the potential for such a state of
illness exists in all human beings. The line between "natural" functions such as excretion that we label as disgusting is contrasted with
the "unnatural" transmission of sexually transmitted diseases in the
marriage bed in a boundary we draw between the "good" and "bad"
objects of desire, and this boundary has no equivalent reality in the
world. Those aspects that society labels as shameful and disgusting,
such as excretion, are, as Freud notes, forces that stand in opposition
and resistance to the libido (*SE,* 7: 159). And yet, regarded as even
more disgusting by Western society, as Freud illustrates in the case of
Dora, for example, are sexually transmitted diseases that are also inti-
mately tied to the libido.

The anxiety about sexually transmitted disease is linked to the fear
of shattering the "good" object of desire. The disgust that arises is of
a violated marriage bed, and this heightens the sense of outrage at the
destruction of the "good" beloved. The difference between Strephon
and Swift's minister is that Strephon benefits from learning about the
"natural." He and Chloe will consummate their marriage and reproduce. His "good" object remains good. Neither adultery nor cuckoldry is possible in their world. The minister is destroyed because he
never acknowledges his unnatural act—the materiality that was responsible for his May/December marriage. He is never aware that
this act is the cause of his pain and his death. Shame and pain are the
two emotions that separate the two actions—excrement is, at least according to Dean Swift, natural, but disease—specifically, sexually
transmitted disease within marriage—is unnatural, like the marriage

in which it occurs. It is evil because it destroys the male and *his* potential progeny. The question of male anxiety about identity and bodily integrity is central to this trope.[9]

The scholarly literature on the violation of the marriage bed, on adultery, at least from Edward Westermarck's late-nineteenth-century study of marriage as the model for sociological study to the present, has focused on the problems of inheritance.[10] Reproduction and property were linked, and the violation of the marriage bed was reduced to the problem of lineage. Adultery was thus merely a problem of defining who would, or at least who should, inherit property and name. With few exceptions, the discussions of the literary representations of adultery have followed this economic model.[11] I would argue that there is a second, perhaps more immediate, problem addressed by the anxiety about the violation of the marriage bed, and that is the anxiety about disease and death. Adultery and virginity become linked concepts. For the purity of the virgin "guarantees" the absence of sexually transmitted illness as well as the ability of the male to pass his name and property down to his "real" heir.[12]

Sex, as Roy Porter and Lesley Hall remind us in their study of sexual knowledge in England, is closely bound to the idea of marriage in European culture: "From the seventeenth century, marriage recurs as a central element in discussions of sexuality. Emphasis on marriage may represent a concession to moral norms: 'for married only' can cover a multitude of explicit detail . . . [moral norms are] presented as being for the benefit of the married, in fact a sound support for monogamy in a dangerous age."[13] Sexuality, or at least the discourse about sexuality, can be fixed within discussions of marriage. Porter and Hall carefully illustrate in their study how knowledge (and myths) about the physicality of sexuality and knowledge (and myths) about infection come to be both mutually understood and constantly separated within the British discourse of uxoriousness. Such a discourse about monogamy masks the anxiety about the violation of the definition in which sex is permitted and healthy within marriage and dangerous and potentially infectious outside of marriage. This myth needs to be reinforced by society to preserve within marriage the one "safe" space for sexuality.

Thus, we have framed our problem—the special question of love, fantasy, trust, and belief in marriage as the prophylaxis against disease. Here marriage comes to be understood as defined by ideas of fidelity and trust as well as love. But marriage is also about creating the illusion of the object of desire's perfection, an illusion that can reach the stage of madness when it does not mature in light of the realities of human desire, physiology, and temperament. How very problematic this is can be judged by Dean Swift's second poem, in which the death of the old man is caused by his marriage—admittedly, in the views of the eighteenth century, an imbalanced marriage, a marriage that was "diseased." Yet both of these poems are readings of a masochistic scenario in which the lover creates an idealized object of desire: Strephon his faultless Chloe, the minister his youthful bride. Each is "betrayed": Strephon in learning that his bride is physical when she urinates, the minister in ignoring his being cuckolded and becoming infected. These are mirror images of the madness of love and the ability to construct an idealized object of desire in one's fantasy. Swift's first poem represses the possibility of disease; his second obsesses about it. The mutual exclusion of these two models of desire illustrate that the representation of pure desire and the healthy body must be separated from the fantasy of corporeal corruption of the body through sexually transmitted disease. This is coupled with a powerful moral lesson (remember that, Swift, too, was a minister). Swift's texts show the tension that can exist when the body of the beloved is imagined as pure, but when the male can never truly know that this is the case.

'As You Like It': Seventeenth-Century Variations on the Theme

Not only are madness, sex, marriage, safety, and illness linked in the ironic world of Swift, they are also linked in a strong Western tradition of comedy. It is in the world of comedy, in Shakespeare's *As You Like It*, that life and love and death and betrayal come to be associated with the idealization of the object of desire and the problem of disgust.[14] For Shakespeare links love, desire, physical illness, madness, and melancholy in complicated ways to reflect the folly of believing that marriage cures all.

As You Like It is a comedy that has recently been of interest because of its complicated pattern of sexual disguise: boy actors play young women dressing as young men. It is a comedy, like all of Shakespeare's comedies, about the problems of generations: the errors of the older generation are made good by the younger generation. The play has, I will try to show, yet one more level of complexity. For it is at the same time a play about love and a play about disease—specifically syphilis—which both comes from and results in melancholy and which is associated with the love madness at the center of this comedy.

The plot of the comedy is rather simple. Rosalind, the daughter of the deposed Duke Senior, and her cousin, Celia, flee into the forest of Arden disguised as Ganymede and his sister Aliena. There they meet Orlando, who has also fled from the "envious court" of Duke Frederick, where he, like Rosalind, was mistrusted because his father, Sir Rowland de Boys, was an opponent of the new duke. Rosalind and Celia take with them the court fool, Touchstone, and find in the forest the men of Duke Senior's court, among them the sad Jaques, the arch-melancholic.[15] After a series of confusions, all is made right. The "real" court of Duke Senior is restored, Rosalind is betrothed to Orlando, Celia to Oliver, his brother, Touchstone to the country maid Audrey. Only the sad Jaques remains isolated in the forest at the close of the play.

As You Like It is haunted, however, by the ghost of illness much like *Hamlet* is haunted by the ghost of Hamlet's father. And it is an illness tied to love, both to the idea of love as the means of creating an idealized object of desire and to the idea of love as that dangerous stage in which, as we have quoted Freud, the "powers of judgment are weakened." Madness is what the fixation on the object of desire causes, and madness is the act created by love. Madness seems to be an illness suffered by the males in the comedy. It may seem at first a pleasant madness, but it is a madness nevertheless. Upon entering the Forest of Arden, Touchstone and Rosalind, disguised as the tall, handsome youth Ganymede, overhear the rustic lover Silvius speak to Corin of his overwhelming love for Phebe, in which his love took the form of "many actions most ridiculous / Hast thou been drawn to by thy fantasy?" (II.iv) Hearing this, the fool Touchstone comments on this theme and on the power of love madness to distort the realities of daily life and make them seem what they are not:

I remember, when I was in love I broke my sword upon a stone and bid him take that for coming a-night to Jane Smile; and I remember the kissing of her batler, and the cow's dugs that her pretty chopt hands had milked; and I remember the wooing of a peascod instead of her, from whom I took two cods, and giving her them again, said with weeping tears "Wear these for my sake." We that are true lovers run into strange capers; but as all is mortal in nature, so is all nature in love mortal in folly. (II.iv)

Here it is the "fantasy" about which Silvius speaks in its most comic reality. For the object of desire that is created has nothing to do with the physical reality of the beloved. The milkmaid is confused with the objects she touches and with all of nature, which become identified with the beloved. She is the "good" object of desire who cannot be anything but perfect.

This reduction of the lover to the fool has its ultimate, masochistic expression not in the comic world of the rustic and the fool but in the discourse of the court and the city. Rosalind, with her ways of the court, identifies with the Arcadian peasant's madness: "Jove, Jove! this shepherd's passion / Is much upon my fashion." Madness and love are intertwined; true love is the madness that creates the object of desire, and yet Rosalind's understanding of love madness and the confusion of the self with the object of desire is cast in quite a different tone.

In the third act, Rosalind (still dressed as the young man Ganymede) confronts her own imagined lover, Orlando, with the charge that he could not love Rosalind since he shows no true madness in his physiognomy:

A lean cheek, which you have not; a blue eye and sunken, which you have not, an unquestionable spirit, which you have not; a beard neglected, which you have not—but I pardon you for that, for simply your having in beard is a younger brother's revenue. Then your hose should be ungartered, your bonnet unbanded, your sleeve unbuttoned, your shoe untied, and every thing about you demonstrating a careless desolation. But you are no such man: you are rather point-device in your accoutrements as loving yourself than seeming the lover of any other. (III.ii)

The lover can only be seen as the mad lover (dressed in the dishabille of madness, which represents the disorder of the body). Rosalind, in male disguise, describes the act of creating the object of desire as the act of madness: "Love is merely a madness, and, I tell you, deserves as well a dark house and a whip as madmen do: and the reason why they are not so punished and cured is, that the lunacy is so ordinary that the whippers are in love too. Yet I profess curing it by counsel" (III.ii). Here the masochistic scenario is stated quite directly. For male lovers should be beaten (as the insane are imagined to be treated) to cure the symptom of their madness, which is their fantasy about the nature of their female beloved. This is represented in their physicality, in their disarray, and the treatment must be a whip or isolation in "a nook merely monastic." They must be made to act "love mad" as an antidote to their love madness. This will "wash your liver as clean as a sound sheep's heart, that there shall not be one spot of love in't" (III.ii).

The male lover's complaint, love madness, arises in the liver, according to Robert Burton's discussion in *The Anatomy of Melancholy*, and is represented by a numbing of the senses as in all madness. But it seems to be clearly gendered. Only men can suffer from it; only they can cure it in other men. The cure, like the illness, has as its primary symptom the inability to see the object of desire as anything but idealized. The inability to measure the reality of the object of desire becomes the symptom, and it is a symptom that leads to other forms of madness. It is the reality of the female beloved that must be restored if the male is to be cured of his illness. Rosalind (as Ganymede) in her rationality mocks such male lovers and warrants that they should be treated like all other mad *men*—with confinement and punishment. And yet she, too, feels desire for Orlando, a desire that constructs him as her love object. Her desire itself may be a type of love madness, as represented by her disguise as a young man. The gender confusion that has been well documented in this drama may well reflect this reading.

Madness, however, is not only represented in the play by these lovers. Love madness in the male is a positive image of insanity. It is the madness associated with the pairing of couples in the comedy, and it seems to be benign because it relates to pleasure. Yet one of the most famous mad men in the Shakespearean comedies, "Monsieur Melancholy" (III.ii), the sad Jaques, is the unifying theme that connects all aspects of the drama. We hear of the melancholy Jaques well before we meet him, for he is described as weeping for the deer, "the poor dappled fools" that his companions have slaughtered. One such deer has only been wounded and seems also to be weeping. Jaques identifies with the wounded deer:

> "Poor deer," quoth he, "thou makest a testament
> As worldlings do, giving thy sum of more
> To that which had too much." Then, being there alone,
> Left and abandon'd of his velvet friend:
> "Tis right," quoth he; "thus misery doth part
> The flux of company." (II.i)

The image of the weeping stag has its analogies in the emblem literature of the seventeenth century.[16] It is the representation of damaged masculinity, and it is also the image of the wounded cuckold, the male who has been damaged by the violation of his marriage bed. The horned stag is a figure that we have already met in Swift's poem. The cuckold is the fool who has trusted the madness of misapprehension and who truly believes in the perfection and cleanliness of the object of desire. Jaques is the male wounded by his beloved, and yet the image is more complicated because the stag he weeps over has been wounded by his fellow male courtiers in the Forest of Arden.

The cuckold's wounding, however, is not merely the wounding of the soul, but also of the body. Throughout the play, Shakespeare does not let us forget this theme. The theme of the horn is echoed often enough in the play as to make it a leitmotiv linking the forest, sexuality, and cuckoldry.[17] Thus Touchstone comments:

A man may, if he were of a fearful heart, stagger in this attempt; for here we have no temple but the wood, no assembly but horn-beasts. But what though? Courage! As horns are odious, they are necessary. It is said, "Many a man knows no end of his goods." Right; many a man has good horns and knows no end of them. Well, that is the dowry of his wife; 'tis none of his own getting. Horns! Even so, poor men alone. No, no; the noblest deer hath them as huge as the rascal. Is the single man therefore blessed? No; as a walled town is more worthier than a village, so is the forehead of a married man more honourable than the bare brow of a bachelor; and by how much defence is better than no skill, by so much is a horn more precious than to want. (III.iii)

Touchstone's ode to horns is echoed in the exchange between Rosalind and Orlando in which Rosalind, still seen by Orlando as his friend Ganymede, recounts the dangers of the marriage bed in terms of the snail's "horns, which such as you are fain to be beholding to

your wives for" (IV.i). Men get their "horns" from their wives' violation of the marriage bed, and these horns are a sign of their madness
of believing in the inviolability of the marriage bed. The final repeti-
tion of the theme of the horn returns to the relationship of sad Jaques
and the wounded stag. As the hunters sing after the kill:

> Take thou no scorn to wear the horn,
> It was a crest ere thou wast born,
> Thy father's father wore it,
> And thy father bore it.
> The horn, the horn, the lusty horn,
> Is not a thing to laugh to scorn. (IV.ii)

But what is dangerous about the violation of the marriage bed and its
results? It is the prospect of death by syphilis, the physical result of
the violation of the marriage bed. For the "velvet" on the stag's
horns—that symbol of spring and sexuality—is also read by Shakespeare in *Measure for Measure* as a sign of syphilitic infection, called
the French pox, as well pain (dolor) and early death.[18]

Jaques has been wounded, like the horned stag, wounded by love.
He is aware that his illness may be directly caused by a woman, yet
her illness has been caused by a man. For the cuckold's status is created by another male's presence in the marriage bed. His illness is
syphilis, and it is this illness that haunts his solitary life. It is an illness,
if the horned image employed is any indicator, caused by a beloved
who has violated the promise of the marriage bed by infecting her
sexual partner. Jaques is the sufferer, like Hamlet, of both physical and
psychological ills.[19] But his world may well lend itself to a rereading.
Jaques's melancholy is thus his means of projecting his illness out of
his body and onto the world. He "will through and through /
Cleanse the foul body of the infected world, / If they will patiently receive my medicine" (II.vii). A cure is to be found within the madness
of melancholy, which sees through the madness of life. Melancholy
now serves as the medicine to cure the foul body world of its infection; it is thus both the symptom of disease and now its cure. And it
is a melancholy caused by Jaques's syphilitic infection. The infection,
as we have seen, seems to be the result of Jaques's love madness, his
reliance on the false belief of his lover's purity. But in the world of the
Forest of Arden Jaques's "illness" is read very differently. It is understood as resulting from his libertine life:

Duke Senior: Most mischievous foul sin, in chiding sin.
    For thou thyself hast been a libertine,
    As sensual as the brutish sting itself;
    And all th' embossèd sores and headed evils
    That thou with licence of free foot hast caught,
    Wouldst thou disgorge into the general world. (II.vii)

Jaques has been cuckolding others and has been punished for it by contracting an illness. He is the libertine who has infected the marriage bed of others and has himself been infected by his actions. Sexual passion must, according to the image in the comedy, construct the pure object of desire. Jaques's lust has not done this. Jaques becomes the exemplary syphilitic in this world of love in *As You Like It*.

That Jaques is syphilitic is accepted in the critical literature on Shakespeare as early as the nineteenth century.[20] But the significance of his syphilis has never been explored. It is a sign of his role as the infected and the source of infection within the sexual economy of the comedy. It is the source of his worldview—his melancholy—and his illness is in turn shaped by his manner of seeing the world. Jaques's syphilis can account for his morose version of the seven ages of man, for as David Bevington argues,

the Duke's point is well taken, for Jaques's famous "Seven Ages of Man" speech, so often read out of context, occurs in a scene that also witnesses the rescue of Orlando and Adam. As though in answer to Jaques's acid depiction of covetous old age, we see old Adam's self-sacrifice and trust in Providence. Instead of "mere oblivion," we see charitable compassion prompting the Duke to aid Orlando and Orlando to aid Adam.[21]

In his soliloquy "All the world's a stage," Jaques speaks of "the lover, / Sighing like furnace, with a woeful ballad / Made to his mistress' eyebrow." This stage of love madness in the male may lead to the fullness of middle age, but the syphilitic male is condemned to die in "second childishness and mere oblivion, / Sans teeth, sans eyes, sans taste, sans everything" (II.vii).

Read as an account of the progression of a syphilitic male's infection from youth through the age of infection into the dotage of tertiary Luis, or even a quicker progression into the rotting of age, Jaques's story signals the most pessimistic course of life and decay. This decay is outlined in the curses of Timon of Athens, who damns the inhabitants of Athens with the symptoms of syphilis (IV.i). Yet it is also Jaques's awareness of himself as infected and as the source of infection, of danger. Shakespeare's syphilitics, unlike Swift's minister, become self-conscious markers of the presence of illness in the world, especially in the world of the comedy.

The relationship between syphilis and melancholy is an old trope in the medical literature of the seventeenth century. Melancholy comes from syphilis, as Robert Burton notes in *The Anatomy of Melancholy*,[22] or predisposes one to syphilis, as Girolamo Fracastoro, who coined the name *syphilis*, notes: "For those whose veins are swollen with black bile and throb with thick blood there is in their case a greater struggle and the plague clings more tenaciously."[23] In his work on contagion, Fracastoro comments that the symptoms of syphilis are melancholy, lack of appetite, thinness, and sleeplessness.[24] Yet there is more to the relationship between the two illnesses than merely causation. Both have their roots in the domination of Saturn in the heavens, and both provide an image of character. The syphilitic, like sad Jaques, rails against his fate: "So someone sighing over the springtime of his life and his beautiful youth, and gazing with wild eyes down at his disfigured members, his hideous limbs and swollen face, often in his misery railed against God's cruelty, often against the stars.'"[25]

Here Jaques's monologues themselves become a sign of his illness. Thus, in Agnolo Bronzino's painting *Venus, Love and Jealousy* (1546) the sign of the violation of Venus's marriage bed and her cuckolded husband Hephaistos is the representation of the black-skinned syphilitic, in pain, his hair falling out; in its parallel piece, *Venus, Cupid, Folly and Time* (ca. 1545), it is the melancholic, in the traditional position, hand on head, into which the syphilitic is transformed.[26] The violation of the marriage bed leads to syphilis and pain.

Jaques's melancholic comments identify the source of his infection as one of the "women in the city." This charge becomes commonplace by the time we get to Addison and Steele's *Tatler*, published on December 7, 1710, with its "Admonition to the young Men of this Town" concerning the dangers of sexually transmitted disease for young men (and the potential loss of their noses).[27] Jaques's melancholy is the result of syphilis and his libertinage and is inflicted on him by an infected woman. But it is his love madness that creates his inability to be unable to distinguish between a proper object of desire (as exem-

plified by the lovers in *As You Like It*) and the "woman of the city."
His wounding results from his presence in another's marriage bed. It
is a sign of his false reliance on the superficial values of the "city," the
place of seduction and disease.

When syphilis is evoked in the world of Shakespeare's dramas, it is
not evoked without at least the mention of an attempted cure. The
common cure for syphilis (as well as for gonorrhea) during the six-
teenth century was mercury. It was, as Porter and Hall note, "a 'cure'
[that] many perceived as worse than the disease, unpleasant, long-
drawn-out, and causing noticeable physical stigmata."[28] And Shakespeare's understanding of the implications of such treatment is clear.
In *Henry V*, Pistol comments about his wife, who is being treated in
the hospital for syphilis: "To the spital go, And from the powdering
tub of infamy / Fetch forth the lazar kite of Cressid's kind" (II.i). The
effects of mercury poisoning (used in the sweating baths) are similar
to those of syphilis itself—the loss of hair, the marking of the skin,
and the development of a stinking breath—and mark one as being
under treatment. These are public signs. Thus, in the eighteenth century, in *Joe Miller's Jestbook*, there are a series of jokes about sore gums,
constant salivation, loose teeth, and the strong metallic smell of the
breath.[29]

Jaques's treatment, however, is to be different. He is aware of his
danger—to the "women in the city." After all the lovers are united and
the court is about to be restored, Jaques separates himself out from
the world made right; he exiles himself. All the male characters, with
the exception of Jaques, have the potential for love and marriage. Yet
the madness that is love, a madness that sees beyond disguise in clothing and beyond gender roles, cannot imagine the betrayal of the marriage bed.[30] And this potential violation is represented in the comedy
by Jaques. He can never marry, for he is marked by another madness,
melancholy, which stems from his libertinage, from his indulgence in
polluting sexuality. The answer to Jaques's madness and infection is
the answer of the leper, whom the syphilitic still mirrors in the seventeenth century. He must be banished once order is restored. He gives
all of the characters their appropriate measure of love, but he remains
alone in the Forest of Arden, "at [the Duke's] abandon'd cave" (V.vi).
Thus, Jaques undertakes his cure of love madness, as Rosalind claims
she was able to do, and changes the "mad humour of love to a living

humour of madness; which was, to forswear the full stream of the world, and to live in a nook merely monastic" (III.ii). Here Jaques also mirrors Timon of Athens's image of withdrawing from human companionship, a companionship he is denied as a syphilitic, and is condemned "to the woods; where he shall find / The unkindest beast more kinder than mankind" (IV.i).

But what of the three pairs of lovers united at the end of the play, with Jaques's blessing? Only Touchstone and his rustic lover are "cursed" with a short stay within the happy madness that is love. But, of course, it was also Touchstone alone who recognized the possibility of corruption within his marriage bed. He states the case for his "love" most directly in the same terms that Shakespeare used for Jaques's melancholy, the image of the horned stag:

> *Touchstone*: Truly, and to cast away honesty upon a foul slut
>   were to put good meat into an unclean dish.
> *Audrey*: I am not a slut, though I thank the gods I am foul.
> *Touchstone*: Well, praised be the gods for thy foulness! Sluttish-
>   ness may come hereafter. But be it as it may be, I will
>   marry thee. . . . Amen. (III.iii)

Audrey may be foul and disgusting, but she is not a slut—at least not now. The fool Touchstone and the melancholic Jaques know that the results of violating the bed of love are disease and death. Here in the comedy lies the potential for betrayal, but it seems to be separated from the other loving pairs. Shakespeare's subtlety here is quite different from Swift's anxiety. He recognizes the potential for death and sex to be closely linked. Certainly, like Swift, he sees it in reducing passion to materiality and commerce. As Dromio of Syracuse says of a prostitute in *The Comedy of Errors*, "She is the devil's dam; and here she comes in the habit of a light wench: and thereof comes that the wenches say 'God damn me'; that's as much to say 'God make me a light wench.' It is written, they appear to men like angels of light: light is an effect of fire, and fire will burn; ergo, light wenches will burn. Come not near her" (IV.iii). Death lies within the action of the unfaithful female lover. It is from her that the illness of melancholy and syphilis spreads. Yet it is also possible in the world of *As You Like It* for lovers to be infected. The prostitute is the woman of the town, but she is never that far from the other objects of desire in the comedy.

All the "pure" lovers are united and the royal court is restored at the conclusion of the comedy. The world turned topsy-turvy is righted again. Only Jaques remains in the Forest of Arden, now the place of exile from healthy humankind. His remaining in the forest denotes the end of the action but not the end of the play. Shakespeare has ended the play in an unusual manner. For the boy actor who had played Rosalind, who was also cross-dressed as a boy, appears on-stage at the conclusion of the comedy and holds her/his epilogue as a man, warning all of the young women of the town against infection by the men. "If I were a woman, I would kiss as many of you as had beards that pleased me, complexions that liked me, and breaths that I defied not" (V.iv), says the young boy who has played Rosalind. Be aware of those men bearing the marks of the treatments for syphilis—bad breath, spotty skin, and thinning of hair and beard. Here the echo of Timon of Athens's curse resounds again: "down with the nose, Down with it flat; take the bridge quite away Of him that, his particular to foresee, Smells from the general weal: make curl'd-pate ruffians bald; And let the unscarr'd braggarts of the war Derive some pain from you" (IV.ii). The smell of the syphilitic, the syphilitic's mottled skin, the loss of hair, the scarred visage—all are public signs of the disease and its mercury cure that make the syphilitic the bearer of the marks of opprobrium. This double-edged warning states the counterlesson. For if Jaques knows that he has been infected (and will infect) through his libertinage in the city, his self-exile in the forest is also in the message that the actor / Rosalind brings. Beware, young women, he says, of licentious men who will infect you and make you into "women of the city." The idealized state of marriage—the resolution of the sexual tensions of the comedy, sex without fear of death—is not a possibility for Jaques (or even, the epilogue whispers, for the lovers). For there are those men, Shake-speare argues in his epilogue, who still live in the cities (unlike Jaques) and can infect you. Beware of these men when you, young women, invite them into the marriage bed. Unlike young men, you do not suffer from love madness, you can make real choices based on the symptoms of your lovers. Shakespeare is thus able to accomplish what Swift could not. He was able to show how very slippery the idealization of the lover can be and how "love madness" can easily become the stuff of physical illness and betrayal.

Conclusion and a New Beginning

The universal preoccupation with the purity of the love relationship, with the anxiety that love and marriage (or at least a permanent relationship based on the madness of love) could lead to death through infection, is a powerful trope of the present age. The age-old suggestion for the control of STDs has again been broached in the era of AIDS—the marriage bed, celibacy, and love. In the 1880s the French physician Alfred Fournier had proposed marriage as the ultimate prophylaxis for syphilis.[31] Recently, the proposal has reappeared as a desire to locate safety, the safety of the idealized object of desire, in the world of marriage.[32] This medical version of the moral obligation to "Just say no" is the simple restatement of the desire for the *guaranteed* purity of the marriage bed that Shakespeare had already shown as impossible, at least in the world of the comedy. Here "love" as the cure for AIDS has become a means to assure public health.

Love has come to be a key word in the most recent public health advertising about AIDS. The Austrian AIDS organization has presented a studied series of "art" posters representing heterosexual and homosexual partners as aestheticized under the motto "Protect Out of Love" [S 25319–24].[33] In the world of the public health advertising poster, "love" is defined as caring and protecting and as the "natural" extension of sexuality. For the hidden message is that the use of condoms is a sign of caring and removes sexuality from a brutal, coarse, ugly, and destructive mode of representation. The pure love of the comedy is the counterpart or antithesis to the sex embodied in Jaques's illness. Today, risk is represented in the broadest possible way. Thus, the image of the healthy, beautiful family is central to AIDS education. The German AIDS-*Hilfe* presents a gender-balanced family (father, mother, one male and one female child) with the motto "Because I Love You" [25182]. A parallel image is to be found on a poster aimed at Native Americans. With a male and female in silhouette is the motto "Love carefully—Preserve your heritage—Know your partner!" [25248]. The elegance of the image, especially the complex lettering of the word *love*, points to the preservation of the "race." The "love" implied is, of course, related to sex, but it is extended to the image of preserving the group. "Love" is caring, and no violation of the marriage bed is permitted, as this will have a negative impact on the isolated world of the lovers. The result of such a violation of the marriage bed is death. A photograph of a shrouded body on a gurney, its feet exposed and presented to the audience in the manner of Andrea Mantegna's Christ, is labeled "Don't Let Love Sweep You Off Your Feet" [28181]. Love comes to be a very dangerous basis for protection from disease.

In the age of AIDS all love relationships become as suspect as in the world of *As You Like It*. Let us turn to the work of the hottest (or at least the most discussed) contemporary British writer, Martin Amis. Amis's work is the thread running throughout this volume, as can be seen in Chapters 7 and 9. As one of the most powerful exponents of contemporary Anglophone culture, he represents the best and the most complex writing of the late twentieth century. Amis's comic novels span the beginning of the age of AIDS. In his first novel, *The Rachel Papers* (1973), the teenage protagonist, Charles Highway, discovers that sex can lead to disease, specifically gonorrhea, but, it seems, only sex with someone who was foreign and who "wasn't very good looking" (89). Having had sex with this foreign, not-very-good-looking girl on a lavatory floor, he develops a severe case of the clap. Foreignness, ugliness, and bodily functions are closely linked in this protagonist's image of the "bad" love object that combines both illness and difference.

Charles Highway spots his "true love," Rachel, at a party and assumes that she is Jewish because of her dark hair and eyes. When this is resolved, when she says that she is not Jewish, his love for her transcends the physical, including the question of disease. Rachel is (ironically) seen as physically perfect. "Neither of us defecated, spat, had bogeys or arses. (I wondered how she was going to explain away her first period, overdue already.) We were beautiful and brilliant and would have doubly beautiful and brilliant children. Our bodies functioned only in orgasm" (180). This mock idealization of the beloved exists until he finds "a stray pair of panties under the armchair. As I lit the fire I picked them up to kiss and sniff at. After I had been kissing and sniffing at them for a while I turned them inside out. I saw: (i) three commas of pencil-thick pubic hair, and (ii) a stripe of suede-brown shit, as big as my finger. 'Fair's fair, for Christ's sake,' I said aloud. 'They do it too.'" (181).[34] Here is the Swiftian awareness, an awareness of the physicality of the "good" beloved, and yet one still quite separate from the foreign girlfriend who infected him. Yet the beloved insists that they use condoms; is this only because she is not on the pill? Well, what of the "huge notice on the mantelpiece" of Rachel's room:

FOR THE LOVE OF GOD DON'T LET HIM TOUCH YOU
HE HAS AN UNUSALLY REVOLTING DISEASE (97)

Amis's *The Rachel Papers*, with all its subsequent scandal, is a novel of sexual self-discovery that centers on the revelation that all human beings, as sexual beings, are also dangerous—dangerous to themselves and to others. Yet it also manages to create a boundary between the "good" (uninfected) and "bad" (infected) objects of desire. The characters of the novel create objects of desire and sex objects that are separate, and yet they are quite aware of the artificiality of these constructions. But this is, again, only within the world of the comic, where satire is the central mode of representation. "Love" makes the object of desire pure, but this purity is always suspended and held up to questioning.

In the age of AIDS, STDs are no longer a joke, even in satirical novels. In 1995, well into the age of AIDS, Martin Amis published his most recent novel about marriage and betrayal, *The Information*.[35] One of the central figures in the novel, Richard Tull, has decided to revenge himself on his friend, the popularly successful novelist Gwyn Barry. To do so he implements a series of minor and rather mordant attacks, one of which concerns a "fan" of Barry who has become enamored with him through his television appearances.

Barry is renowned in England, or at least on English television, for his "uxoriousness," his happy and loving marriage to Lady Demeter (35, 42). Theirs was "a match made in heaven" (65). This also seems the case in Tull's often-repeated expressions of sexual desire for his wife, Gina. Marriage is the state of perfect desire, or so it seems in the novel. One must remember, however, that in Britain the ghost of the 1937 divorce law reform was still haunting popular consciousness.

Marriage could be annulled if one party could be shown to have married while "suffering from communicable venereal disease."[36] In Amis's novel the protagonists' marriages represent the idealization of marriage, yet they are constantly shown to be the source of danger. The anxiety about infection lurks always in the background.

Tull proposes to have the seventeen-year-old Belladonna seduce his rival Barry, in order to besmirch his friend's reputation. And Belladonna, tricked out in punk dress and black eyeliner, is indeed "deadly" (67). Hers is not the illness of literary biography that Tull is condemned to spend his time reviewing, such as that of William Devenant, who "got a terrible clap of a black handsome wench that lay in Axe-yard . . . which cost him his nose" (95). For such risks to the poets in the age of AIDS are minor. In the age of penicillin, syphilis holds few fears.

Tull fantasizes that he had acted upon Belladonna's sexual invitation and allowed her to perform fellatio upon him: "There was one favorite in particular: the kind of sexual intercourse that involved not an exchange of bodily fluids so much as a full transfer" (135). This is the image of safe sex (at least for the male). Safe sex is the major subtheme of this novel of the 1990s. Sex, disease, and the violation of the marriage bed have now become the theme that links Eros and Thanatos, love and death. For, as it turns out in the course of the novel, Belladonna is revealed as being HIV-positive: "She ain't mega-well. She's *positive*, man" (339), says the boyfriend who had initially approached Tull to sell him the information regarding Belladonna's fantasies about his enemy. Thus, the marginal attempt at muddying Barry's name by associating him in a sexual adventure with a minor turns out to be a question of life and death. The adventures in the realm of seduction were indeed flirting with the potential for infection:

"You remember that weird little sister I brought round to see you—Belladonna?" He waited, with his head down. "What happened?"

"That would be telling now, wouldn't it."

"Naturally." He waited. "You didn't fuck *her*, did you?"

"Are you out of your mind? Or do you just think I am. A little spook like that. . . . I need that. Not to mention the risk of disease. . . . No. I just let her give me a blow job." (357–58)

Barry then turns, in what appears to be a moment of concern, to his friend and asks: "*You* didn't fuck her, did you?" (358) This moment of concern is the final twist to the plot. It is not Tull's "trap" that is the center of the novel, but rather his friend's behind-the-scenes manipulation of Tull's life. For, as the novel unravels, it becomes evident that it is indeed Barry who has been directing the action all along. He has been in control of Tull's life in every detail. He is anxious when his "friend" informs him about Belladonna, not because of his potential infection from her, but because he has been having weekly sex sessions with Tull's idealized wife, Gina. These meetings, paid for and delivered, have enabled Tull to write his final, awful novel. And the final scene of Amis's novel is the staged discovery by Tull of this fact when he walks in on his wife performing fellatio on Barry. It is the same position that enables the infection to spread only one way—according to the myth created in the text—from the man to the woman. It is precisely what Tull imagines doing with Belladonna. There is no safe haven for the anxiety about sex and disease in the age of AIDS. The safety of the marriage bed in the age of AIDS is only conceivable in terms of black humor.

The violation of the marriage bed is a source of humor from the seventeenth to the twentieth century. Cuckolds are funny, at least to male readers, who, idealizing their own narcissistic pleasure, can never image being anything but the seducer. The humor of sex is tied to the idealization of the object of desire created by the male—the beautiful woman, pure beyond belief, who could never be anything but faithful. The antithesis, the woman who infects, lies on the other side of that arbitrary boundary. She is the destroyer of men. Yet it is the male, too, who infects, who corrupts. This is not the stuff of humor—it is the anxiety of the male who imagines himself being infected in order to infect. The social conventions of marriage are thus the fantasy construction in which safety lies, and this safety shields the male from the world of illness, the world of disease. Purity in the marriage bed is the idealization of the object of desire as beyond infection, beyond disease, beyond the aging process, beyond death! Here we can remind ourselves of Otto Kernberg's description of the ages of sexual passion that end in the acceptance of decay and death as part of the natural process of aging together. The narcissistic projection of the idealized self onto the world and its concretization as the object of desire exclude all of these possibilities.

Three variations on a theme—Shakespeare's plays, Swift's poems, and Amis's novels—point to the anxiety about disease that lies within comic representations of the marriage bed. Not just anxiety about future lineage defines the dangers. The cuckold dies from his cuckoldry, betrayed by the love object he has constructed in his love madness. The male's anxiety about not only his heirs but also his own body, at risk for infection from the women of the city, is placed within the comic world. It is that aspect of this world that denies the power of satiric distancing, where the anxieties of the body transcend the framing power of the genre. Jaques remains isolated by his libertinage in the forest; Swift's minister dies of his cuckoldry; Amis's failed writer sees his ideal object of desire vanish as he observes his friend having oral sex with his wife. In all cases the object of desire—the male's fantasy of the woman as idealized figure—comes to be revealed as the castrating adulteress who carries with her the potential for the male's destruction. And yet in all these images the dichotomy of the infecting woman and the infected male is undercut to show us how all participants are involved in the dance of sex and death, blinded by the self-delusion of the purity of the marriage bed. Love + marriage = death.

CHAPTER THREE

Max Nordau, Sigmund Freud, and the Question of Conversion

Freud and Nordau: A Question of Honor

On September 28, 1902, Sigmund Freud wrote the following letter to Theodor Herzl, addressing him more as one of the major journalists of his day than as the intellectual formulator of modern political Zionism:

Following the recommendation of your editorial colleague, Mr. Max Nordau, I am having you sent . . . a copy of my book on the interpretation of dreams which appeared in 1900 along with a modest lecture on the same topic. I cannot know whether you will have the same impression, that the volume would be of use [for a review] as Mr. Nordau believes that it would, but I hope that you in any case keep it as a sign of the high regard which I— like so many others—bring to the poet and the fighter for the human rights of our people.[1]

The mediator in Freud's attempt to get a review of his new book placed in the *Free Viennese Press* was the sometime correspondent, sometime vice president of the Zionist Congress, sometime physician, and full-time writer Max Nordau (1849–1923). Nordau's role in formulating the goals and agendas of modern Zionism is relatively well known through the work of Shlomo Avenari and recently through the work of Hans-Peter Söder, who has explored the relationship between Nordau's cultural criticism and his ideas of health and illness.[2] Nordau's central role was in the debate about modernism as a form of "degeneration" (the title of his best-known work, published in 1892), which was the topic of a strong critical literature at the turn of the century. Indeed, even George Bernard Shaw provided a critique of Nordau's writing.[3] My own work over the past decade has reflected on the role that Nordau's ideology of the body played in understanding the reconstructive work of Zionism in creating a "new" Jewish body. The focus of my present examination of Nordau and Freud will be the question of the ideology behind Nordau's identifying the sick Jew and specifically the role that contemporary definitions of racial identity had in shaping their understanding of the Jew. Central to Nordau's and Freud's model of the "sick" Jew is the fin-de-siècle Jewish image of the Jewish convert. For the model of conversion, of shifting from one mode and model of identity to another, is central to any understanding of the dangers that await the Jewish psyche. This fin-de-siècle reversal of the age-old topos of the diseased Jew, a topos at least as ancient as the sermons of St. John Chrysostom in the fourth century, makes not the Jew, but the convert, the emblem of disease.[4] Conversion was understood by Jewish physicians at the turn of the century as a sign of illness, a sign of the mental confusion inflicted upon the Jew by the pressures of modern life. According to this argument, conversion turns Jews, who are predisposed to illness because of two thousand years of trauma (so claims the Swiss-Jewish psychiatrist Rafael Becker), into sick Jews.[5]

How can one become whole and healthy? How can one shed the trauma of one's Jewishness? By the end of the nineteenth century, the answer is clearly that one cannot—the Jewishness of the body and the psyche is indelible. The hatred of the Jewish body is also a disease. But what if one could become totally different and thus stop being the cause of the Other's illness, namely, antisemitism? An older model, the model of religious conversion, which had haunted the Jews for almost two millennia, was consistently present in European society from the time of the early Church. Conversion was a central theme of the Jews of the nineteenth century. In the period following the Jewish Enlightenment of the late eighteenth century, the *Haskalah*, or conversion, seemed to be a civil (rather than a religious) alternative; Heine could speak of conversion as the "entrance ticket into European culture."[6] However, by the end of the nineteenth century, conversion was no longer seen as a viable alternative. The earlier model permitted converts to acquire social and institutional status. Indeed, Sigmund Freud's uncle by marriage, Michael Bernays, the famed professor of German at the University of Munich, converted in order to be granted a chair.[7] At the close of the century, such status was not sufficient in the eyes of "scientific" antisemites to mask the essence of the Jew. Older views such as those of Theodor Mommsen[8] or Heinrich Treitschke,[9] which demanded that the Jew become a Christian in order to become a full-fledged German, ring strange in fin-de-siècle scientific ears more accustomed to hearing the Jew contrasted with the "Aryan" rather than with the "Christian." Indeed, the call of converts, such as that of the anonymous author of a pamphlet published in 1880 that "there is only one solution for the Jewish question, the turning of the Jews to their true King, Jesus Christ," sounds, by the end of the century, hopelessly antiquated.[10] Rather, it is clear that conversion was understood as an illusion, a desire to cure what could not be cured. As A. A. Brill noted, conversion occurred as a result of a "special emotional state": "Some like Heinrich Heine—a most sensitive poet—accepted baptism as a salvation for his Jewish disabilities."[11] It is the transformation of conversion from a religious to a medical category that was significant to Jewish scientists at the fin de siècle.

What must be understood is that the promise of conversion also presented a complex model that combined images of cultural and biological integration. The assumption was that the elimination of all the social barriers between Jews and Christians would eliminate the mutually exclusive sexual selectivity of both groups. Thus, in a letter of November 12, 1861, the Polish-Jewish sociologist Ludwig Gumplowicz wrote about civil emancipation to his friend, the Galician-Jewish nationalist Philipp Mansch:

Civil marriage! My reply: that is supposed to be part of our striving—that has to come. You have read the motion of the Commission for Religion—decided by Smolka. You are finding that "religion is no obstacle to matrimony!" . . . Give me your word that we shall marry the most beautiful Christian girls—alias *shikses*—in case that motion becomes law! I am joking and yet the matter is no joke. The day is not far when even this last wall of separation is bound to fall—and we are compelled to take leave from this shadow of our nationality which is long decayed but which for centuries keeps creeping after us like a vampire, sucks our blood and destroys our vitality.[12]

The diseased Jew can only be cured by removing *him*self from the source of disease—his Jewishness—and this can only be accomplished by complete biological integration. But Gumplowicz's first point for the regeneration of the Jews, the means by which the final goal, intermarriage, could be accomplished, was the "acceptance of the language of the people among whom one lives." Abandoning the language of the Jews, a language that defined the limitation of the Jew's psyche, was closely associated with abandoning the sexual selectivity of Jewish marital practices. For the Jewish liberals of the mid-nineteenth century, all roads led to acculturation, and the ultimate form of acculturation was sexual symbiosis.

Convert, the society in which the Jew lived had seemed to say, stop being a Jew, and you will become a full-fledged member of the majority. Traditionally, Jews were no more accepted as Christians than as "Aryans" at the close of the nineteenth century. Indeed, one of the pamphlets written against the very idea of Jewish political emancipation in Vienna in 1782 was entitled "The Baptized Jew: Neither Jew nor Christian."[13] But the promise still existed. What, then, did conversion mean in Freud's culture? It has been claimed that "the stern voice of Freud's conscience . . . prevented him from taking the assimilationist path"[14] and that he, "like every Jew who has been set apart, yearned unconsciously to become part of . . . [the Christian] world."[15] Even Ernest Jones, who dismissed such speculation, noted that Freud "for five minutes toyed with [the] idea" of converting to Protestantism, as such a conversion would have enabled him to avoid a religious marriage ceremony.[16] Protestantism was the preferred religion for Jewish converts in Vienna because one was legally considered a Christian while not being a Catholic. Such a conversion was understood as not demanding the same sense of religious conviction as becoming a Catholic in apostolic Vienna. As Moritz Saphir, the famed mid-nineteenth-century Hungarian-Jewish newspaperman (himself a double convert) observed, "When I was a Jew, God could see me, but I could not see Him, then I became a Catholic and I could see Him, but He could not see me. Now I am a Protestant and I don't see Him or He me."[17] But this was a mid-century view. By the turn of the century many Jews avoided converting, even in this most superficial manner. For by the fin de siècle, especially in the world of medicine, even this mode of conversion becomes a pathological sign.

Nowhere in the cultural tradition of fin-de-siècle Jewish letters in German is this better exemplified than in Max Nordau's drama *Dr. Kohn* (translated into English as *A Question of Honor*) (1899).[18] This drama presents the conflict between the converted Jew and his prospective Jewish son-in-law, a conflict that reflects the heightened discourse about the immutability of Jewish racial identity at the turn of the century. It is vital to note that the drama reflects on the fact that in the twenty years at the conclusion of the nineteenth century, the very meaning of conversion has changed. When, in the 1880s, Julius Christian Moser (né Moses) approached the father of his intended, a general, there was little question that he would be well received. He was very wealthy, a convert out of nationalistic sensibilities, and he had just been awarded an Iron Cross for his bravery in the field (90–91). When Dr. Leo Kohn, who has just won an international medal in theoretical mathematics, approaches Moser for the hand of his daughter some two decades later, the world has radically changed. The meaning of conversion has changed, and the Jew's body has become the sign of immutability. In this world the anti-semites have "a keen scent [to] discover the Jewish strain here" (11), they "smell the gang, at once, in every dilution" (11). They see the "Jewish face" (11), and, indeed, see in Kohn's courting of Christine Moser a "great delusion. His conduct has always seemed strange. There is a peculiar expression in his eyes. Only it is very unpleasant that his mania assumes this form" (89). It is not only the gaze of the Jew but even the "flat foot of some Oriental" (13) that marks him.[19] This difference appears in the offspring of mixed marriages: "So he has Jewish blood. . . . I really ought to have suspected it—there is something cringing about the fellow—certain suave, humble gestures, which struck me at once" (12). Indeed, Christine Moser's decision to marry Leo Kohn is understood by her mother's brother, a pastor in the Protestant Church, as a sure sign of her Jewishness coming to the fore: "There must be something in Christine that attracts and encourages a Jew. I am perfectly sure that, in spite of the brazen effrontery of this race, this Oriental would never have dared approach a Christian girl of pure descent" (104). No conversion helps: "A Jew is a Jew. The sacred rite of baptism, even when it is received with devout faith, will probably save the soul, but will not wash clean the base, impure blood" (103). Moser truly believes that "baptism makes a Jew a Christian"; his brother-in-law agrees but notes that "it never makes an Oriental a German" (118). Beneath the veneer of Christianity, "the Hebrew's real face sneers at me—in all its hideousness" (124). It is this biological difference that Nordau saw as part of the discourse about Jewish identity at the fin de siècle.

Conversion cannot blot out the difference attributed to the Jew. But Nordau also saw this difference as inherent to the Jew because of the Jew's social status. Thus, Julius Christian Moser, who appears to be a Christian in every one of his attributes, reveals his Jewish nature early in the drama through the language of his body: "Moser [*With a Jewish gesture, bowing his head and raising both hands with the palms flat and turned outward.*] Good Lord—command!" (23). The gestural language reveals the hidden Jew, only masked through baptism and intermarriage. (Nineteenth-century anthropology regarded such gestural language as a sign of being "primitive.") For Leo Kohn, "Judaism is indelible. We may regard it as an honor or as a stain, but we cannot get rid of it" (78). As the quintessential antisemite said to the German-Jewish writer Jacob Wassermann in the 1920s, "Whether, after conversion, they cease to be Jews in the deeper sense we do not know, and have no way of finding out. I believe that the ancient influences continue to operate. Jewishness is like a concentrated dye: a minute quantity suffices to give a specific character—or, at least, some traces of it—to an incomparably greater mass."[20]

Moser still regards Judaism as a religion; Kohn understands it in racial terms. For Moser "Judaism consists of blowing ram's horns on certain days, in gnawing indigestible bread at certain seasons, and in uttering a repulsive jargon" (79). Religion, like language, is a social convention for Moser that can be shed. And his experience of the late nineteenth century was that Jews were assumed (at least by other Jews) to be capable of altering their internal psychological makeup as directly as they could alter their external social presentation. For Kohn, two decades later, the Jew's language mirrors his psyche in an intense and direct manner. This language is the window into the mind, not merely a social convention like dress or manners. Language marks the Jew and language represents the mental status of the Jew. The Jew is revealed as a member of a race, but not in terms of his fixed physiognomy—rather in terms of his mental status. Thus, Leo Kohn's parents, Amschel and Nancy Kohn, are revealed as orthodox, Eastern Jews, who "speak the Jew Jargon" (112). Kohn himself comments that they are "both Jews of the old type, who speak the disagreeable Jewish German and will not give up their strange customs" (39). His mother "wears a wig" (112) and his father wears "*a long black coat, with a long grey beard, and a little greasy skull cap*" (145). Here the social conventions of the Eastern orthodox, with all their religious requirements, mark the Jew as different for Nordau. For his character Kohn, these qualities, as disagreeable as they seem to him, shape his mental state as a Jew. No conversion can mask the Jewishness of these Jews or of their offspring. They remain different in the eyes of Moser (and indeed, in the eyes of Nordau), at the very end of the drama, after the death of Kohn in a duel with Moser's "Christian" son: "It was right of me to renounce Judaism. I should like to doubt it when I talk to your uncle; but when I see old Kohn before me, I am sure of it again. That is a different order of mankind, with which I have nothing more in common. But it is still my flesh and blood, though no longer my soul, and this I ought to have taught my children" (170).

Conversion, in the words of one of Nordau's antisemites, results in a "sham Christianity . . . an abominable masquerade, and [it] really ought to be punished, like the unlawful wearing of a uniform" (19). The only answer for the Zionist Nordau, at least in 1899, was the establishment of a secular Jewish identity separate from that of the German Aryan. Moser had converted during the Franco-Prussian War, for he had found himself isolated from his fellow soldiers who sung Lutheran hymns while he "stood apart in silence. . . . When I returned from the campaign, I was baptized; not because I believed in Christianity, but because I wished to be and to live like all other Germans, distinguished from them at no hour and in no custom" (74–75). Twenty years later, Kohn cannot consider this alternative, for when "we go out into the world, German to our fingertips, German in everything we love and hate, they suddenly thrust us back, crying scornfully: 'You are no Germans, and there is no way for you to become so; you are aliens, and aliens you will remain forever'" (75).

Moser's conversion robs him of his status as a man and as a father. He acknowledges at the conclusion of the play that he has too often ab- dicated his role in the family to his Christian brother-in-law and has sought invisibility as a human being to avoid being seen as a Jew (122, 80). Kohn refuses to do this. He remains a Jew, not a religious Jew but a national Jew, and this will restructure his body, his manhood: "If the Aryan thrusts back the Semite, and shuts him out of the Aryan race of humanity, the Semite must seek to become a virile man as a Jew. And virile manhood requires a consciousness of nationality which the individual acknowledges to himself and others" (76). Kohn is a Zionist in everything but name. He advocates a new nation as well as "recalling our forgotten language" (77). Here Hebrew, the new (old) language, provides a new manner of experiencing the world, a means of establishing or at least fixing the new virile man- hood that the German Jew (such as Moser) is clearly lacking. Yiddish shapes the old Jew and provides that Jew with an awareness of Jew- ish identity; the new Jew must transcend that initial identity and re- place it with a new, healthy mind and language. German, the lan- guage in which Nordau is writing, plays absolutely no role in this process since he does not consider it to be an appropriate language for the Jews. It is merely a transitional tongue, through which the au- thor can persuade his audience of its own lack of identity and lack of virility. This conflicted sense of the role that language and identity play in the drama, as in relationship to the audience's sense of its own role, is but a structural mirror of the inner conflict of the plot itself.

The inherent confusion in Nordau's play lies in the role that inter- marriage can play in the creation of this new, virile Jew. Moser con- fronts Kohn on this issue, noting that "a mixed marriage, in which you will remain a Jew and a Kohn, does not fulfill its purpose. You do not mix, you maintain the separation" (81). This is, however, a "bour- geoisie tragedy," as its subtitle announces, and Nordau is able to evoke the basic conventions of this Enlightenment genre. Kohn's an- swer falls back on the discourse of Romantic love; he acknowledges "a certain mental inconsistency . . . I love Fräulein Christine, my love is the most absolutely personal thing about me, a thing with which neither my forefathers nor my race have any connection" (83). But, of course, they do. And Nordau resolves this as German dramatists had been resolving the problem of such truly "mixed marriages" across racial (not religious) lines since the eighteenth century—the member of the "inferior" or "different" race must die.[21] (The nineteenth-century model is certainly the death of Rebecca, the daughter of Isaac of York, in Sir Walter Scott's *Ivanhoe* [1820], which precludes any misalliance with Ivanhoe.) In the end, Kohn's love for Christine is impossible, given the absolute boundaries drawn between Jew and Aryan in the drama. Even questioning these boundaries leads to the belief that Kohn is simply "manic," suffering from a "great delusion" (89). His madness is that of the feminized Jew, the Jew who has lost his virility, who is mad like a hysterical woman. As Nordau wrote to Wanda von Sacher-Masoch on June 5, 1885, about one of her novellas:

Your character Leona is the most comprehensive image of a modern hysteric, as it is to be seen in the despair of the family and the pure pleasure of the alienists and neurologists. There is only one thing wrong about your image: this type of mad woman, who cannot formulate an integrated thought can never love. They sometimes evidence sensual excitement, they often have moods, they are shameless and uncaring about the opinion of the world (as long as one cares about them!) That is the sole goal of their mad activity, but they love only one thing: themselves.[22]

In Nordau's play this is how Christine's two brothers, the offspring of the mixed marriage, are represented. But the psyche of the sister, who falls in love with Leo Kohn, is no less damaged. Kohn's love for Christine Moser, and hers for him, falls into the realm of the pathological as both confront "natural" boundaries between the Jew and the Aryan and desire to commit an unnatural act—miscegenation, in the racial terminology of nineteenth-century science. Their egoism is a pathological sign since it violates the absolute boundary established to define the Jew. The answer that Kohn suggests—that each retain his or her identity, that each remain in their own race so that their love will transcend even this difference—is confronted with his political agenda, the separation of the Jew from the body politic in Europe and the establishment of a Jewish national state. A Jewish national state in which the non-Jewish offspring of mixed marriages dominate is hardly a workable ideal. For the very fact that the children of Leo Kohn and Christine Moser would be non-Jewish by Jewish convention (as her own mother is an Aryan) would vitiate Nordau's image of the Jews as "a separate people" (77). This confusion of identity and goal underlies the conflict in the drama.

The theme of the drama becomes explicit within the nosological categories of nineteenth-century medicine. For the pun on conversion—the conversion of real memories into hysterical symptoms and the conversion of Jews into Christians—is paralleled here.[23] The model evolved by Freud and Joseph Breuer in the *Studies in Hysteria* (1895) built on the work of Jean-Martin Charcot, with whom both Freud and Nordau studied (*SE*, 2:7). Both Freud and Nordau attempted to avoid labeling the Jew as mentally ill because of his or her inherent nature or predisposition. Rather, they saw universals of experience (trauma) as the cause of the mental aberration of all human beings, including Jews. They believed that it was indeed the history of the Jew that drove him or her into acts of self-destruction, such as conversion and mixed marriage. Jews, like hysterics, suffer from reminiscences—or as the Italo-Jewish forensic psychiatrist Cesare Lombroso put it, Jews suffer from the "trauma of memory," which alters their behavior.[24] The trauma is the way Jews are treated in Western culture; the symptom is the desire to become invisible. Invisibility means either converting within the public sphere or deluding oneself into believing that there is a truly private sphere in which racial categories have no meaning.

The death of Kohn, which concludes the drama, presents a "resolution" to the question of intermarriage and conversion. But this resolution, like Moser's confusion at the end of the drama and his daughter's despair at being rejected by Leo Kohn's parents as a Christian, simply turns into reflections of the basic hysterical nature of the Jew (and his own offspring). Intermarriage and conversion are impossible and lead to death—if not the death of the individual, then, at least in the discourse of the late nineteenth and early twentieth centuries, the death of the race. Intermarriages are dangerous because they are fundamentally diseased, if not infertile. This view was common in the 1890s and after. In 1894 the philo-Semitic publishing house of J. Schabelitz in Zurich published a pamphlet with the title "The Decline of Israel," written by a "Physiologist."[25] For this scientist-as-author, the Jews as a religious community no longer existed at the fin de siècle. And thus the race itself was in danger of vanishing, for "the purpose of religion is the preservation of the race."[26] Even mixed marriage would not retard this process, for "individual marriages between Jews and Christians have little purpose physiologically and are of importance only when they lead to the addition of new blood under new circumstances. Presently this is not imaginable, since the general, national practices are now to be found among the Jews and influence their progeny exactly as they influence those of the Christian population."[27] It is not prejudice that will lead to the disappearance of the Jews (whether this is good or bad is never quite clear), but rather, the nation with which "they mix and which permits their characteristics to become lost."[28]

The widely circulated fin-de-siècle view that the Jews were in danger of vanishing was best known through the work of Felix Theilhaber in 1911.[29] Theilhaber's work on the "decline of the Jews" (its title was a prefiguration of Oswald Spengler's *Decline of the West* of 1918) presented the demographic case for the disappearance of the Western Jew in greatest detail. He accepted most of the negative evidence, including the greater incidences of disease and insanity, as signs of the Jew's degeneration. Indeed, he relied heavily on the medical authorities in evaluating the clinical status of the Jews as the object of special study, without ever drawing their findings into question. Medicine had a much greater authority for him than did other arenas of proof, such as social statistics. Central to his argument was the decline in the Jewish birthrate, which he blamed on late marriages, the emancipation of Jewish women, and mixed marriages. According to Theilhaber, mixed marriages had an especially low rate of reproduction. Indeed, he noted, if it were not for the "primitive sexuality of the *Ostjuden*," the statistics about the birthrate of the Jews in Germany would be even worse.[30] Theilhaber's view of the eventual disappearance of Western European Jewry was anticipated by the founder of German-Jewish demography, Arthur Ruppin, in 1904.[31] Ruppin warned that "there is the danger of gradual extinction" of the Western European Jews while the birthrate of Eastern European Jews continues to rise.[32]

Nordau, the Hungarian Jew, saw the potential disappearance of Western, acculturated Judaism as a reality; his Jewish critics in Germany saw things quite differently. They attacked the play vehemently, which Nordau saw as a pathological response. He wrote to Gustav G. Cohen in Hamburg on November 2, 1898, that "your comments [about *Dr. Kohn*] have to give me recompense for all of the vile insults of the critical vermin (all without exception Jews)."[33] Among these critics were the popular philosopher Fritz Mauthner and the famed literary historian Ludwig Geiger. For the overall tenor of German-Jewish culture during this period saw the debate about intermarriage as ill-suited to take place on the German stage. And Nordau's Jewish critics were especially upset at the setting of the confrontation about the social role of the Jew on the fin-de-siècle stage. But it was the undermining of a traditional theme of nineteenth-century bourgeois theater, the story of the ill-fated lovers, which engendered the most criticism. For Leo Kohn's marriage plans had to be frustrated. This is very much in terms of the Romeo and Juliet theme of the play, which was much loved on the German stage of the late nineteenth century.

But the ostensible theme of the drama, the difficulty of marriage between a Jew and an Aryan, reveals itself to be but window dressing. Nordau's hidden theme is the immutability of Jewish identity and the impossibility of any interracial marriage. The model for the failed attempt is not the relationship between Leo Kohn and Christine Moser, but the marriage of Christine Moser's own parents, which leads to the completely confused identity of the children. For all three children—the two sons, who become virulent antisemites like their uncle and their fraternity brothers, and the daughter, who is completely unclear about who she is—reflect the model that the children of mixed marriages are neurotic. For as the products of a mixed marriage, all these children are disturbed because they cannot acknowledge their confusion over their own hidden identities.

Nordau's views on marriage between Jews and Aryans reflect his literary construction of national identity. His own relationship to a non-Jewish Danish woman (Anna) who had borne him a child (Maxa) a year before their marriage seemed not to be reflected in his rejection of mixed marriages. In his memoirs, which were rewritten and partially compiled by his widow after his death, Nordau's drama is represented as an objection to mixed marriages "in German society, which is still dominated by anti-Semitism. His own marriage—which was in no way diminished in relationship to race and religion—permitted him to recognize that a mixed marriage could be harmonious, but elsewhere, such as in Germany, he saw such cases as unsuccessful."[34] Nordau's own ambiguity (and/or that of his Aryan, non-Jewish widow) saw the problems resulting from mixed marriages as existing exclusively in German society, with its powerful image of the primitive nature of the Eastern Jew. Nordau was an Eastern Jew, and he saw this image as reflecting on his control of his own sexuality. It was only in this construction of Germany that all his own anxieties about his identity as an Eastern Jew could be played out safely. His own mixed marriage becomes a surrogate for his ability to transcend the identity superimposed upon him by the German literary culture with which he closely identified.

The Mind of the Jew

The question of conversion and the definition of the Jew that were made ambiguous in Nordau's *Dr. Kohn* appeared in quite another context during World War I. Nordau, in *Dr. Kohn*, identified the double bind of the modern Jew, a double bind that leads to madness and death. But what is the nature of the psychic processes that enable the Jewish psyche to become so deformed? In 1918, driven from Paris as an enemy alien (because he was born in the dual monarchy), Nordau took refuge in Madrid. There he provided the *American Jewish Chronicle* with a detailed reading of the "Psychology of the Anti-Zionist," as his article was titled.[35] Nordau saw the anti-Zionist as still captured by the mentality of the ghetto: "They tremble before their own shadow and are permanently haunted by the dread lest the people in the midst of which they dwell might come down upon them when they least expect it, deprive them of their rights, expel them" (8). The result of the Jews' inherent insecurity and their dependency on the national identity of the people among whom they live is that the Jew has "a complete inner estrangement from his stock, the extrication from every tradition, the eradication from the historical past, and a dismal impoverishment of his subconscious, the principal contents of which are formed by hereditary concepts and collective imagination, and our impulses for action" (7). This definition of the Jew is very much in line with Freud's own comments.

In 1926, Freud stated in an address to the B'nai B'rith, upon being honored for his seventieth birthday, that being Jewish is sharing "many obscure emotional forces (*viele dunkle Gefühlsmächte*), which were the more powerful the less they could be expressed in words, as well as a clear consciousness of inner identity, the safe privacy of a common mental construction (*die Heimleichkeit der gleichen seelischen Identität*).["][36] His contemporaries, such as Theodor Reik (along with Freud and Eduard Hintschmann, the only psychoanalysts to be members of the B'nai B'rith) "were especially struck" by these very words as the appropriate central definition of the Jew.[37]

Freud's version of the ethnopsychology of the Jew twisted Gustav Le Bon's claims concerning the biology of race.[38] It evoked the Lamarckianism of William James's view of the transmission of "the same emotional propensities, the same habits, the same instincts, perpetuated without variation from one generation to another."[39] The uncanny nature of the known but repressed aspects of an individual's psyche—about which Freud wrote in his essay on the uncanny—haunted Freud's image of the internal mental life defining the Jew. (Here it is the "uncanny" [*unheimlich*] that domesticates the "canny" [*heimlich*] nature of Jewish identity.) One of Freud's models is the ethnopsychology of the Jew, that is, that there is a racial memory existing in each generation. He observed (concerning "the uncanny associated with the omnipotence of thoughts") that "we—or our primitive forefathers—once believed that these possibilities were realities, and were convinced that they actually happened. . . . As soon as something actually happens in our lives which seems to confirm the old, discarded beliefs we get a feeling of the uncanny."[40]

It is the affirmation through daily events—such as the exposure to antisemitism—that revivifies the group memory, confirming the "common mental construction" of the Jew. This does not take place on the rational level, but within the unconscious. As Freud wrote to his Viennese and Jewish "double," Arthur Schnitzler, "Judaism continues to mean much to me on an emotional level."[41] It was the return of the repressed—not the ancient traditions of religious identity, but the suppressed discourse of antisemitism, expressed by Freud within the model of racial memory—that haunted Freud. He, like Nordau, articulated this discourse of the Jew's difference within the phylogenetic model of the inheritance of racial memory.

Nordau's "anti-Zionist" lacks any connection to this Jewish psyche. In denying the Jewish psyche, the anti-Zionist becomes the lying Jew of the antisemitic stereotype: "They falsified our opinions, distorted our ideas, threw suspicion on our motives, spread lies about our ways and aims, and libeled our person" (7). The anti-Zionists remain "crippled Ghetto souls" who suffer from a "cowardly anguish" (8). They can only "whine and abuse" (8). For their imagination is affected by the suffering of the European Jews of the Middle Ages:

> In their feeling, their imagination, they live in the middle-age, somewhere about the eleventh century, and their permanent nightmare is that a Jewish Palestine, a Jewish nation in a Palestinian Jewish country, might give the impulse to withdraw from these "free men" the tolerance in the free countries. . . . They are panic-stricken and revive in their imaginations the scenes their ancestors have passed through during the crusades in the Jewries of Rhenish towns. (8)

Thus, Nordau's Jews remain fixated at an earlier stage of development. They are pathological because their Jewish consciousness was shaped—and remained shaped—by the experience of European Jewry. Nordau was implicitly evoking the return to the model of the Jewish national consciousness during the period of a Jewish national state. This return to Zion—as a secular state of mind—was for Nordau a definition of the healthy Jew. For Freud the "common mental construction" of the Jew encompassed all positive aspects of cultural identity. Both Freud and Nordau defined conversion as a psychological process of devaluation of the self: for Freud as for Nordau these are pathological states. Nordau saw the anti-Zionist as the convert, not as a convert to Christianity, but as a pathological Jew who has been so cowed by the experience of German antisemitism (and that is *his* example) that he is unable to function as a healthy member of modern society. The healthy Jew is the Zionist; the sick Jew the anti-Zionist, who has been corrupted by the Christian world. All returns to the model of the convert as "pervert." And both of these Eastern Jews, Max Nordau and Sigmund Freud, position themselves carefully within the constraints of the scientific debate about race at the fin de siècle, transforming the debate into a positive discourse about Jewish identity.

Freud and the Idea of Conversion in Psychoanalysis

The rejection of conversion by even "godless" Jews such as Max Nordau and Sigmund Freud seems to point to the need to comprehend the separateness of the Jew as positive. Being centered within one's race came to have a positive quality, since escaping one's racial fate was an impossibility. As we have discussed, the labeling of converts as "sick" becomes a widely used trope of the fin-de-siècle. Indeed, there is a large literature that discusses the question of conversion and the resulting mixed marriage in purely medical/pathological terms.[42] Conversion is rarely, if ever, understood as an act of belief.[43] It is a sign of psychopathology.

Fritz Wittels, who later became Freud's first biographer, authored a study of the "baptized Jew" in 1904. Wittels stressed the fact that the Jew's desire for baptism was a neurosis and rejected conversion as a matter of convenience.[44] The German-Jewish novelist Ernst Lissauer commented that "baptism, following the bureaucratic rules which declare the Jewish faith as an obstacle to promotion, is merely joining the state church, it is an official, not a confessional act."[45] For Wittels, such a "baptized Jew" was a congenital liar who showed a form of "ethical insanity." Or, as the French historian Anatole Leroy-Beaulieu wrote in 1893, "the de-judaised Jews are, in too many cases, lacking in moral feeling."[46] The implications of the Jew's *Mauscheln* (or speaking German with a Yiddish intonation or vocabulary), the corrosive and corroding nature of the Jew's discourse, has pathological significance here as a sign of the "diseased" Jew, the Jewish convert. But for Wittels it was not enthusiasm that marked the psychopathology of conversion, but rather, the highly manipulative, self-serving rational psyche of the convert. Thus, although he excluded only artists and lovers from the psychopathological category of the convert (because they are irrational anyhow), he saw all other converts as suffering from a form of mental illness.

For Wittels, the baptized Jews were similar to Lombroso's born criminals. They showed an innate pathology: "He lies without having the feeling that it is something dishonest."[47] Wittels did believe, in the abstract, that a Jew could convert for reasons of belief. But he attested to knowing no one of this type personally.[48] True believers are usually the ill, women, and children.[49] The ultimate form of the convert is the self-hating Jew, the outsider, who hates the duplicity of his fellow Jews. The self-hating Jew internalizes the "sense of the slave" that stigmatizes the Jew in Christian society.[50] "Such rabble only poisons the well."[51] This view was echoed in the image evoked by the German-American psychiatrist Ernst Harms, who reported

the case of a Jew whom he saw in an asylum "in the state of almost total amnesia, who kept on crossing himself. I was assured that he was
not Catholic, but had great difficulties in socialization." For Harms,
this image of the demented Jew crossing himself was proof of the
"impossibility of adapting to a new system, as the conscious mind is
still bound to the older life-forms."[52] The conflict that results in the
self-hating or mad Jew is between the innate "common mental construction" of the Jew and his desire to submit to the societal pressure
to convert and stop being a Jew. Because this is impossible, given the
innate nature of the Jew, the sole resolution is madness.

At the meeting of the Viennese Psychoanalytic Society on December 9, 1908, Wittels recounted a case of a patient who had come to
him specifically because of Wittels's publication of his work on baptized Jews, Jews trying to pass as Christians. The patient was a young
man of about thirty who suffered from "anti-Semitic persecution, for
which he holds his inconspicuously Semitic nose responsible. He
therefore plans to have the shape of his nose changed by plastic
surgery."[53] Wittels and his patient lived in an age that embraced the
semiotics of the nose, according to their contemporary, Rudolf Kleinpaul. Every race could be read in the nose, including the "Jewish
ram's nose."[54] Wittels attempted to persuade him that his anxiety
about his nose was merely a displacement for anxiety about his sexual
identity. "This the patient declared to be a good joke." The obvious
analogy in Wittels's suggestions does not occur to him. If a patient
comes to him expressly because of his writing about the neurosis of
conversion, if he wishes to have his nose rebuilt to hide his Jewishness, then the question of his own "paranoid" relationship to his circumcised penis, that invisible but omnipresent sign of the male's Jewishness, is evident. Freud picked up on this directly and noted that
"the man is evidently unhappy about being a Jew and wants to be
baptized." "At this point Wittels remarks that the patient is an ardent
Jew. Nevertheless, he does not undergo baptism. In this fact lies the
conflict that has absorbed the meaning of other conflicts." To be a
Jew and to be so intensely fixated on the visibility of that identity is
to be ill.

Wittels then revealed the name of the patient to the group, and
Freud recognized from the name that the patient's father was an engaged Zionist. Freud then read the patient's desire to unmake himself

as a Jew as a sign that he was rejecting his father. Freud, however, did not comment on the link between strong Jewish identity and the rejection of the visibility which that identity entailed. There was a real sense that the Jewish body, represented by the nose, could never truly be changed.

Conversion becomes a sign of pathology that has its roots in the "common mental construction" of the Jews. This view was seconded by the physician Felix Goldmann in Oppeln, who in 1912 provided a historical study of the pathology of conversion among the Jews.[55] Goldmann not only listed in great detail the infamous history of baptized Jews, who were active in attacks on Jews and their religious and social institutions, but he also attributed the reappearance of the "blood libel" in the nineteenth century to two baptized Jews, Paulus Meyer and "Dr. Justus," that is, Aaron Brimann. Goldmann raised the question of the pathology of these actions and pointed to a series of such figures who were active in the antisemitic movement of the times, such as Robert Jaffé (a co-worker of Theodor Fritsch, the editor of the most notorious antisemitic newspaper at the turn of the century) and Maximilian Harden (born Isidor Witkowski), editor of the muckraking journal *The Future*. Goldmann saw these converts not only as unethical and immoral but as diseased.

This creation of a pathologized, lying Jew, a Jew whose diseased psyche is exposed in his words as well as in his actions, is reflected in Freud's image of the Eastern Jew. This image of the Eastern Jews' difference is also reflected in Max Nordau's representation of Leo Kohn's parents in his 1899 drama. And it is, of course, the enthusiastic Eastern Jew who forms the basis for the popular Christian image of the convert. In a letter written to Wilhelm Fliess during April 1898, Freud referred to his brother-in-law, Moriz Freud (a distant cousin who married his sister Marie), as a "half-Asian" who suffers from "pseudologica fantastica."[56] He is "half-Asian" because he is from Bucharest, and the disease he is said to suffer from is the psychiatric label for those mythomaniac patients who lie in order to gain status. "Pseudologica fantastica" is a syndrome in which "an extraordinary vanity forms the motor, the need for the extraordinary, the need to appear more than one is, to have experienced more than one has, more than one can experience in the course of daily life. . . . The pleasure, which accompanies such vacillation, is so great that it cannot be controlled, even when the substance of the lie is immediately evident; it is simply impossible for such characters to stay with the truth."[57] Sufferers of this condition commit acts such as stock fraud, confidence games, "lying and swindling"—all traditionally associated with Jews in the forensic literature of the period.[58] The sign of this form of madness can already be found early in the developmental cycle "when teenagers and high school students send themselves anonymous love letters, correspond with one another with pompous sounding pseudonyms, indulge in secret societies, etc." Such a diagnosis "in ethically inferior individuals . . . predestines the individual to the speciality of a common criminal, as an international confidence man." It is such an individual who can be converted to Christianity.

But such a description—from the scientific claims of psychoanalysis, to the youthful correspondence between Freud and his childhood friend, Eduard Silberstein (often written in schoolboy Spanish and signed with their highly literary pseudonyms), to the "scientific congresses" of Freud and Wilhelm Fliess—seems to take the hidden measure of another Eastern European Jew, Sigmund Freud. Indeed, the proposal at the turn of the century that there was a typical "Jewish psychosis" was couched in terms that are redolent of Freud's representation of his brother-in-law. This psychosis consisted of a markedly "Jewish argumentativeness" as well as an overly critical rationality that "draws everything into question."[59] Equally important, Freud diagnosed the three daughters (his cousins) as "hysterical," "the youngest, a rather gifted child, severely so. I doubt the father is innocent in this case either." The father's "guilt," like the guilt Freud attributed to his own father, lies in his Eastern Jewish identity, in the taint of Jewishness passed on from one generation to another.[60] Hysteria is a potential reflex of being an Eastern European Jew (like Freud and his cousins), and it manifests itself in hysterical actions—such as conversion.

Freud rejected conversion, even though he was tempted by its promise. His fascination with conversion—as a personal as well as a professional choice—stayed with him his entire life. He himself noted this in his own interpretation of his Hannibal dream.[61] But Freud never converted, and indeed, he stressed this fact in his autobiography. What did conversion mean for Freud? In a letter to Max Graf, the father of "Little Hans," Freud argued that having Graf's son baptized would not change his essential "Jewishness": "If you do not let your son grow up as a Jew, you will deprive him of those sources of energy which cannot be replaced by anything else. He will have to struggle as a Jew, and you ought to develop in him all the energy he will need for that struggle. Do not deprive him of that advantage."[62] Being a Jew is being a member of a race, possessing a "common mental construction." In a powerful letter from Paris in 1886 to his fiancée, Martha, Freud recounted that he found himself confronted with his own Jewish identity, as an inheritance of "all the obstinate defiance and all the passions with which our ancestors defended their Temple." He saw himself as a "Jew, who is neither German nor Austrian."[63] If anything, the pressures he perceived in the world of science made it clear to him that conversion was neither a practical nor a realistic alternative to remaining a "godless Jew."

Freud's own most detailed analysis of the meaning of conversion appeared in his analytic response to a letter he received from an American colleague upon the publication of his interview with the German-American newspaperman George Sylvester Viereck in 1926. The letter, as Freud described it, recounted a conversion episode in which the American physician, as a young medical student, was confronted for the first time with a corpse in the dissecting room, overcame his horror of death, and accepted the truth of Christianity. Such tales were typical of the conversion literature of the period. What made this story unique was its medical setting.

Freud answered this missive by stating that he had never heard such an "inner voice" and that at his advanced age, if God did not hurry, "it would not be my fault if I remained to the end of my life what I now was—'an infidel Jew.'"[64] (The latter phrase Freud cited in English from the physician's letter. Freud's own sense of a lack of religious mission is echoed in the opening of his *Civilization and Its Discontents* [1930].)[65] The tone of Freud's response was ironic; but his correspondent's response was anything but: "In the course of a friendly reply, my colleague gave me an assurance that being a Jew was not an obstacle in the pathway to true faith and proved this by several instances. His letter culminated in the information that prayers were being earnestly addressed to God that he might grant me 'faith to believe.'"[66] Here the conflict is outlined: the Jew who did not see his Judaism as a religion but as a "common mental construction" was confronted by a Christian who not only wished him to convert, but who presented him with cases of Jews who have converted. Thus, we have an answer to the immutability of the racial definition of the Jew—Jews who can truly become Christians in spite of their Jewish mindset.

Freud's response to this call for conversion was to examine the conversion episode as a neurotic break and to relate it to the Oedipus complex. As we have seen, the medical literature of the fin de siècle viewed the convert as a psychopath. The American physician's faith had been cast in doubt when he saw the body of a "sweet-faced dear old woman" brought into the dissecting room. Freud read his response to "the sight of a woman's dead body, naked or on the point of being stripped" as a "longing for his mother which sprang from his Oedipus complex." (One also sees here Freud's own childhood experience with his family servant and his belief that she attempted to convert him.) The physician's oedipal experience triggered anger and fear of his father, which was translated into a rejection of the deity. This displacement into the discourse of religion had nothing, according to Freud, to do with the rational mind: "The conflict seems to have been unfolded in the form of a hallucinatory psychosis: inner voices were heard which uttered warnings against resistance to God."[67] Conversion becomes a psychosis, reflecting the universal model of the Oedipus complex, and resolves itself in the "complete submission to the will of God the Father."[68]

Here the tensions concerning the nature of the Jew's conversion are laid out in detail. True conversion, as advocated by enthusiasts, is at best a neurosis; Jewish converts who dissimulate conversion are pathological. Conversion is a symptom of psychopathology, at least if we follow Freud's rhetoric. His own attraction to the prospect of conversion, at least as a child, was itself tied to the image of an old woman seen naked. In his reading of Freud's paper, Theodor Reik stressed the "intimate connection between the peeping impulse and desire for knowledge, the investigatory impulse."[69] But we can also evoke the special status of both Freud and Reik, who were seeing as scientists rather than as children or as Jews.

The very scenario that Freud evokes is not only a personal one, but given his own professional identification with the dissecting room, one that reflects his own sense of professional identity and the antisemitism that he associated with his medical career.[70] Freud's response not only rejected religious faith—this was to be expected—but cast the very idea of conversion in the pathological terms of the medical literature of his day. The image of the psychopathological convert was evoked by his correspondent's serious claim that his racial identity as a Jew would not stand in the way of his conversion. The "common mental construction" of the Jew appeared in the most direct manner unaffected by the argument. Freud was quite prepared to turn this claim into the material for analysis of the neurotic text.

Freud's reading during this period concerned the link between conversion and the pathological Jew. In his library is the German translation of the Soviet Slavist Leonid Grossmann's documentary study of the relationship of Fyodor Mikhaylovich Dostoyevsky to Abraham Urija Kowner, a.k.a. Albert Kowner.[71] (This volume was part of the series of Dostoyevsky translations for which Freud's own "Dostoyevsky and Parricide" had served as introduction to an earlier volume.)[72] Kowner, an Eastern European Jew born in Vilnius, was raised within the strict tradition of Eastern Jewish orthodoxy. Like many Eastern European Jews for whom the Enlightenment ideal of acculturation still existed in the mid-nineteenth century, he painstakingly (and against the wishes of his family and community) acquired a Russian education. He became a journalist, one of the few professions open to (and strongly associated with) the Jews. In 1871 he moved to St. Petersburg, where he became extremely well known as an advocate of liberal causes. In 1875 he was arrested for, and convicted of, passing a bad check for 160,000 rubles; he was sent to prison and then into exile in Siberia. From Siberia he wrote to Dostoyevsky, whose powerful antisemitic views had been echoed in his own journalism. Given the nature of Kowner's crime and the length, detail, and intensity of his correspondence, he would have fit the contemporary clinical definition of the individual suffering from "pseudologica fantastica." He was a "mad" Jew, and he showed it in all of his actions and statements.

Dostoyevsky entered into a public exchange of letters with Kowner, who converted to Dostoyevsky's political and religious views. Kowner was dismissed by his Jewish contemporaries as a "convert, a braggart, and an apostate," but remained a presence in Russian intellectual life until the beginning of the next century.[73] Kowner served the Russian intelligentsia as an example of the Jew who achieves insight into his own Jewishness yet still remains Jewish in all his qualities. The editor of this volume, Leonid Grossmann, labeled him the Russian equivalent to Otto Weininger, who had also acquired true insight into the "common mental construction" of the Jew.[74] Freud would have read this case quite differently—as an example of the impossibility of conversion. He would have counted Kowner as a self-destructive, self-hating, insane Jew. But he would have also sensed the interchangeability of Kowner and all Jews. Not only does he come to represent the intellectual Jew in Dostoyevsky's text, but "when Kowner's portrait was published in a widely circulated German magazine [*Kladderdatsch* (May 23, 1875)], a totally innocent Jew was arrested in Berlin."[75] All Jews come to be seen as criminals. Their criminality is written on their physiognomy. It is precisely the image of the Jews as inherently visible in Western society—no matter how they attempt to mask their invisibility—that is reflected in Max Nordau's drama *Dr. Kohn*.

Freud was not the only Jewish psychoanalyst confronted by the psychic conflicts arising from conversion. In Theodor Reik's 1914 version of the case of "Dora," his pseudonym for his fiancée, the nature of religious interest and psychopathology were linked. Dora's father was a "fanatical anti-Semite" and her mother "an apostate from Judaism."[76] Both opposed her relationship to the Jewish psychoanalyst. Reik needed to understand their feelings, "hypothesizing that the anti-Semitism of persons with neurotic tendencies is due in large measure to a transference of hostile feelings from their closest relatives (father, wife, etc.)." In other words, the father's all-consuming hatred of him was the result of his relationship with his own father or with his converted Jewish wife, as Reik later surmises in his autobiography.[77] This is the origin of the neurosis that is labeled anti-semitism. Unlike such neurotic antisemites, Jews themselves have split the "ambivalent attitude meant for the father. The deprecatory and antagonistic tendency now is directed against the religion, which is regarded as obsolete and superfluous, while the affectionate and delicate current flows toward the Jewish people to which the young Jewish generation in Western countries adheres with great pride (Zionism, Jewish nationalism.)" Reik sees the rejection of religious identity as part of the splitting of the healthy from the unhealthy self.

The healthy Jew is the national rather than the religious Jew. Religion in all forms is unhealthy. But Reik's example is one in which the hatred caused by the wife, a convert, is transferred to the Jews as a group. Antisemitism is an Aryan disease. Here the cause of this disease, unlike in Freud's comment, is the convert, the "apostate." She becomes the source of the antisemite's hatred; her failure causes the rejection of the Jews. According to Reik, the Jew's (always the male Jew's) religious identity is shaped by this "relationship with his father." Reik's view of the convert is that her presence has destroyed his relationship with his potential father-in-law.

Freud's own views echoed this position. In a discussion with Professor S. Ehrmann after a meeting of the Vienna Lodge of B'nai B'rith, Freud got into an intense discussion with a lodge brother who advocated conversion as a personal act, if it enabled one to "fulfill life's goal, one which would otherwise have to be abandoned," such as "assuming a leadership function in the arts, sciences, or politics." Freud dismissed this out of hand, noting that such an act was never a private one since it "endangered the common interest." It was unfair for the state to demand "that a member of a specific confession of a tribal community . . . deny his origin and his belief" without demanding this action from everyone. Such a demand would create "a common right *via facti* which would be a denial of the rights of everyone."[78] This is Nordau's claim when Leo Kohn confronts the president of the university who has denied him a professorship in mathematics because he will not convert: "We imagine that, in our character of human beings, we have a full claim to all human rights, and you are convinced that you are showing us a favor when you recognize Jews as human beings. Your silent assumption is that the Jew does not possess the dignity of human nature naturally, but obtains it first when your favor explicitly bestows it upon him" (45). Freud's refusal to permit any type of conversion was an acknowledgment of the strengths of the Jews' "tribal community" as a collective. He was not opposed to mixed marriages, but he thought that they should not lead to conversion: "a Jew ought not to get himself baptized and attempt to turn Christian because it is essentially dishonest, and the Christian religion is every bit as bad as the Jewish. Jew and Christian ought to meet on the common ground of irreligion and humanity. Jews who are ashamed of their Jewishness have simply reacted to the mass suggestion of their society."[79] Freud rejected Judaism as a religion at the same moment when he saw the immutability of a "common mental construction" of the Jews. Intermarriage could no more obliterate this construction than could conversion.

Freud's attitude toward the nature of the convert and the meaning of conversion paralleled that of Max Nordau. The emphasis on a secular Judaism of the spirit, in which neither conversion nor intermarriage is permitted, is central to both of their views. Each sees the question from the standpoint of Eastern European Jews who, by the rigid standards of the times, could never truly become part of Western culture. For both, and for many other Jews of fin-de-siècle medical culture, their alienation is not a reflection of their bodies—that is, of their biological identity as Jews—but of their psyches, the ethnopsychology of the Jew. In this way the fantasy of the immutability of Jewish character negatively projected onto the heterogeneous mass of European Jewry by the antisemitic rhetoric of the fin de siècle is transmuted into a positive sense of the "common mental construction" of the Jew. And yet the conclusion drawn from this is precisely that which is seen as the cause of the psychopathology of the Jew: marriage within the race or faith. Having a solution that negates the source of the psychological problems of the Jew presents a trope of resistance for Nordau and Freud. The Jewish mind, established through this model of sexual selectivity, can even transcend the trauma of the ghetto. Freud and Nordau see marriage outside the race as the sign of the psychopathology of the Jew.

CHAPTER FOUR

Salome, Syphilis, Sarah Bernhardt, and the "Modern Jewess"

A Problem with the Gendering of Stereotypes

One of the most fascinating problems with tracing the stereotype of the Jew in fin-de-siècle German culture is the evident difference that gender makes in the visibility of the Jew. Among Jewish and non-Jewish writers there is no question that representations of Jewish men are immediately and always identifiable. The stereotypical representation of the male Jew may try to hide or disguise his identity, but eventually, for good or for ill, he is revealed. In this German fantasy of difference, whether positive or negative, the Jewish male body is indelibly marked and is therefore always recognizable.[1] And it seems to make little difference whether the authors employing these stereotypes are male or female, Jewish or non-Jewish. The stereotypical representation of Jewish women, on the other hand, seems often to be ambiguously identifiable.[2]

When Jewish women are represented in the culture of the turn of the century, the qualities ascribed to the Jew and to the woman seem to exist simultaneously, and yet they seem mutually exclusive, much like M. C. Escher's merging and emerging image of fishes and birds: when we focus on the one, the other seems to vanish. It is clear that neither the qualities ascribed to "sexuality" nor those ascribed to "race" are primary in the construction of these images. Rather, qualities from each constructed category reinforce those ascribed to the Other. Central to the arbitrary but powerful differentiation between the stereotype of the Jewish man and that of the Jewish woman is the different meaning of male and female sexuality at the fin de siècle. And yet, these very qualities ascribed to sexuality are analogous to those ascribed to "race."

What I will be illustrating in this essay is the construction of antithetical images of the male and the female Jew at the turn of the century in German culture. The relationship between the stereotype of the Jew (defined as male) and that of the woman (as parallel categories to the Christian and the male but different from the male Jew) becomes a central element in the structuring of Jewish identity. Neither one of these images reflects an unmediated conceptual category. Each is constructed to present a means of influencing aspects of a world understood as out of control. It is not that these two stereotypes are equivalent, even though they undergo certain similar shifts at the close of the nineteenth century. The feminine is primarily an inclusionary stereotype. Woman is not the opposite of man, but rather, is reduced to his complement. For, in the eye of the male, there can be no reproduction without woman; thus, woman must be in many ways a protected category. The stereotype is that women are weak, while men are strong; they are intuitive rather than intelligent, and so forth. It is only in the work of a very few individuals of the time, such as Arthur Schopenhauer or P. G. Möbius, who either did not wish to, or could not, sustain relationships with women, that the woman becomes a totally expendable category.

By the nineteenth century, the fixed relationships of the empowered male to the stereotype of the woman (as a conceptual category) had indeed become strained. Rather than being perceived as purely inclusionary, threatening aspects of this category come to be marginalized. Thus, the intellectual woman, seen as the antithesis to the reproductive expectations of the male, is viewed as sterile; the prostitute, seen as a threat to the male because of his anxiety about sexually transmitted disease, is viewed as destructive, as criminal. But these conceptual categories, extensions of the image of the introjected "bad" Other, are always linked to the image of the "good" (m)Other, as the stereotypical caregiver. Here is where the inclusionary image of the woman is most powerful.

Jews, on the other hand, have been historically classified as an inclusionary category with a status analogous to that of the woman. (The "Jew" is always defined as a masculine category.) As long as Christians viewed themselves in some way as the extension and fulfillment of the Jew, they needed the Jew to be within their conceptual framework. The Jew was that historical element against which they could define themselves; the Jew was that which they had been and were no longer. The "Synagogue" was thus old, while the "Church" was young. But even this theological model always portrayed the female Jew as inherently different from male Jews, yet also different from the ideal feminine. Vicomte Chateaubriand wrote, in his *Essay on English Literature* (1825), that "Jewesses have escaped from the curse of their race. None of them were to be found in the crowd that insulted the Son of Man. . . . The reflection of some beautiful ray will have rested on the forehead of Jewesses."[3] "I hate Jews because they crucified Christ," said the anti-Dreyfusard Paul Bourget at the end of the nineteenth century. "I adore Jewesses because they wept for him."[4]

However, with the secularization of the image of the (male) Jew (now the antithesis of the constructed image of the Aryan), there is no longer any need for the parallelism of the Jew to the Christian. The Jew becomes an exclusionary category. The (male) Jew defines what the Aryan is *not—and never will be*. The Jew becomes the projection of *all* the anxieties about control within the Aryan. There is no need to "protect" aspects of this image, as there is no necessary link between the male Jew and the Aryan male like there was between the male and the female.

Indeed, even as the categories of the "prostitute" and the "bluestocking" at the fin de siècle came to represent those aspects of the feminine that provoked anxiety (and that are therefore masculinized), the circumcised Jew came to represent the anxiety-provoking masculine.[5] This image of the Jew was also closely tied to anxiety about syphilis, for circumcision was understood in nineteenth-century discourse about hygiene as a prophylaxis against sexually transmitted diseases. The male Jew becomes inherently "bad" as the image of those projected aspects of a world out of control and threatening to the integrity of the Aryan. As a result, the difference of the Jewish male body and mind from those of the Aryan becomes absolute within the Western tradition. One can observe how the very body of the male Jew becomes the image of the anxiety generated by the potential sense of the loss of control, a loss that replicates and evokes the initial construction of the division between the "bad" and the "good" Other.

The male Jew's compromised masculinity, his "femininity," is one of his defining qualities. He is not quite a man, and yet, certainly, he is also not a woman in the inclusionary sense. He is constructed as a "third sex." The male Jew is thus separate and distinct from either the internal representation of masculinity or of femininity. And, indeed, when we examine Jewish self-representations of masculinity at the turn of the century, the problem of self-questioning of masculinity seems always to be present. Yet the femininity of the Jewish woman, that anomalous category of the fin de siècle, seems to be accentuated in this model. The Jewish woman is essentially the exclusionary feminine or its countertype. As in the German proverb "God created the Jew in anger; the Jewess in wrath," the Jewess is even worse than the Jew.[6] Antisemites such as H. G. Nordmann could write, in 1883, that "the Jewish nature of a woman is even more repellent than that in a man, it is even more unfeminine than it is inhumane."[7]

I intend to examine the construction of the image of the Jewish woman in this double perspective and to ask under what circumstances do her "Jewishness" and her "femininity" become her defining moment. To do so I will construct a set of specific moments in one of the master narratives of this stereotype at the fin de siècle, the story of Salome. I want to understand how the exclusionary stereotype of Jewishness, with its evocation of the "third sex," is transmuted into an image of the feminine. I shall examine how antisemitic turn-of-the-century non-Jewish male authors construct the image of Salome as the essential "woman" and simultaneously evoke this image in representing the essential "Jew." This will lead me to ask how such a conflation of images was dealt with by a Jewish woman writer of the turn of the century in her construction of the "modern Jewess." These alterations and this transmutation are two constant and interrelated markers of difference in fin-de-siècle German and Austrian thought—the nature of the Jew's language and its function as a marker of Jewish sexuality—and they serve to mask and highlight the difference in the gendering of the stereotypes.

Salome and Syphilis

In 1930, Hans F. K. Günther, one of the leading anthropologists of the Weimar academy, published his full-scale *Anthropology of the Jews*.[8] Günther had begun work on this topic in an appendix to an earlier work on general anthropology (first published in 1922), which saw the Jews as a specific subset of the human race deserving or requiring special consideration. Although much attention had been given to the anthropology of the Jew in Jewish, non-Jewish, and indeed in antisemitic writing at the fin de siècle, Günther's work came to be regarded as the standard work on the anthropology of the Jews, especially in the Third Reich. This work consisted of a survey of the history and culture of the Jews as well as a detailed presentation of the physical anthropology of the Jew. As with most nineteenth- and early-twentieth-century anthropologists, Günther focused on those qualities of all Jews, both male and female, that set the Jew apart from all other human beings. Thus, in his chapter on the special nature of the Jewish voice, Günther observed that the speech of the Jew, male or female, is set apart from that of all other peoples. The *Mauscheln* of the Jews, according to a standard German dictionary cited by him, is the "presence in language of unique Jewish elements."[9] In the same paragraph, Günther called upon the theologian Johann Jakob Schudt, the late-seventeenth-century Orientalist who was *the* authority on the difference of the Jews for his time and who saw *Mauscheln* as the "unique accent of pronunciation and elocution of language which betrays a Jew the moment he opens his mouth."[10] The language of all Jews, male and female, as much as any other physical sign, marked Jewish difference at the fin de siècle.

But the most important authority for Günther's proof of Jewish difference was Richard Wagner, who characterized the special language of the Jews as found especially in the "song, as the song is the language spoken in the most extreme passions."[11] The world of German high culture in the nineteenth century was seen as the least accessible sphere of society open to Jews. Wagner explained *Mauscheln*, especially in musical form, as the sign that all Jews, male and female, no matter how long they have lived in a land, will always speak its language as an outsider. For Günther, the specific nature of Jewish speech revealed itself especially in the sung voice, an example not only of Jewish difference but also of its difference in a world—that of the arts—to which the Jews cannot belong. Günther found the clearest representation of Wagner's theoretical statement in a later musical text. It is Richard Strauss's opera *Salome* (1905), specifically the "contested conversation among the five Jews, which is an attempt to represent the *Mauscheln* of excited Jews in artistic form" (255).

Günther thought not only that all Jews spoke differently because of the "alien" world of European high culture in which they could not truly function but also, according to a medical authority of the day, because their "muscles, which are used for speaking and laughing, are used inherently differently from those of Christians, and this use can be traced . . . to the great difference in their nose and chin."[12] The difference of the Jew's language is reflected in the special nature of the Jew's body—a major factor in the structuring of Günther's argument. Language use, especially language use as it relates to high culture, reveals (because of the very truth value of high culture) the essential nature of all Jews, at least according to the neoclassical aesthetics to which much of German conservative society of the fin de siècle subscribed. Thus, the Jew's language is a marker of the Jew's difference from the male "Aryan" (Günther himself), who clearly, in the writing of his scholarly monograph, had control over the discourse of science and culture.

Without being familiar with Günther's argument, I independently reconstructed the image of the corrosive, contentious, debating male Jew in Strauss's *Salome*.[13] But there is a corollary question that stems from Günther's reading (and my reconstruction of its context): Why are only the males, the five argumentative Jews and King Herod, seen as racial representatives of the Jews in Richard Strauss's opera? Or rather, why are the other members of the royal family, Herodias and Salome—Jews by inheritance and ritual in the legend—not represented or understood by Strauss's German contemporaries as Jews?[14] The very claim that the voice of *all* Jews marks the Jew as different should include Salome and Herodias in the category of the Jews. This exemption of the female court members from consideration as prototypical, stereotyped Jews clearly reflects an early-twentieth-century German reading of Strauss's *Salome*, which is remarkably different from the American reception of the opera. Richard Aldrich, the first *New York Times* reviewer, commented that all of *Salome* was "a picture set in the time of Jewish decadence and the Roman domination."[15]

I would like to argue that the German reading of Oscar Wilde's *Salome* did contain a stereotypical image of Salome and Herodias as Jewish women. Yet the reading of this image was so closely linked to the general qualities ascribed to the "feminine" at the fin de siècle that later writers such as Hans Günther could not see the specially Jewish aspects of the figures.[16] Here we have a classic case of the simultaneous yet exclusionary existence of two related images of difference — the femme fatale and the *belle juive* — which usually function in two different cultural contexts, the one misogynist, the other antisemitic. The danger of the Jewish woman is analogous to that danger ascribed to the "bluestocking" and the "prostitute." In Strauss and Günther's reading of Oscar Wilde's drama, what dominates the representation of the women is their femininity. Prior to Strauss's setting of his edited version of a contemporary translation of Wilde's drama, there was a widely read drama, Oskar Panizza's *The Council of Love* (1895), in which the figure of Salome was introduced as an image of female corruption closely associated with, yet contrasted to, the image of the Jewish male. It is in this text that the implied qualities of the "woman" and "Jew" present in Strauss's reading of Wilde can be examined.

The Salome legend as the representation of the Jew and the woman is at the center of one of the central tropes of Panizza's *The Council of Love*, perhaps the most scandalous text of the German fin de siècle. In 1895, the publication of his play led Panizza to be sentenced in Munich to a year in prison for blasphemy. This trial became one of the most talked-about scandals in the literary world of the time, and it made the text an underground best-seller, at least among the intellectual avant-garde of the time. The play, according to its author, is a satire on religious belief.[17] Set in the Renaissance, it represents the introduction of syphilis into the world through the agency of Salome, who is the chosen vehicle through which the Devil corrupts the flesh. While his play ostensibly attacked all religious belief, Panizza used many of the contemporary images of the Jews to characterize even Christian icons such as God the Father and Jesus. (This was very much in line with Nietzsche's attempt to see Christianity simply as an extension of Rabbinic Judaism.)

Panizza, trained as a physician at the University of Munich, was, like so many males at the turn of the century, syphilophobic.[18] Using the model of the exclusionary stereotype of the Jewish male, he constructed the diseased male Jewish body as even more repellent than his fantasy of his own diseased body. In his drama, the Devil, the eventual seducer of Salome, is visible as a Jewish male whose corruption is written on his body. "The Devil stands before them, leaning on one foot and supporting the other with his hands. He wears a black, close-fitting costume, is very slender, close-shaven with a fine-cut face, but his features wear an expression that is decadent, worn, embittered. He has a yellowish complexion. His manners recall those of a Jew of high breeding. He leans on one foot, the other is drawn up."[19] The "yellowish" skin color, the limping leg, and the degeneracy of the Jew form Panizza's image of the seducer of humankind.

The Jew's yellowish skin is part of the standard image of the diseased Jew. Johann Jakob Schudt, Günther's seventeenth-century authority, cited the male Jews' physical form as diseased and repellent: "Among several hundred of their kind he had not encountered a single person without a blemish or other repulsive feature: for they are either pale and yellow or swarthy." [20] Schudt saw the diseases of the Jews as a reflex of their "Jewishness," of their stubborn refusal to acknowledge the truth of Christianity. But skin color reappears two centuries later as a marker of the ill Jewish male. This yellow skin later marked the bearded "friend in Russia" in Franz Kafka's tale "Judgement" (1913), where "the jaundiced color his skin had begun to take on seemed to signal the onset of some disease."[21] The male friend from Russia bears the qualities of illness, including his yellowed skin, associated with the diseased Jew.

The limping Jew, as I have shown in detail elsewhere, is a sign of the exclusion of the Jewish male from qualities associated with the masculine at the fin de siècle.[22] Panizza's Devil as Jew as Devil clearly limps:

> The Devil turns on his right heel, smiles sardonically,
> and shrugs his shoulders. He feigns regret. Very much
> the Jewish merchant. A painful moment. . . .
> *Mary*: By the way how is your foot?
> *The Devil*: Oh, so-so! No better! But no worse, actually! Oh,
> god! (Hitting his shorter leg a blow.) There's no change
> any more! Blasted thing!
> *Mary* (in a lower voice): Your fall did that?
> (The Devil, not reacting, is silent for a while; then he
> nods gravely.) (91–92)

The trope of the limping Devil and the limping Jew are interchange-able at the turn of the century and are here set within a secularized (and anti-Christian) theological model of the Jewish disavowal of God/Christ. At the fin de siècle, it is the syphilitic who limps, as the Parisian neurologist Joseph Babinski was to show in 1896, when he proved that a diminished plantar reflex was a sign of neurosyphilis. But within the related images of the lame Jew and the limping Devil, the association with the gait of the syphilitic was already well estab-lished in late-nineteenth-century culture.

Panizza's limping Devil is revealed to be a syphilitic Jew. The male Devil is thus a prefiguration of the central theme of the play: the in-troduction of syphilis into the world of the Renaissance. He is already infected with his "disease," his Jewishness, and he will spread it throughout society through the creation of an appropriate medium. Syphilis, which was actually understood as a Jewish disease as early as its first modern outbreak in the fifteenth century, is introduced into Panizza's debauched world of Renaissance Rome and the history of the West by the Jews—in this case, by the Jewish male Devil.[23]

Syphilis is written on the male Jew's body, revealing his corrupt soul. But it is not just the Devil who is a corrupt Jewish male, but all the figures of the "Jewish" Bible. And in this reading the New Testa-ment is just as Jewish as the Old Testament. Panizza's image of all the male figures in the pantheon of the gods stresses their visible defor-mities. God the Father is the limping, syphilitic Jew whose tubercular son, Jesus Christ, has inherited his disease and shows symptoms of lo-comotor ataxia and mental deficiency. Panizza employs much of the vocabulary that categorizes the hidden nature of the Jew in the medical science of the fin de siècle. God "has a backward curvature of the spine. . . . He coughs. His throat rattles. He gropes His way awkwardly, leaning forward, dragging His feet" (19). Just as the Jew is immediately recognizable, so, too, will the syphilitic be, who as of that moment in the play exists only within the vocabulary of images that its author used to characterize the "Jewish male." Mary, therefore, is spared any overt pathological physical characterization.

For Panizza, the new disease of syphilis, too, will be written on everyone's body, as men are seduced and infected and in turn infect women. It will be a visible sign of their corruption, of their "Jewification" (to use one of Adolf Hitler's favorite words):

> *The Devil* (sneering): In a matter of six weeks they won't recognize their own bodies! Their hair will fall out! Their eyelashes will fall out! Their teeth will fall out! They won't be able to chew, and their joints will be sprung! Inside of three months their entire body surface will look like a sieve and they'll go window-shopping to see the new styles in human skins! And I don't think that the fear will remain only inside their hearts! The stench of it will seep out through their noses, and their friends will exchange glances, and the ones that are in the first phase of the disease will laugh at those in the third or fourth! A year later their noses will fall off into their soup, and then it'll be the rubber-goods department for a new one! (128–29)

The traditional evil smell of the Jews, the *foetor judaicus*, and the Jew's nose are all echoed in the Devil's construction of this new disease, which will expose the inner corruption of each human being for all the world to see.

The vehicle of this destruction of Western society through syphilis, according to Panizza's construction, must be a woman. The Jewish Devil is made to seek after the perfect "mother" for this disease. He calls the roll of the women he finds in Hell, and all of them have one thing in common—they are mute. Helen of Troy will not do. She is a "poor simple thing" (106) who does not think. Héloïse had indeed "seduced her teacher," but "out of love," and is therefore eliminated (108f.). Agrippina is a plotter and murderess but has no "artistic drive," no "authentic naïveté," but merely "limitless ambition" (111). It is only Salome, the Jewish princess, who fulfills the Devil's every need. His exchange with her is interesting enough to reproduce in its entirety:

> Tell me, pretty child, you were at Herod's banquet?
> (She nods affirmatively.)
> You danced, didn't you?
> (She nods.)
> Why?
> (She doesn't know.)
> Was it because pretty young girls always like to dance? And because you had taken dancing lessons?
> (She nods.)
> Everyone applauded?
> (She nods.)
> And so Herod said you could name your own gift?
> (She nods.)
> So you said you wanted a head?
> (She nods.)
> A man's head?
> (She nods.)
> A real man's head that was still alive?
> (She nods.)
> Why?
> (She doesn't know.)
> For a toy?
> (She hesitates and finally nods affirmatively.)
> So Herod sent you into the prison with the hangman and there he cut you a head?
> (She nods.)
> It happened to be the head of John the Baptist?
> (She nods indifferently.)
> They laid it on a platter and you brought it back into the banquet room?
> (She nods.)
> The blood ran into the platter until the platter was full?
> (She nods.)
> You got your fingers wet?
> (She nods vigorously.)
> Did you like that or didn't you?
> (She nods yes.)
> What do you mean, yes? Did you like it or didn't you?
> (She rubs her hands together.)

You mean you got a kick out of it?
(Her affirmation is very clear.)
You must have very sensitive fingers!
(No answer.)
And then, then you gave the head to your mother as a gift?
(She nods.)
Why?
(She shrugs.)
It was already dead?
(She nods sadly.)
Yes, amputated heads don't last very long! Now, tell me, did you care about any of the people? Was there any one that you loved?
(She doesn't know what to say and finally shakes her head no.)
Did you love Herod?
(No.)
Saint John?
(No.)
Your mother?
(She shrugs, then shakes her head no.)
But you did like your sliced-off head?
(She nods very definitely. The Devil suddenly jumps up.)
You're it, my child. . . . We have great things to do together, you and I! You will be the mother of a magnificent race which no aristocracy will ever equal. Your children won't have blue blood or red blood in their veins. It will be a far more remarkable kind of blood! You're the only one of your kind in my whole, huge realm! (111–15)

All the rhetoric that Panizza places in the Devil's mouth is racial rhetoric. It evokes the debate about the special status of the Jewish sexuality at the fin de siècle, specifically sexual selection ("inbreeding") and its pathological results. The daughter born of the pairing of the Devil and Salome is syphilis incarnate. She is called simply "the Woman," "a young blooming creature with black hair and deep black eyes in which a smouldering sensuality, as yet only half awakened, is apparent" (121). And she is silent. It is the silence of the woman that represents the language of destructive femininity in Panizza's world; it masks the *Mauscheln* of the Jew. She is seen as essentially female in her silence, not as Jewish.

If the body of the Jewish male is indeed marked and made visible by the signs of his pathology, the woman's beauty and silence are visible signs of her danger to all human beings.

Salome quietly begins to spread her disease with her seduction of the pope and then "to the rest of the human pack" (140). It is vital to note that, while Salome is in no way to be distinguished from the other women in Hell by her gestural language, her daughter—the daughter of two Jews—seems to bear the visible marks of her difference. And her visibility seems to mark her as a corrupted and corrupting Jew. Her physiognomy is overtly that of the *belle juive;* the dark hair and black eyes are the salient markers of this beautiful Jewess in European, but especially in nineteenth-century German-language, drama. One thinks immediately of the physiognomy of the seductive Rahel in Grillparzer's *Die Jüdin von Toledo.* Or, indeed, one thinks of Merimée's if not of Bizet's Carmen, whom the narrator first takes for a Jew. Yet this visibility is in no way signposted for the reader/audience by Panizza. Unlike with his representation of the Devil, whose Jewish identity is manifest, Panizza never overtly characterizes either Salome or "the Woman" as a Jewish woman.

The image of the "dark" woman, while echoing the Western trope of the "blackness" of the Jews, is also a sign of the femme fatale. (Thus, Bizet's representation of Carmen is clearly as a "gypsy" and not as a Jew.) It is not an exclusionary sign of the ugly and the pathological, but rather an inclusionary sign—for even the dark woman here is an object of desire, unlike the yellow, limping Jewish Devil. It would be counterproductive to characterize her otherwise, since her inclusionary "feminine" qualities are needed to make "the Woman" an object of desire, an object that the Jew cannot be. (One can speak here of the attractiveness of difference, but "the Woman's" difference is clearly distinguished from that of the male.) This inclusionary stereotype enables the seduction of all the men in the papal court to take place. Salome and "the Woman" must be attractive to the males they are to seduce. And yet, the selection of a Jewish mother and a Jewish father produces a Jewish daughter, a fact that we, the reader/audience, intuitively know and yet repress. Her Jewishness (read: her pathology) is represented by her visibility as a woman, a visibility very different from that of her "father," the Devil, and very similar to that of her mother, Salome. The trope of the inheritance of Jewish identity through the mother is here reversed: here the feminine is her maternal inheritance. Her visibility to the audience as "the Woman" triggers the male (or at least Panizza's) anxiety about syphilis, about the presence of this hidden, dangerous aspect of the stereotypical feminine. Here, the Escherlike image of the Jewish woman is evoked: Is she primarily a woman or primarily a Jew? Both images are present, yet they are constructed so that one must function as an inclusionary stereotype (the woman) while the other (the Jew) signals this as an impossibility.

A counterimage from the time can highlight how highly contextualized Panizza's (and Strauss's) images of Salome are in the fin-de-siècle antisemitic discourse of difference. No such hint of this double image of the Jewish woman appears in a contemporary "Jewish" version of the Salome legend. The Viennese poet Ignatz Kohn's "Salome" (1902) appeared in the leading secular Jewish periodical *East and West*:

> Jochanan, I love you,
> My soul longs for you,
> Pain-bringing pain redeemer
> Jochanan, I love you.
>
> Deep in my soul there is a yearning.
> Look! I am beautiful and young . . . so young!
> Dreams go through my soul,
> That let me sense what is.
>
> Before me life extends blooming.
> Look! I am beautiful and young . . . so young!
> Before me I see a life of pleasure,
> But I thirst for pain and suffering.
>
> Pain, I greet you! I want to kiss you!
> My soul wants to sip on pain
> Jochanan; my soul loves you,
> Jochanan, I want your life.
>
> I don't care if people curse me!
> I want to see God bleeding in you,
> My soul cramps and cries,
> My soul jubilates in pain.
>
> Jochanan, I love you,
> My soul longs for you,
> Pain-bringing pain redeemer
> Jochanan, I love you.[24]

For Kohn, Salome is purely the feminine. No Jewish overtones are permitted in her representation—she is "beautiful and young . . . so

young" and her monologue (echoing Wilde's last monologue for Salome) is an outpouring of her destructive adoration of the body of
John the Baptist. The poem was accompanied by an engraving of Peter Paul Rubens's fulsome image of Salome bearing the severed head
of John the Baptist. While dark-haired and dark-eyed, Rubens's image, like that of Kohn, evokes the feminine and excludes any image of
the Jew. His positionality as a Jew permits Salome only to represent
the destructive feminine.

Sarah Bernhardt and the Disease of the Jew

The contradictory image of the Jewish woman found in Panizza's
drama draws on the general image of the *belle juive* at the fin de siècle. Yet there was also a real Jewish woman of the time who, more
than anyone else, came to represent the symbolic embodiment of this
destructive stereotype. That woman was Sarah Bernhardt (1844–
1923), Oscar Wilde's original Salome. Sarah Bernhardt's association
with the Salome tradition created a public scandal almost as widely
spoken of in Europe as the scandal surrounding Panizza's arrest for
blasphemy. In June of 1892, Bernhardt had begun rehearsals for Oscar Wilde's drama at the Palace Theater in London.[25] Within the
month, the examiner of plays for the Lord Chamberlain denied his
approval for its performance, since it represented biblical figures on
the stage. Wilde's anger at this was extreme; indeed, he threatened to
renounce his British citizenship and become a citizen of France. And
for a moment, this British theatrical scandal linked the figures of Salome and Sarah Bernhardt. In fact, one of the original reviewers (in
the *Times* of February 23, 1893) erroneously implied that the drama
had been written for Sarah Bernhardt. Even though Wilde had not
written his play for *La Divine Sarah*, she truly seemed to be the role's
ideal embodiment.

Sarah Bernhardt's image was most complex and diffuse, and one
powerful aspect of it, in Germany as well as in France, was its antisemitic overtones.[26] In France, Marie Colombier had published her *Les
Mémoires de Sarah Barnum* (1883), which depicted Sarah Bernhardt as
an ugly, money-hungry, sexually promiscuous, and destructive Jewish woman. She was also understood as the exemplary tubercular Jew.
For the historian Anatole Leroy-Beaulieu, in 1893, saw in the face of

all Jews, "those lean actresses, the *Rachels* and *Sarahs*, who spit blood, and seem to have but the spark of life left, and yet who, when they have stepped upon the stage, put forth indomitable strength and energy. Life, with them, has hidden springs."[27] It is Sarah Bernhardt and Rachel Félix (1820–58) who represent the face of the sick Jew. At about the same time, the anonymous *Sarah's Travel Letters from Three Continents (America, Europe and Skobolessia)* appeared in German.[28] In the German context, this text (which seems to be completely independent of the Colombier volume) presented a specific voice and image of Sarah Bernhardt that can lead us to a deeper understanding of the cultural discourse about the repression of the Jewish element of Salome. Written by the minor Viennese playwright and editor Ottokar Franz Ebersberg, it purported to be a series of letters from Sarah Bernhardt to her admirers (especially to Benjamin Disraeli) and from them to her.[29] Given the convention of the time, discourses among Jews overheard by non-Jews were assumed to reveal the Jew's hidden nature. Here, Günther's image of a specifically Jewish language is linked to the character of the Jews: Jews lie to non-Jews but tell the truth among themselves. According to these letters, Sarah Bernhardt was the "most notable embodiment of the Semite" (133) and represents all Jewish "racial qualities" (20). Sarah Bernhardt's language in her letters reveals her true nature. Her language is Jewish, unlike the mute discourse of Panizza's Salome, which is identical in form, if not in content, to all the other women that the Devil evokes before choosing her.

Two specific moments in the text are of interest. The first comes in the sixth letter to Disraeli, dated from Indianapolis on February 26, 1881. "Sarah Bernhardt" presents her insight into the nature of the Jewish woman, and the tradition into which she sees herself fitting, to her Jewish correspondent Disraeli. She recounts that she had been studying the accounts of the Wandering Jew, but truly to understand her people she had to turn to "her own sex: To the Misses Esther and Herodias 'of the Persian and Jewish ballet,' to the beloved of the Polish king Casimir and the 'Little Dove' of the Nordic Kings—was it not Jewesses who accomplished everything and forced themselves into the tent of the enemy, and if flattery did not succeed, killed them as Judith did the stupid Holofernes?" (60) She follows this with an account of Jewish women who were prominent (or, rather, infamous) in her own time, such as Anna Kaulla, Heine's friend, or Madame Friedman Persigny, the Prince Persigny of Paris's daughter, who was accused with her father of embezzlement. Indeed, even women whom the author does not believe to be Jewish, such as Sophie Arendt, the author of a widely discussed book on the loves of the Jewish Socialist Ferdinand Lassalle, acquire Jewish characteristics by their very association with Jews. Being a seductress is contagious and marks one as a Jewess.

But such seductresses are dangerous—they kill non-Jewish men like Holofernes. (The confusion between Judith's beheading of Holofernes and Salome's demand for John the Baptist's head is a set topos of the fin de siècle.)[30] Sarah Bernhardt's catalogue begins with Esther and Herodias, the mother of Salome, who are described as dancing girls, a euphemism of the late nineteenth century for prostitutes. (In the Salome legend, the dance of Salome is often attributed to Herodias.) The catalogue ends, however, with the actual killing of a non-Jewish male. Non-Jewish males are at risk when they are exposed to Jewish women. Thus, the association of Sarah Bernhardt with the Salome legend is fixed as the history of the Jewess as sexual seductress. She is as dangerous as she is seductive—she is the essential *belle juive*.

But Bernhardt's association with the image of Salome does not rest on this rather oblique single entry in her catalogue of the *belles juives*. Rather, the volume concludes with the twenty-second letter written by her to the most famous Viennese artist of the fin de siècle, Hans Makart. He is accused by Bernhardt of having withdrawn his portrait of her from the major art exhibition of the year. He is not Jewish, so her letter to him is both duplicitous and contains intended multiple meanings. *La Divine Sarah* condemns him for having withdrawn the painting, noting that he himself had praised the picture as having been painted in "a true passion." She believes that he withdrew the portrait because some "high personage" commented to him, "You are now painting trash" (176).

But the prime reason it was withdrawn seems to have been the portrait's color. The image itself was jaundiced. The accusation that the picture was *too yellow* evokes not only all the images of decay and degeneration evoked by yellow in general at the turn of the century, but also the parallel image of the diseased and "yellow" Jew. (One needs only to remember *The Yellow Book,* whose color evoked the very spirit of the self-conscious degeneracy of the fin de siècle.) And Sarah Bernhardt observes,

Yellow on yellow was the color of Henri Regnault, the late master from Paris, when he painted his Salome—shouldn't the famed Sarah not also be permitted to be yellow? . . . Yes, Mr. Makart, even though my statue has been rescued from the Ring Theater fire, my portrait must now be driven away. And yet my head and arms are so beautifully made up, the gown, the table cloth, the embroidery, the palm fan, everything is so beautifully yellow. Take assurance that I, too, have become truly yellow from gall, because you, whom I held to be my friend, betrayed me, after you painted me yellow. (177)

And so the volume ends—a banal ending, perhaps, and yet one that ties the image of Sarah Bernhardt to Makart's fin-de-siècle "modern" excesses and to the image of a Salome painted in the corrosive colors of the degenerate. (Makart is retrospectively associated with the full-blown academic, historical painting of fin-de-siècle Vienna; yet in the 1880s, he was considered to be the most "modern" of painters.) The disease of the male Jew is literally marked on her yellow skin and is reflected in her ventriloquized, Jewish voice in these letters.

It is clear that the image of Sarah Bernhardt in this text generates a further exclusionary category of the female. And it is made exclusionary through its association with the image of the Jewish male. Bernhardt as the exemplary Jewish woman is represented as the diseased Salome, the destructive seducer, but she also has all the overtones of the "bluestocking." Her image in this text is "mannish" in her demand for control over the world, but this is also Jewish. She represents herself as the very embodiment of the modern woman—whom the minister who refused to officiate at her wedding believed to be really a boy in disguise. He refuses to marry the lovers because there is not to be any "confusion about the sex of those about to be married" (174).[31] According to her own account in the text, she does not "withdraw with the other women when the gentlemen begin to smoke and drink their sherry" (3). She represents precisely the anxiety about the "modern woman" that is associated, as early as 1849, with the emancipation of women. Louise Otto-Peters writes that "emancipated women are the sexually ambiguous type [*Zwitterwesen*] such as George Sand or Louise Aston, dressed like men, smoking cigars, hair cut short, praising free love. This is imported from France by the Young Germans

who praise the 'emancipation of the flesh.'"[32] This description replicates almost verbatim the image of Bernhardt presented in this text.
Bernhardt's seemingly "feminine" nature masks a masculine one, that
of the fin-de-siècle image of the lesbian as cryptomale.

The Jewishness of Bernhardt provides for an ambiguous masculinity—making her a "third sex." And this is associated in a direct manner with her "modern" image as Salome, the Jewish princess whose
visible yellow skin reveals her as diseased and corrupt—as a Jew.
Bernhardt is Salome, and Salome is diseased in more than one way.
The visibility of Salome and Bernhardt reflects a specific debate about
the sexuality of the Jew. For the Jewish female becomes the destructive seducer—the parallel image of the Jewish male (as, for example,
in Panizza's image of the Devil). And this primacy of the stereotype
of the Jew is reflected in her language. *La Divine Sarah* is the embodiment of the sexuality of the Jew and, therefore, of the modernity that
this sexuality comes to represent. Imagining Bernhardt playing Salome on the London stage was the perfect meshing of the role and
the performer. For in this match of the emancipated Jewish actress
and the destructive biblical Jewess, the very nature of the Jew as the
corrupter of the non-Jewish world was embodied.

The "Modern Jewess" as Seen by a "Modern Jewess"

After the turn of the century, the discourse about the destructive Jewish female as the epitome of the modern woman becomes commonplace. It becomes so common, in fact, that modern Jewish women
were constrained to explore the very meaning of this stereotype in
terms of their own self-representation. From the externalization of
these stereotypes of the Jew and the woman in action, we can turn to
the programmatic presentation of the "modern Jewess" by Else
Croner, published in 1913, which offers a summary of the discourse
about modernity and the Jewish woman.[33] (Croner use the term *modern Jewess*, and I shall use it when referring to her construction.)

Sarah Bernhardt was represented as the quintessential modern
woman in the stereotypical discourse of the late nineteenth century.
Croner's account of the "modern" Jewish woman focused on two aspects that construct the representation of Bernhardt in Ottokar Franz

Ebersberg's text—the sexuality of the Jewess and its relationship to the representation of the special language of the Jewess as the sign of the modern. Croner's text presents a post-1900 attempt on the part of a self-identified Jewish woman to construct, and thus rescue, the image of the Jewish woman as different from both the antisemitic image of the male Jew and the misogynist image of the woman. She wished to construct an image in which both qualities are visible simultaneously. Her construction of an independent image of the Jewess was an act of resistance, given the invisibility of the Jewess in the culture of the time, as can be seen in the popular German reception of Strauss's opera.

If there is something masculine and destructive in the stereotype of the Jewish woman at the fin de siècle, Croner's image provides a countertype. She constructs an image, according to Croner herself, of the "modern Jewess" who is defined by her heterosexuality. In this regard, she is the "most feminine of all women." The shift between the older reality of the Jewess in the ghetto and that of the "modern" Jewess is marked by the abandonment of early marriage as a means of channeling her sexuality. She "matures earlier" than all other women. In the social structures of the ghetto, this maturity was recognized and controlled through the institution of early marriage. She has a "greater hot-bloodedness, liveliness, and sensibility," which "is the result of [her] early development." And this is because she is constituted as biologically different. She is an "Oriental" (74). All these images provide a positive reevaluation of precisely those negative qualities traditionally associated with the image of the modern woman (more intensive sexuality) and the Jew (destructive sexuality).

By the time the Jewess entered into sexual maturity, she was already married, and this early marriage "allow[ed] her to avoid side steps and mistakes but also robbed her of the individual choice and an erotic life full of play and pleasure" (72). And one might add to this what one constantly finds in the medical literature of the period: that such an early marriage enabled her to avoid exposure to syphilis and its consequences. Thus, the Jewess in the ghetto, according to Croner, was sexually less liberated, yet sexually more fulfilled, than her non-Jewish contemporaries. And she was at less risk for disease. Croner thus answers the long association of Jews with sexually transmitted disease by evoking the sexual practices of the Jews, practices that are often associated with the very image of the pathology of the Jews.

According to Croner, with civil emancipation and the introduction of "Western norms" of sexual behavior, the Jewish woman began to marry later and later. She became more like her non-Jewish counterpart, who married on or after the end of her second decade. Yet unlike her "occidental" counterpart, all of her "Oriental" being is sensual and sexual. For the Jewish woman, there is no rejection of the flesh. " 'To marry is good, not to marry is better' is a New Testamentary idea unknown in the Torah and Talmud" (74). Her desire is to "marry and reproduce." Her drives are purely biological. She is an "individual of reproduction and completely intuitively desires the preservation of her species" (76). Thus Croner answers the charges, made by a number of her contemporaries such as Otto Weininger, that the biological imperative to reproduce is central to all women. Here, however, it is linked to the sexual selectivity of the Jews.

According to Croner, the modern, emancipated Jewess had the potential to develop in two radically different directions. At this juncture, this German-Jewish author projects all the negative images of the Jew and the woman outside herself. She has begun to construct the image of the Western Jew as the romantic reversal of the standard stereotypes of the woman and the Jew. She now places the originally negative images outside her own self-definition. She places them in the East among the Eastern Jewish women. The Russian Jewess is the destructive seductress. She traps her object—Jew or non-Jew— without "shame or propriety, she masters and tortures him, drains him of the very marrow from his bones and eventually drives him 'through her life' to death" (76–77). Once she abandons the confines of the ghetto, the Russian Jewess, unlike the German Jewess, is given no alternative in her culture but to revert to a more primitive and intuitive sexuality.

The German Jewess, even with her "greater sensuality," is regarded quite differently. She, too, abandons the religious strictures of the ghetto, but she replaces the rules of religion with the "intellect" that governs her sexual life. There is no intuitive sexuality among German Jewesses. "The Jewess is not 'Gretchen' and 'Klärchen.' She is always the queen of love; she and not the man grants, makes happy, heightens. Here, her character is close to that of the American woman. An

American Käthchen of 'Heilbronn' is as unthinkable as a Jewish 'Klärchen'" (78). The passive, dependent image of the woman is foreign to the Jewish woman in the West ("America"). Her heterosexuality is under the control of her rationality at all times. It is less passionate and, therefore, more controlling of the male. Croner's dichotomy between destructive and acceptable independence becomes the difference in the image of the Eastern and the Western Jewess. Everything destructive and corrosive in the sexuality of the Jewish woman at the fin de siècle, with Sarah Bernhardt and Salome, is projected onto a construction of the Eastern Jewish woman. Here, the position of the acculturated Jewish woman becomes the antithesis of the universalizing image of the female according to fin-de-siècle thinkers such as Otto Weininger, whose image of the female is, in point of fact, identical to that of Croner's Eastern Jewess.

Croner's need to split this stereotype is further reflected in her attempt to adapt and refunction the stereotypical image of the language of the Jews as a sign of the "modern Jewess." But if the representation of female sexuality is restructured, so, too, is the universal stereotypical attribute of the Jews' language. The language of the Jewish woman becomes the focus of the anxiety about the sort of control attributed to the sexuality of the Western "modern Jewess"—cold and controlling. The language of the "modern Jewess" is "elastic to the point of disconnectedness, sensible to the point of nervousness, and elegant to the point of glossiness" (91). Here, all the anxiety about pathology ("nervousness") is articulated in a context of the heightened risk for mental illness on the part of Jews, which was a commonplace image of the Jews at the fin de siècle. This nervousness was understood as a sign of her moving into the competitive world of "modernity." Her ghetto ancestry, where her ancestresses spoke "a bad, clumsy German," is behind her. Indeed, she is, at least in her writing, the new master of the language and she "exceeds many German women in glossiness and grace of style" (92). But there still remain clear signs of her racial difference in her biology, her intonation, and her choice of words. Her larynx, practiced in pronouncing hard, guttural sounds for a thousand years, is used to these sounds, and their echo is still to be heard in her pronunciation of German. Her "Hebrew larynx unintentionally transfers these sounds into German" (92). Her pronunciation is "jumpy, disjointed; her sentences remain

often incomplete, entire words and syllables are swallowed, the concluding syllables are only hinted at, and the intonation only margin-
ally sketched in" (93). Here, the counterdiscourse is repressed and
projected by Croner: that it is the sexuality of the Jew that (in terms
of racial-biological argument) is inherently different. This image, tied
to the image of the circumcised male Jew, is placed onto the very
voice of the "modern Jewess," who comes to be vacuous in her
modernity. Her choice of words becomes banal. She calls everything
"neat" (*großartig*). Needless to say, this description of the slangy, hy-
peranxious, visible (or rather, audible) language is tied to the prototypical "Jewish princess"—the classbound image of the Jewish
woman as parvenu, which reappears in the United States after World
War II.[34] But it is a language written on the body. It was this gendering of the Jewish voice that was understood by Günther and the
physical anthropologists to be a universal sign of the Jew. This language is the antithesis of the controlled, incisive, and academic language that Croner herself employs in her own writing. Here the questions of the nature of the Jew's body and the Jew's language are
linked in the representation and projection of the "modern Jewess" as
an object beyond the text (and its author).

Just as the sexuality of the "modern Jewess" (both Eastern and
Western) is different from that of the non-Jew, so, too, is her language. (At this point, the "modern Jewess" becomes the object of investigation and a category that excludes the author.) While there is
only a little trace of *Mauscheln*, there are still some remnants of the
language of the ghetto left in her language, such as the use of "German-Jewish" words that give an "intimate but not always proper and
resonant-beautiful tone" (94–95). Here, the sexual difference of the
Jewish woman, her improper intimacy, is displaced by Croner onto
her larynx to be articulated in the description of her language. But
Croner further distinguishes one aspect of the language of the "Western modern Jewess" from that of the "Eastern Jewess." What clearly
remains different and visible are her gestures: she has a "greater power
and rapidity of gesture." Among the German Jewesses (who are not
as "Oriental" as the Eastern Jewesses), gestural language is a sign of
the oppression of the Jews in the West. (According to Croner, true
"Orientals" use minimal gestures.) She had to "catch the ear of her oppressor" (95). The inherited characteristics of oppression continue to

shape the very language of the emancipated Jewish woman. The image of the Jewish woman and her gestural language seem fixed. When the Nazi-Germanist Wilhelm Stapel imagines Heinrich Heine's "Lorelei," he "feels immediately the words flowing into his arms, a compulsive shrugging of the shoulders as the hands move apart: a typical Jewish gesture."[35] The stereotypical nature of the Jew is articulated in the visibility of the Jew. Jewish women become visible through their language, even as Jewish men are visible through their deformities. Croner returns at this moment to the counterargument against this quality of difference being the result of biological predisposition. She evokes the history of the oppression of the Jews as an explanation for their difference, and thus recapitulates the liberal promise of the Enlightenment: become like us and we will treat you as we ourselves wish to be treated. Croner's construction of the "modern Jewess" is an attempt to come to terms with the qualities that embodied the double image of Jew and woman at the fin de siècle.

An analogy to Croner's argument can be found in the controversial 1930 essay on female masochism by Sigmund Freud's Jewish analysand Helene Deutsch.[36] Deutsch, building on work by Freud and Karl Abraham, accepted the view that female masochism was the psychological reflex of the reproductive biology of the female. Her essay concludes, however, with an analysis of the historical shift in the meaning of the woman's body at the turn of the century. Women of the nineteenth century were able to repress their anxiety about their bodies in a denial of the sexual: "If questioned about the nature of their experience in coitus, they give answers which show that the conception of orgasm as something to be experienced by themselves is really and truly foreign to them." These women receive pleasure only in giving pleasure to the man as "they are convinced that coitus as a sexual act is of importance only for the man. In it, as in other relations, the woman finds happiness in tender, maternal giving." But this stage has now been replaced by that of the "modern woman," whose sublimations "are further removed from instinct." This is the result of "social developments and that is accompanied by an increasing tendency of women towards masculinity." This echo of an earlier attack on the masculinization of the "bluestocking" points toward the gradual sublimation of the masochistic aspect of the female psyche. She and her heirs demand to be freed of the pain associated with reproductive sexuality: "Perhaps women of the next generation will no longer submit to defloration in the normal way and will give birth to children only on condition of freedom from pain." Anesthesia becomes the answer to the biology of pain which, according to Deutsch, is the condition of all women. At this point in her argument Deutsch, who is writing about the condition of all women, makes a move into the future, in which women will have to generate symbols to compensate for the absence of those painful experiences that represent the masochistic nature of the feminine: "And then in after-generations they may resort to infibulation and to refinements in the way of pain—ceremonials in connection with parturition." Female circumcision and birthing ceremonies are the counterimages of the male Jewish symbolic world, with its stress on male circumcision and the ritual of manhood, the bar mitzvah. But it also extends the idea of circumcision as a magical prophylaxis against sexually transmitted diseases. "Infibulation" becomes a symbolic extension of marking the body as a sign of health. Deutsch reverses Croner's reading. She moves from the universal quality of masochism in all women and reveals it to be an encoded reading of the female Jewish body and the female Jewish mind. Her claim that masochism is "the most elementary force in feminine mental life," and that it is a biological quality of all female experience, reveals itself to be an encoding of the claims about the female Jewish body and psyche, a body suffering from the social repression of the Jews in Western culture. This is a parallel movement to Croner's: Deutsch, assuming a biological universality of all women, comes to read the body of the woman as the body of the Jew; Croner departs from "culture" as the formative force in the "modern Jewish woman" and shipwrecks on the reef of "nature."

In my fantasy, I imagine how Else Croner would have read Salome. On the one hand, she would have seen Salome as a "modern" woman, as an "Eastern Jewess" stripped of her racial identity and reduced to the elemental forces of the feminine, and on the other, she would have seen her as a "Western Jewess" attempting to capture the eye of her oppressor through the gestural language of her dance. Croner constructed her image of the "modern Jewess" as a representation of the woman as Jew within the discourse of an age that could focus on either Jews or women. As a German-Jewish woman, she was still constrained to separate this image from her own image as a *Jew and as a woman.* Here is where Salome lurks in Croner's perspective—as a Jewish woman in the East, but only from the Jewish female perspective. The "Oriental," gesticulating, sexually destructive, de-centered image of Panizza's Salome, with all its associations with the contemporary antisemitic discourse, is subsumed under Croner's image of the modern Jewish woman, but it is distanced in every way from her. Here, the problem of the construction and externalization of stereotypes in culture becomes a way to measure the limits of this "double vision" that constructs the image of the Jewish woman but rarely permits it to be seen in its totality.

CHAPTER FIVE

Zwetschkenbaum's Competence
Madness and the Discourse of the Jews

The Question of Competence as a Central Theme in Albert Drach's 'The Long Report About Zwetschkenbaum'

The central question in Albert Drach's 1938 novel, *The Long Report About Zwetschkenbaum*, is the relationship between discourses of power and those individuals dominated by those discourses.[1] The central discourse satirized in the novel is that of the legalistic language of the Austrian legal bureaucracy and its object, the Eastern European Jewish itinerant who is caught in its grasp. Drach's novel is remarkable because of its sustained representation of the discourse of power and its revelation of how powerless those in power truly are. They are powerless because of their own subjugation to the system of laws that controls not only their actions but also their very modes of thought and expression. The language of the novel is literally the language of the legal system, but it is placed in the mouth of the weakest and most powerless representative of that system, the assistant prosecutor in training. The contrast, at least for the Jewish-Austrian lawyer Albert

Drach in the late 1930s, is the language of the Eastern European Jew, a language that is understood, by the system in which his protagonist finds himself, as the discourse of the insane.

Early in the novel, after Zwetschkenbaum is arrested for stealing plums from an orchard, the question of whether this itinerant wanderer is capable of understanding the charges brought against him arises. The question of competence becomes the thread that is spun through all of Drach's representations of discourses of power and powerlessness in this novel. For competence, the legal concept of whether an individual comprehends the charges brought against him/her, is the salient metaphor for all the representations of the discourses of power. According to Austrian criminal law, an individual who "does not have the use of reason," is intoxicated, is younger than fourteen years old, is unable to understand the act as a crime, or who undertakes the act out of compulsion or self-defense has not committed a crime.[2] Such individuals are incompetent. (And the list has broader significance, as we shall see.) Austrian law, unlike German law, does not demand that a concept of "disease" be evoked in order to judge an individual's competence. Thus, determining the mental status of an individual does not necessarily mean labeling him or her as suffering from a specific form of mental illness. Who is competent, and who is competent to judge competence, is the key to deciphering the functions of language in this novel. For competence is, in reality, the test of whether the individual examined can use language within socially accepted boundaries; he or she is tested by the examiner's supposedly correct use of language. Competence presents a complex image of the power of language to deform understanding as well as to mask it. Thus, being drunk and underage—two forms of powerlessness—are recognized by the courts as signs of diminished capacity. It is in the incompetents' ability to manipulate language that their difference from the competent adult is to be found. The unstated addition to the categories of competency described in Austrian law are those individuals who are incompetent because they belong to certain groups. These groups are understood as so inherently different from those defining competency that they are by definition incompetent. From the standpoint of an Austrian Jew looking at a world haunted by the specter of antisemitism, it was clear that the Jew belonged in this category. And Drach, well-educated in the meaning of forensic evidence from his university studies, would have seen the language of the Jew, represented by Zwetschkenbaum's *Mauscheln*, as a sign of the incompetency of the Jew. In Drach's novel, the lawyer and the accused speak two very different languages, not merely the language of Austrian legalism versus the Yiddish (or *Mauscheln*, speaking German with a Yiddish intonation and vocabulary) of the Eastern European Jew, but also the language of power and powerlessness. Of course, only one of these discourses, the language of law, appears on the page. Zwetschkenbaum's language is always "translated" (often incorrectly) into this jargon in order to be understood by the fictive reader of the report, the court.

The language of the Eastern Jew in Drach's German-speaking world is *Mauscheln* (speaking with a Jewish accent) or *Jüdeln* (speaking with Jewish words).[3] (These terms are clearly pejorative. *Mauscheln*, in its original usage in German, means to counterfeit.) His language retains the "unique lisp or disgusting language, which, even if one should shut one's eyes and without seeing the physiognomy, would enable one to recognize the Jew."[4] This special sign is embedded in the Jew's language—no matter what language he speaks. "The average German," a German-Jewish commentator noted, "regards Jewish language and dress not only as 'strange,' but as a caricature, a ridiculing of his own language and dress. The Jewish language is, to him, 'German in an ugly disguise.'"[5] This view mirrors the views of Arthur de Gobineau, the most important theoretician of race in nineteenth-century Europe, who claimed that one of the salient features of the Jews was their lack of an "ancestral language." According to Gobineau, Jews have never had a real language; even Hebrew was simply borrowed from the "black Hamites." "Jews used the tongue of the country where they settled, and, further, these exiles were known everywhere by their special accent. They never succeeded in fitting their vocal organs to their adopted language, even when they had learnt it from childhood."[6] And Gobineau, in turn, reflected the views of the eighteenth-century physiognomists, such as Johann Caspar Lavater (quoting his friend, the poet J. M. R. Lenz): "It is evident to me that the Jews bear the sign of their fatherland, the orient, throughout the world. I mean their short, black, curly hair, their brown skin color. Their rapid speech, their brusque and precipitous actions also come from this source. I believe, that the Jews have more gall than other people."[7] Or as Georg Buschan noted in the 1920s, the Jews in Europe speak a "grotesque mix of Old Franconian dialect mixed with Jewish linguistic elements."[8] It is this link between language and physiology that marked *Mauscheln* as a pathological sign in the medical discourse of the period. By the mid-nineteenth century, this attribute, while part of the overall caricature of the Jew in Western Europe, is powerfully associated by Western Jews with the Eastern Jews, who had maintained Yiddish as their primary language.

Zwetschkenbaum is an Eastern European Jew who understands little German. He is constrained to sign the initial report of his crime in "Hebrew characters" (17) because his own linguistic competence is that of a speaker of Yiddish. Given this caveat, we can turn to Zwetschkenbaum's mental status examination by the court-appointed psychiatrist, Dr. Herbert Zoltan Ondoraki (20–22). Such examinations have been standard within European (and American) court systems from the middle of the nineteenth century to the present, whenever a judge or prosecutor believes that an accused is unable to understand the charges brought against him/her. The questions that Ondoraki asks are "common" ones, that is, they presuppose no specialized knowledge—at least according to the lawyer or the physicians. For these questions reflect the world of power that sees this milieu as universal. But, of course, they not only require highly specialized knowledge but are cast in a language that is complex in its euphemistic restatement of the "evident." The questions initially posed are the following: What is your name? What is the capital of Austria? On what river is the capital? None of these are answered directly, but with illicit head shaking and "complicated and repulsive gestures" (20). Here Zwetschkenbaum's Jewish consciousness is misunderstood as a sign of mental incompetence. A Jew's name is not the same as that of a non-Jew, since Jews traditionally use patronymics. Thus the ongoing confusion about Zwetschkenbaum's name, about his brother's name, and about the fact that Zwetschkenbaum may not be his name at all, reflects the examiners' difficulty in understanding the differences in the onomastics of Eastern European Jewry and the social pressures under which the acquisition of a name placed an individual. Gesture, the mark of the primitive in the anthropology of the early nineteenth century, delineates a sublinguistic response (at least in the eyes of the examining physician).[9] Lenz comments on the Jews "brusque and precipitous actions," which becomes a sign of mental disorder.

When none of these questions provokes any answer that is useful in judging Zwetschkenbaum's competency, the examining physician moves from questions of "education and instruction" (20) to purely natural questions, such as the difference between men and women. Zwetschkenbaum "blushes" at this indelicate question and can only answer that "men are circumcised and women are not" (20). Finally, the question turns to the accused's understanding of his crime. He is accused of stealing plums—does he know what a plum is? Zwetschkenbaum's remarkable answer is that it is a "laughing winged animal whose wings shine in the sun" (21).

All the accused's answers point toward an inability to understand not only what he is asked but anything at all. His answers reflect his lack of intellectual capacity, his underlying mental illness. We, the readers of this satire, know that Zwetschkenbaum's answers or lack thereof make perfect sense. Why should he know the geography, political or natural, of Austria? Such details are understood, even by the examining physician and prosecutor, as reflections of the individual's education, not of the individual's competency. It is possible to not know that Vienna is the capital and that it lies on the Danube and to still be sane, especially in the world after the dissolution of the "k.u.k." monarchy. Vienna had stopped being the center of civilization as the power brokers know it, but no one bothered to inform them of this fact.

Zwetschkenbaum's responses to the natural questions are more complicated, for his answers to these questions seem quite off the mark. Is the sole distinction between men and women the mark of circumcision? Certainly this question points to the difference in the form of the genitalia, since only infant male Jews are circumcised. But it also points to the discourse about circumcision in German and Austrian culture that Drach would have felt was central to his own identity. For a male Jew, the central distinction between male and female is the representation of the covenant. But by the late 1930s and 1940s, the meaning of circumcision in Austria (as well as in Germany) had taken on quite a negative tone. One can turn to one of the most widely read sexologists of the beginning of the twentieth century, Paolo Mantegazza (1831–1901), for a "liberal" reading of the meaning of circum-

cision in the culture in which Drach wrote. (Certainly antisemitic representations were even cruder and more offensive.) The controversial
centerpiece of Mantegazza's work is his trilogy on love and sex, *Physiology of Love* (1872), *Hygiene of Love* (1877), and *On Human Love*
(1885).[10] Cited widely by sexologists from Cesare Lombroso, Richard
Krafft-Ebing, Havelock Ellis, and Iwan Bloch to Magnus Hirschfeld,
Mantegazza remained one of the accessible popular sources for "scientific" knowledge (and misinformation) to the educated public at the
turn of the century.[11] If we turn to the chapter after the one on "per-
versions" in Mantegazza's study of the anthropology of sexual practices, we come to a detailed discussion of the "mutilation of the genitals," which recounts the history of these practices among "savage
tribes," including the Jews.[12] Indeed, only in Mantegazza's discussion
of the Jews did the text turn from a titillating account of "unnatural
practices" into a polemic (echoing Spinoza's often-cited comments on
the centrality of circumcision to the definition of the Jew)[13] against
the perverse practices of that people out of their correct "space" and
"time"—the Jews, whose correct space was understood to be the Holy
Land and whose correct time was the age of the Bible:

> Circumcision is a shame and an infamy; and I, who am not in the least anti-
> Semitic, who indeed have much esteem for the Israelites, I who demand of
> no living soul a profession of religious faith, insisting only upon the brother-
> hood of soap and water and of honesty, I shout and shall continue to shout at
> the Hebrews, until my last breath: Cease mutilating yourselves: cease im-
> printing upon your flesh an odious brand to distinguish you from other men;
> until you do this, you cannot pretend to be our equal. As it is, you, of your
> own accord, with the branding iron, from the first days of your lives, proceed
> to proclaim yourselves a race apart, one that cannot, and does not care to, mix
> with ours.[14]

Jews, in Vienna as elsewhere in German-speaking Europe, looked
upon their bodies as the objects about which the debates over the
meaning and source of health and disease were held. The primary
means of avoiding these confrontations was to understate the meaning of circumcision. This avoidance was also reflected in the debates
about the need for circumcision among acculturated Jews in Vienna.
The extraordinary anonymous tale of "Herr Moriz Deutschösterreicher," written in the mid-1940s, begins with the argument between
the father and the mother of this "Mr. Average Austrian Jew":

Moriz Deutschösterreicher was born on June 2, 1891 in Vienna. His mother did not want him to be circumcised: "It's crazy, Sandor, to purposely violate my child, think about when he goes into the army and they all have to bathe naked together, or what if he marries a Christian, how embarrassing. . . . If you are dumb enough and don't have him baptized, don't do this to him. Does one have to send such a poor worm with such a handicap into the world?" She cried day and night. But it didn't help a bit. Sandor agreed with his old mother—by himself he would have perhaps hesitatingly agreed, because he did not place much store in such things.[15]

Circumcision has no positive meaning in this context, except as a means of pleasing someone of an older generation. For the prototypical Eastern European Jew, such as the accused in Drach's novel, such self-doubt did not exist. But within Drach's sense of the difference between his world (the world of Austrian legal culture) and that of his protagonist, the issue of circumcision is central. It is stressed in the physician's reading of Zwetschkenbaum's responses. For, according to his analysis, Zwetschkenbaum can only "distinguish between the sexes by means of a totemic mutilation" (22). Indeed, he seems to have no interest in sexuality except where it reflects specific "rituals of his tribe" (23). This view adheres completely to the science of his time.

One final question should be asked about the implications of the mental status examination: Why does Zwetschkenbaum define the plum (that he is accused of stealing) as a bird? It is reported that he later tells the jailer that he had misunderstood the physician, whose missing eyeteeth had caused him to mispronounce the word (*Zwetschken*) as the name of a bird (*Spätzchen*) (21). (One might also add that the usual Yiddish word for plum is *Flaum*.) Here, the classic mispronunciation of German words by Yiddish speakers, the *Mauscheln* that marked the discourses about Jewish difference for centuries, is projected back onto the Austrian physician. The jargon of the lawyer in which the entire novel is written is, of course, the most evident form of a linguistic corruption, which reflects the mental decay of its user. Following Karl Kraus's view of the relationship between language and thought, or at least between impure language and muddled thought, Drach turns the table on the Aryan image of the Jew, presenting the discourse of the interrogator as corrupted by his own power in the world. This reversal of the meaning of the Jew's discourse and the discourse of the law is missed by the evaluators (but not by the reader), and Zwetschkenbaum is diagnosed with a case of "moral insanity," representative of his whole community, that is, the entire race (23).

This diagnosis is at the core of Drach's novel. For it is not the Jew who is mad; it is all the Jews who are insane. Whatever Zwetschken-baum had answered in his mental status examination would have re-vealed the madness that was inherent in being a Jew and that was ex-acerbated in the "rudimentary, retrogressive nature" of the protago-nist (23). According to the science of the time, Jews are mad simply because they are Jews, and this becomes most evident in the most primitive of Jews—the Jews from Eastern Europe.

The Discourse on the Madness of the Jews

Jews were understood to be statistically and individually at greater risk for mental illness. The statistics presented by nineteenth- (and in-deed twentieth-) century writers on the topic of the mental instabil-ity of the Jews may not, of course, reflect any specific predisposition of the European Jewish community to mental illness. These statistics, cited over and over by mental health practitioners during this period, most probably reflect the higher incidence of hospitalization of Jews for mental illness due to their concentration in urban areas, which, un-like rural ones, are not as tolerant of the presence of the mentally ill. Also, urban Jews had developed a better network for identifying and treating illness, including mental illness. The overt social pressures that were mounting against the Jews, and that were often repressed by acculturated Jews anxious about their status in European society, may well have increased the amount of psychic pain these individuals had to bear. It is also quite possible that some Jews in Western Euro-pean urban areas, especially those who were displaced in Eastern Eu-rope and were forced to flee west, experienced trauma caused by their flight. The sense of community, coupled with the impression that the mentally ill were unable to function within urban society, may have led to more frequent hospitalization, and thus to the much higher statistical incidence of psychopathology among the Jews. Jewish communal organizations certainly subscribed to the view that Jews were at greater risk for mental illness. The Bureau for Jewish Statistics, for example, published a detailed study in 1918 in which the greater frequency of hysteria and neurasthenia among German Jews was detailed.[16]

By the 1880s linking the Jew with psychopathology was a given in anthropological circles. In the Parisian Anthropological Society, the Prussian census of 1880 was the point of departure for an even more detailed debate on the psychopathologies of the Jews. Again statistics were used to stress the greater occurrence of mental illness among the Jews. The comments on the etiology of the mental illness were more diffuse. M. Zabrowski blamed the mental illness of the Jews on their ecstatic preoccupation with mysticism and the supernatural, a clear reference to the Eastern Jews, whose presence was felt even more in Paris following the assassination of Alexander II in 1881 and the resulting forced immigration.[17] Here the echoes of the underlying rhetoric about conversion and the inherently unstable nature of the Eastern Jew surfaced. He and M. Sanson also stressed the curative role of agricultural employment and the absence of Jews in this field. The "cosmopolitanism" of the Jews, the pressure of the fields in which they were occupied, formed part of this reason. But M. Blanchard simply stated that "hysteria and neurasthenia are more frequent among the Jewish race than all other races." Thus, it is no longer simply mental illness, but rather "hysteria and neurasthenia" that are typical of the Jew. The source of these illnesses, according to Sanson, was endogamous marriage.[18]

The view that Jews are especially prone to hysteria and neurasthenia through inbred weakening of the nervous system appeared in canonical form throughout Jean Martin Charcot's *Tuesday Lessons*, such as the one for October 27, 1888.[19] In it Charcot described "a case of hysterical dyspnea. I already mentioned that this twenty-year-old patient is a Jewess. I will use this occasion to stress that nervous illnesses of all types are innumerably more frequent among Jews than among other groups," a fact that Charcot attributed to inbreeding.[20] Charcot saw "the Jews as being the best source of material for nervous illness."[21] (Charcot had a number of Russian male Jews suffering from hysteria and neurasthenia as his patients. Their case notes are among his unpublished papers in Paris.) Charcot lectured on the predisposition of Jews to specific forms of illness, such as diabetes, where "the exploration is easy" because of the intermarriage of the Jews.[22] In an off-the-record remark, "a French physician," most probably Charcot, commented, "In my practice in Paris, . . . I have the occasion to notice that, with the Jew, the emotions seem to be more vivid, the sensibility more intense, the nervous reactions more rapid and profound." And this leads to the "vital sap ris[ing] from his limbs, or his trunk, to his head [and] . . . his overstrained nervous system is often apt, in the end, to become disordered and to collapse entirely."[23] This view was certainly present in mainstream German medicine. The anthropologist-physician Georg Buschan, whose first position had been as an asylum physician in Leubus in 1886, stressed, in an address to the Organization of German Psychiatrists in Dresden on September 21, 1894, the "extraordinary incidence" of hysteria among European Jews as a sign of their racial degeneration.[24]

One of the most striking documents of the period is one of the major dissertations written, with Charcot, by Henry Meige, the physician who succeeded him as the editor of the Salpêtrière journal. In Meige's dissertation of 1893 on the Wandering Jew in the clinical setting of the Salpêtrière, the image of the Jew and the gaze of the Jew become one.[25] Meige attempted to place the appearance of Eastern European (male) Jews in the Salpêtrière as a sign of their inherent instability. In his dissertation he sketched the background to the legend of the Wandering Jew and provided (like his supervisor Charcot) a set of visual "images of Ahasverus."[26] He then provided a series of case studies of Eastern (male) Jews, two of which he illustrated. The first plate was of "Moser C. called Moses," a forty-five- or forty-six-year-old Polish Jew from Warsaw who had already wandered through the clinics in Vienna and elsewhere.[27] The second plate was of "Gottlieb M.," a forty-two-year-old Jew from Vilnius, who likewise had been treated in many of the psychiatric clinics in Western Europe.[28]

Given the extraordinary migration of millions of Eastern Jews through Western Europe toward England and America beginning in the early 1880s, the appearance of these few cases of what comes to be called "Munchausen syndrome" should not be surprising. Without any goal, these Jews "wandered" only in the sense that they were driven West, and that some should seek the solace of a clinic where they would at least be treated as individuals, even if as sick individuals, should not make us wonder. The treatment of Jews, especially those who passed through Germany, was aimed at making them feel diseased and dirty. Herded into barracks, stripped, showered, their clothes disinfected—they were marked as disease carriers.[29] What is striking is that Meige provides images and analyses that stress the pathognomonic physiognomy of the Jew—especially his eyes.[30] The images stare at us madly, informing us of their inherent hysterical pathology. For the fixed, staring gaze of the Jew is itself a pathological sign. The Jew is the hysteric; the Jew is the feminized Other; the Jew is seen as different, as diseased. This is the image of the hysteric with which the Jewish scientist was confronted. He was to see himself as the Other, as the diseased, but most important, as the feminized Other, the altered form of his circumcised genitalia different from other men's and understood as analogous to the form of female genitalia.

By 1890 Charcot's view had become commonplace in European psychiatry. Standard German psychiatry textbooks of the period cited it regularly. Georg Burgl's 1912 handbook of forensic medicine stated quite clearly that "the Jewish race has a special predisposition for hysteria." For Burgl this predisposition was a result of the degenerative nature of the Jew and was marked by "physical signs of degeneration such as asymmetry and malocclusion of the skull, malocclusion of the teeth, etc."[31] The visibility of the Jew was identical to the visibility of the degenerate, their signs and symptoms pointing to their susceptibility. And it is in the world of Eastern Jewry that the most salient examples of such forms of mental illness are to be found.

Eastern European Jews and Mental Illness

Cesare Lombroso, the Italian forensic psychiatrist whose name is linked to the concept of "degeneration," which he helped forge, was also a Jew. After authoring a number of studies on the degeneracy of the prostitute and the criminal, Lombroso was confronted with the charge that Jews, too, were examples of a degenerate subclass of human being, a class determined by their biology. Lombroso's answer to this charge, *Anti-Semitism and the Jews in the Light of Modern Science* (1893), attempted to counter the use of medical or pseudoscientific discourse to characterize the nature of the Jew. But Lombroso also accepted the basic view that the Jew was more highly prone to specific forms of mental illness. He quoted Charcot to this effect, but saw the reason for this tendency not in the physical nature of the Jew but in the "residual effect of persecution."[32] Lombroso accepted the view that some type of degenerative process, which caused the predominance of specific forms of mental illness, exists among all Jews. What differentiated his view from that of the others was what he believed to be the cause of this process. In rejecting the charge of inbreeding, Jews such as Lombroso were also rejecting the implications that they indulged in primitive sexual practices, practices that violate a basic human taboo against incest. Confusing endogamous marriage with incestuous inbreeding was a result of scientific discourse that desired to have categories circumscribing the explicit nature of the Other. The Jews are mentally ill, they manifest this illness in hysteria and neurasthenia, and the cause of their mental illness is their sexual practice, or their mystical religion, or their role as carriers of Western cosmopolitanism. All of their mental instability can be attributed to their corrupt discourse. Their illness is literally inscribed in their corrupt use of language.

Other Jewish commentators on the nature of the mental illness of the Jews took similar positions. Moses Julius Gutmann, who wrote extensively, beginning with his 1920 dissertation, about the predisposition of the Jews to various illnesses, including mental illness, wrote an extensive study of the mental illness of the Jews in 1926.[33] Gutmann, too, saw the Jews as especially predisposed to specific forms of illness. He considered specific forms of mental illness among the Jews to be the result of the early marriages among Eastern Jews, which permitted individuals to pass specific forms of mental illness on to their offspring before they themselves manifested any symptoms. The assumption was that these individuals would not have reproduced had they waited until they were older to marry. The Jewish physician Max Sichel, a member of the staff of the psychiatric clinic at the University of Frankfurt, while understanding the exogenous causes of mental illness such as the transition from the closed world of the ghetto to the competitive world of modern society, also stressed the endogenous aspects of the Jews' constitution as a major factor in their illness.[34] Sichel accepted the immutability of the racial characteristics of the Jew. As with all the work of Jewish physicians, he affirmed the reality of Jewish mental illness, while believing it was triggered "by the constant persecution and mental torture, by the eternal struggle for naked existence and for daily bread,"[35] and in doing so he accepted its inheritability, even if just over a limited span of generations. But Sichel, like most of his contemporaries, also believed that interbreeding played a major role in transmitting and causing such illnesses.[36]

Bertha Pappenheim, the Anna O. of Sigmund Freud and Joseph Breuer's *Studies in Hysteria*, critiqued the

absence among Galician Jews of the most primitive concepts of child care, nursing care, and the care of newly delivered women, indeed the absence of any knowledge of infection or even disinfection. . . . The spas, hospitals and mental asylums, the institutes for the blind and the deaf-dumb show a high percent of Galician Jews. Today many of these diseases are labeled as hereditary, which have their sources in the ignorance of the simplest hygienic rules and the exercise of other activities detrimental to health.[37]

The attempt to dismiss all disease, even mental illness, as having a biological cause (here in the environment rather than in the individual) simply places the blame for Jewish illness on the world of the Eastern Jew, which is distant from the charge of Jewish racial susceptibility for hysteria. The image of the Eastern Jew as "filthy" (set in contrast to the cleanliness and orderliness demanded of the Jew) simply transfers the locus of anxiety about the risk of madness from Western Jews (always fearful they are not quite clean enough) toward the East. In 1930, in a handbook entitled *Hygiene and the Jews*—one of the products of the Hygiene Exhibitions held in Germany since the fin de siècle and during which there was usually a Jewish pavilion—there appeared a historical essay on "why the Jews of Poland were 'filthy.'"[38] Here the comments of Bertha Pappenheim were placed in the mouth of the eighteenth-century city physician of Warsaw, August Ferdinand von Wolff, the son of a baptized Jew, the physician Abraham Emanuel Wolff.

From the standpoint of Western Europe in the early twentieth century, Eastern Jews were at special risk for mental illness either because they were so unlike Western Jews (as seen from a Jewish point of view) or because they were so essentially Jewish (as seen from an Aryan, racialist point of view). Beginning in the mid-nineteenth cen-

tury, statistical studies of the East began to document higher incidence of mental illness among Eastern Jews. Josef Czermak, using admission figures for a hospital in Moravia during 1857, showed that for
every 10,000 Catholics there were seven Catholic patients admitted
for some form of mental illness; for every 10,000 Jews, there were 22
Jewish patients admitted.[39] Parallel findings were seen in the Baltic
provinces of Russia. In 1914 H. Budul studied the frequency of certain mental illnesses in Dorpat (Tartu) in Estonia. There he found
that Jews suffered more than comparative groups from manic-
depressive illness and hysteria.[40] Harald Siebert conducted a similar
study in Latvia, in which he found that Jews were racially predeter-
mined for hysteria. He made an interesting distinction, however, de-
claring that "for the educated class one finds primarily nervous disease
among women; for the lower classes, among men."[41] Certainly the
major figure to deal with the mental illness of the Eastern Jews was
the Jewish psychiatrist Hermann Oppenheim, Karl Abraham's cousin
and the widely cited author of a standard psychiatric textbook of the
late nineteenth century.[42] His essay on the psychopathology of the
Russian Jews is without a doubt the most widely cited and authoritative work in the field. Published in a *Festschrift* for August Forel, the
essay begins with the complaint that "from year to year the growing
hoards of patients from Russia come to us for advise and cure."[43] The
"us" is the Western physician. Oppenheim stated quite directly that it
was "well-known that Jews have a predisposition for neurosis and
psychosis." He made an unstated distinction between the collectivity
of the Eastern Jews, whose social milieu triggers their innate predisposition to mental illness, and the individual Western Jew, such as he,
who may be tainted but who has not been exposed to the circumstances that trigger the illnesses.

What is striking in Oppenheim's account is the role that the voice
as a sign of the sensibility of the patient plays. He notes that even
"with the simplest test for sensitivity with needle pricks the patient
cries out: 'Gewalt, Gewalt!' Certainly cowardliness, the fear of pain
may play a role, but more evidently this cry seems to me a statement
of the horrid path of suffering of this people, i.e. this race."[44] In another case study he described the visit of a Russian-Jewish singer who
had imagined a change in the quality of her voice upon the death of
her husband. She appeared to be a hysteric, according to Oppenheim,

because the only sign of her putative aphonia was a slight nasality in her voice. This he notes "was in intimate relationship to her mental state."[45] The image of the female seems to subsume the image of the Jew, and yet, for Oppenheim, the voice of the Eastern Jew permeates even the veneer of high culture. The altered voice of the Jew was a sign of the Jew's pathological relationship with the discourse of high culture.

The relationship between mental illness and the disruption of discourse has its roots in late-nineteenth-century medicine. The neurologist who listened to his hysterical patient or who diagnosed "general paralysis of the insane" because of the patient's monomaniacal tirades, or the psychiatrist who was able to characterize the discourse of the patient suffering from "dementia praecox" as "word salad," centered their perception of illness on the nature of the patient's language. Alterations in the nature of discourse were understood to be basic signs of pathology. Indeed, in the closing decades of the nineteenth century, these alterations came to be considered the primary signs of psychopathology. How a patient spoke was important, and incompetent discourse was a sign of psychopathology.

For the medicine of the fin de siècle, race was a major force in shaping the form, appearance, and symptoms of both neurological and psychological illness.[46] Indeed, Richard Gaupp, in his inaugural lecture as the professor of psychiatry at Tübingen in 1907, saw as one of the most needed goals of contemporary psychiatry "the clarification of the influence of race and morals, of climate and life style" on the appearance and frequency of mental illness.[47] Thus, we come to see that Adolf Hitler's views on the diseased nature of the Jewish psyche were in line with many of the mainstream views in the Viennese academy.

The Viennese psychiatrist Alexander Pilcz, a pupil of Heinrich Obersteiner and Julius Wagner-Jauregg, authored one of the period's standard handbooks on racial psychiatry.[48] Pilcz received his doctorate in 1895 and was the acting chair (*locum tenens*) for the "First" Department of Psychiatry at the University of Vienna from 1902–7, when he became director of the mental hospital Am Steinhof. (The "Second" Department of Psychiatry came to be the primary one. It was chaired by Wagner-Jauregg.) Pilcz was one of the most visible members of the psychiatric faculty of the University of Vienna during the first decades of the twentieth century. In Pilcz's work the question of the Jewish predisposition to manic-depressive psychosis was spelled out in detail: "In conclusion, I would like to present a personal observation, which is evident from the material presented here as well as from my private practice. It seems to me that there is a very high incidence of Jews among those patients with periodic insanity. It is noticeably high in regard to the relationship between Jews and the rest of the population."[49] Pilcz then elucidated six of the cases in his study of Jews suffering from mental illness. Of these cases four were men and two were women. No other "racial" category (such as Hungarian or Czech) was mentioned in any of his other case studies. He used phrases such as "possessing an extraordinary dialectic and sophistry" in describing the Jews' symptoms, terms taken from the antisemitic rhetoric of the day. Pilcz's study sought out the Jews as a visible "race" marked by a high rate of mental illness. For him, it was clearly the biological predisposition of the Jew that was evident in these cases.

One needs to understand Pilcz's views as a reflection of mainstream Viennese medicine during the period.[50] In 1901, Pilcz, then on the staff of Wagner-Jauregg's clinic in Vienna, published a widely cited essay on the occurrence of mental illness among Jews in the popular *Viennese Clinical Survey*. In it Pilcz stressed the great number of Jews who showed up in his study of periodic mental illness. It was for him a question of race. Pilcz stressed that he could not sort his sample by religion, for "even though those of the Jewish confession overlapped completely with those of the Jewish race, it is evident that not all patients who were Christian could be seen as Aryan."[51] Thus, he placed "baptized Jews in the rubric of Jewish patients." According to Pilcz, one's "race" is inescapable. The Jews' madness is an inherent racial quality. Pilcz presented his own clinical findings, noting that in Vienna, from January 1, 1898, to August 1, 1901, 1,219 patients were admitted, of which 134 (10.99 percent) were Jews. According to the 1900 census, the population of Vienna at the end of that year was 1,648,335, of which 146,136 (8.86 percent) were Jews. Now it is clear that Pilcz defined the Jews in the clinic by race; in the 1900 census they are defined by religion, that is, Jewish converts would be found not among the 8.86 percent but among the remaining population. The diseases for which Pilcz saw the highest occurrence among Jewish patients were drug addition (two out of six or 33.3 percent), neurasthenia (25 percent), and "periodic insanity" (manic-depressive psychosis—26.08 percent). The etiology of the Jews' madness, he noted, citing Krafft-Ebing and Theodor Kirchhof, lies in their inbreeding. This essay was popular enough to warrant translation into French in 1902.[52]

Pilcz lectured widely in Vienna on this topic.[53] In 1906 Pilcz, by then the assistant chairperson of the psychiatric clinic, published a detailed monograph on "comparative racial psychiatry."[54] He introduced this monograph by noting the positive reception of his earlier study on the madness of the Jews.[55] In this more extensive study, which also included anthropological data on non-European groups, Pilcz focused on the racial groups in the Austro-Hungarian Empire: Hungarians, Germans, "North Slavs," and Jews. According to his findings, Jews suffer from progressive paralysis (final stage of neurosyphilis), dementia praecox (schizophrenia), paranoia, and periodic psychosis (manic-depressive disorder) more frequently than from any other mental and neurological illnesses, and more frequently than all other groups. Under hysteria Pilcz simply noted that "since Charcot" the "especially strong predisposition of the Jews for hysteria has been known."[56] Likewise, he believed that Jews make up the majority of neurasthenics[57] and that they reveal a tendency toward "hereditary-degenerative psychosis."[58] He argued, citing medical and anthropological authorities, that the incidents of mental illness in Palestine were equal to those in Europe. And he closed with the statement that "since the heightened disposition is also to be found in women, it cannot be the exhausting mental life, the *struggle for life* [in English], the damage of 'civilization,' which can explain the prevalence of the Jewish insane."[59] It is race and nothing more. Pilcz has provided us with a theoretical model for the transmittal of such tendencies (relying on the view of Wagner-Jauregg), in which he stressed the forms of mental illness that can be carried from generation to generation.[60] He noted that the "hereditary-degenerative" mental illnesses, in their form and their cause, are uninfluenced by external causes. The question of proximal cause of any disease was for him secondary, except, perhaps, for those mental illnesses that could be traced to neurosyphilis. Pilcz preached the dogma of the racial transmission of mental illness to students and faculty throughout the first decades of the twentieth century. On February 10, 1927, he lectured on this topic to the 24th International Course for Continuing Medical Education held by the medical faculty.[61] There he stressed the existence of an Eastern European Jewish psychosis.

In Vienna there was a Jewish attempt to answer Pilcz directly. Ignaz Zollschan, a physician-anthropologist whose work was widely read at the turn of the century, argued that "many authors have painted the future of the Jews in the blackest colors because of the great number of the mentally ill to be found among them. . . . All of the biological advantages and disadvantages of the Jews are the result of inbreeding. . . . The Jew has an especially fine and sensitively organized nervous system. He responds with sensitivity to stimulation more than the nerves of the robust peasant, and can thus hardly be considered neurasthenic."[62] This seems to dismiss the Jews' "mental illness" as an artifact of their more highly developed nervous system, and yet the power of the epidemiological literature of the period did not leave Zollschan unaffected. Zollschan, who persuasively argued for a single, pure Jewish race, still accepted the statistical arguments that Jews do frequently suffer from different types of mental illness. Among other sources, he cited the Prussian census, which "proved" that Jews had twice as high a rate of mental illness as did Aryans (five cases per one thousand of the population as opposed to two and a half cases per one thousand). His rationale was complicated, and it returns us to the earlier discussion of the frequency of syphilis among the Jews and its relationship to the nature of the Jew's body. Zollschan carefully argued that the higher incidence of "mental illness" was in fact a higher rate of progressive paralysis. Citing Pilcz's study of racial psychiatry, he noted that of the cases of mental illness in Prussia from 1898 to 1900, 20.5 percent were of progressive paralysis. He tied progressive paralysis to syphilis directly and saw the increased rate of mental illness as a reflex of the increased rate of syphilitic infection. But why would Jews have a high rate of syphilitic infection? Zollschan, echoing the work of Iwan Bloch, argued that a group's first exposure to a new disease creates greater damage than a group's long exposure to the disease. The Jews, having been sequestered in the ghetto and practicing early marriage, were simply shielded from the ravages of syphilis until civil emancipations. "Syphilitic infection is endemic among the Jews only as a result of their assimilation." This is a powerful metaphor for Zollschan, whose Zionist agenda was the preservation of the pure race of the Jews from the contamination of mixed marriages and assimilation. But even here Zollschan made one further attempt to provide a rationale for the insanity of the Jews. A thousand years of mental toil, "the extraordinarily difficult struggle for existence, the haste and hunt for daily bread" also contribute to the neurosis of the Jew. (These arguments were repeated verbatim by Felix Theilhaber in the *Jewish Lexicon* in the late 1920s.)[63] In other words, everything that is associated with the Jews' life in the Diaspora leads to their diseased mental state. The sole cure, a political state, will "preserve the individuality of the race" and provide a cure for the Jew's madness.

In the course of the nineteenth and early twentieth centuries, a number of approaches were taken to the myth of the mental illness of the Jews. European biology, especially in Germany and France, served to reify accepted attitudes toward all marginal groups, especially the Jews. The scientific "fact" that the Jew was predisposed to madness would have enabled society, acting as the legal arm of science, to deal with Jews as it dealt with the insane. However, the reality was quite different. While the fantasy of the privileged group would have been to banish the Jews out of sight and into the asylum, the best it could do was to institutionalize the idea of the madness of the Jews. The popular wisdom was that Jews, like women, possessed a basic biological predisposition to specific forms of mental illness. Thus, Jews, like women, who were also making specific political demands on the privileged group at the same moment in history, could be dismissed as unworthy of becoming part of the privileged group because of their aberration. Like the American slaves, who were labeled mad because of their desire to escape from slavery, Jews, by acting on the promise made to them through the granting of political emancipation in the eighteenth century, proved their own madness.[64] Jewish professionals, in accepting the rhetoric of nineteenth-century medicine, needed to limit the applicability of this model to themselves. They saw in various subgroups of Jews (the merchant Jew, the Eastern Jew, the disenfranchised Jew, the immigrant Jew) those groups most at risk. They removed themselves from the category of those endangered and freed themselves from the potential curse of the Jews' madness.

Conclusion: The Narrative Voice as the Voice of Unreason

It is in this context of the image of the mad Jew that Albert Drach's question about the competence of the Jew must be read. Is Zwetschkenbaum mad? In the novel, the general consensus among the other inmates in the lunatic asylum is that he is sane and being held in a world that is mad. The use of the asylum as a representative of the world's madness is an ancient topos. Drach uses it here to ask who is truly mad—the victim or the system? But there is a further and more important qualification in Drach's work, one that reveals the specificity of his own time and place. The madness of the Jew is the central question here. As Drach has the narrative voice state, "Why is this Jew here [in the asylum]? Is he crazy? No! He is here, because he is a Jew" (52). He is not "morally insane" (23) nor is he "paranoid" (35). He is a Jew caught in a system that reduces him to the object controlled. Is he mad? No, he is a Jew, and that is the equivalent of madness. The Jews' madness is their natural state, as the physician argues so ably in the novel: "It must be clear to the judge that Zwetschkenbaum is a Jew, and therefore thinks differently than normal Christian men" (92). And what is a Jew?—"a madman, someone possessed" (92). In its most sophisticated form, this madness appears as genius; in its most primitive state (as in the case of Zwetschkenbaum) it remains simply insanity.

This, of course, is the ironic twist in Drach's novel. Drach draws all of the discourses that evolve within this world of power, including that of Zwetschkenbaum, into question. We only see Zwetschkenbaum through the eyes of the prosecutor; his words are always rephrased, translated, or explained by the figures of power in the novel. Never does his discourse appear unmediated. This is very different from the other great representation of a mental status examination in the literature of the "k.u.k." tradition, Jaroslav Hasek's novel of the early 1920s depicting the adventures of the "good soldier Svejk." Josef Svejk's mental status examination takes place after he, too, falls into the hands of the police. In his interrogation, it is the doctors who are incompetent, or at least less competent than he. But unlike Drach, Hasek has his psychiatrists ask impossibly "technical questions," such as how deep is the Pacific Ocean or is radium heavier than lead, questions that would have never really been asked in such a context. There is a substantial difference between asking what is the capital of Austria and requiring someone to determine what the multiplicand of 12,897 times 13,863 is. Hasek's questions are a parody of the mental status examination; Drach's reflect the "reality" as well as its misinterpretation. Hasek's psychiatrists find that "Josef Svejk . . . expressed himself in terms such as 'Long live our Emperor Franz Joseph I,' which utterance is sufficient to illuminate the state of mind of Josef Svejk as that of a patent imbecile." This parodic response is the unquestioned result of their mental status examination.[65] But in this examination, Svejk is clearly the one in control. He sees their examination as nonsense and responds in kind. When asked how to "calculate the diameter of the globe" he responds with a joke as pointless as the question asked. This non sequitur is taken as a sign of his stupidity by the "experts," while we as the readers understand it as a sign of his command of the exchange.

Zwetschkenbaum is never in control, and he knows it. Svejk's subsequent sojourn in the madhouse is further proof that it is not the madman who is mad, but his keepers. It is not the madman's discourse that reveals him to be insane, but the keepers' discourse that discloses their madness. For this is a world in which not everyone is mad, where there is a real boundary between the sane and the mad. Svejk is the baseline for the possibility of sanity in this world. Hasek postulates the naïveté of Svejk as the sanity of truth. Drach does not permit such as easy reversal of roles. For he knows that, like it or not, Zwetschkenbaum is part of this world once he enters it and is formed by it. The discourse about Zwetschkenbaum's sanity is highly charged; it is always debated, even though the assumption of those in control of this world is that, by the very fact of his identity as a Wandering Eastern Jew, he is mad. And Zwetschkenbaum responds in kind. His naïveté is formed by the world in which he lives. He is a true victim of that world, not at all Hasek's wise fool. (One might note that Hasek's actual experience of such an examination and the resultant incarceration in an asylum was on the receiving end; Drach would have experienced such a process, if he ever did, as a lawyer. Hasek was a non-Jew and Drach a Jew, which added further differences to their perspectives.)

The discourse of law and its relationship to medicine is revealed in both of these novels as faulty. But for Drach, it is not merely the power of the examining physicians and their sense of what is right and wrong that is at stake. Unlike Hasek's representation of the mental status examination, it is not the wise fool versus the foolish wise person that is at the center of the representation of difference. Rather, it is the sense, written on the body of the author himself, that the law sees him as a Jew as different from all other categories constructed in his world. (Given Hasek's own antisemitic representations in his novel, this view could well have been shared by him.) Forensic psychiatry was itself a form of madness, because it rested its premises on the faulty notion of the inherent difference of the Jews, and not just because it was a means of societal control. For Hasek, Svejk's madness is a sign of the ability to undermine the system from within. No such ability exists for the Jew, whose essence is labeled as diseased and mad. The law, as Drach so strikingly reveals, becomes complicit as society, too, sees the Jew as inherently different. But it is not the discourse of the Jew that finally reveals itself to be the benchmark of madness, but the authoritative voice of the narrator. The voice of madness is embodied in the voice of the narrator. Much like the voice in Vladimir Nabokov's *Pale Fire*, which makes use of the conventions of literary criticism to reveal its own madness, so, too, does the narrative voice reveal its own culpability. The question of competence is shown to be relative, and the entire debate about the madness of the Jews, so central to the medical discourse of the early twentieth century, is revealed to be merely a device for controlling those elements seen as "foreign" in Austrian society. Drach's world is one in which discourse does reveal the underlying motivation, not of the Wandering Jew, but of the world of political power.

CHAPTER SIX

Otto Weininger and Sigmund Freud

Race and Gender in the Shaping
of Psychoanalysis

The Body of the Jew

In the summer of 1904, the Berlin ear, nose, and throat specialist Wilhelm Fliess wrote a sharp note to his friend and colleague Sigmund Freud, accusing him of having leaked Fliess's concept of bisexuality to Otto Weininger, either directly or through Freud's patient, the psychologist Hermann Swoboda.[1] Freud replied to Fliess that he had totally repressed Weininger's visit to him. In a later letter to David Abrahamsen concerning Weininger, Freud noted that he had seen Weininger's book only in manuscript, as a draft of the dissertation, which totally avoided the discussion of the "Jewish Question."[2] While for Freud Fliess's accusation concerning Weininger marked the end of his "homosexual cathexis" to Fliess, his memory of the matter reflected the intense antisemitism of Weininger's text.[3] For Weininger's juxtaposition of the "sexual" and the "racial" linked two aspects of the Jew long related within medical science in the popular culture of fin-de-siècle Vienna. In 1904 Otto Weininger (and the views that he espoused) came to have a role in Freud's locating a sense of his own identity as a Jewish male.

Otto Weininger published his revised dissertation, *Sex and Character,* in 1903, and he killed himself shortly thereafter in the house in Vienna in which Beethoven had died.[4] Weininger's book both became an immediate best-seller and established him as a serious contributor to the discourse about the relationship between race and gender at the beginning of the century.[5] *Sex and Character* is a work of intensive, undisguised self-hatred that had an unprecedented influence on the scientific discourse about Jews and women at the turn of the century. The book was fundamental in shaping at least some of Freud's attitudes toward the nature of the body, especially the question of bisexuality and its relationship to the concept of polymorphous perversity. More specifically, it also shaped his understanding of the complex relationship between his "racial" identity as a Jew and his "sexual" identity as a male. It is in the image of the Jewish body that these two definitions of identity meet. Freud's incorporation of Weininger's image in his work is parallel to a number of other fin-de-siècle thinkers whose reading of Weininger also repressed the question of the relationship of sexual identity to sexual anatomy. Thus, the lesbian feminist Charlotte Perkins Gilman saw Weininger's work as a major contribution to the science of gender.[6] And Ludwig Wittgenstein, the homosexual "partially Jewish" Catholic philosopher, accepted and incorporated aspects of Weininger's philosophy into his worldview.[7]

Central to Weininger's study of the relationship between the masculine and the feminine was the dichotomy between the Jew and the Aryan.[8] What contemporary science saw in the form of the body, Weininger saw in the structure of the psyche. Weininger's work, while in no way innovative, summarized the view of a psychological spectrum that runs from Jewishness at one end to the Aryan mind at the other. His polemical restatement of Schopenhauer's cranky views on women as biologically inferior simply extended the category of the "feminine" to the Jew. This scale was parallel to that on which the "masculine" and the "feminine" served as the antithetical points. For Jews and for women such a view of bisexuality or "biracialism" meant that the biological antithesis between the self and the Other should have vanished. For Weininger, the converted Jew, it meant that he saw himself as less Jewish than the arch-antisemite Richard Wagner, whom he labeled as "having an accretion of Jewishness in his art" (305). Jewishness is a mind-set; for Weininger it did "not refer to a nation or to a race, to a creed or to a scripture. When I speak of the Jew I mean neither an individual nor the whole body, but mankind in general, in so far it has a share in the platonic idea of Judaism" (306). Weininger constructed the image of the Jew like that of the woman: as an inherently negative quality of the psyche, as needing to be transcended. It is this linking of the Jew and the woman that is reflected in Freud's work.

Weininger served Freud as a touchstone for the definition of the diseased Jew, the antithesis of the Jewish physician, whose role is to heal. For Freud, Weininger's disease is his self-hate, both as a Jew and as a homosexual; the proof of his disease was his suicide. It is not surprising that Weininger appears in Freud's work in the context of the debates about sexual identity.

It is in a footnote to his argument about castration anxiety in his account of the 1909 case of Little Hans that Freud cites Weininger's text and his life as exemplary cases of the internalization of self-hatred. In the case of Little Hans, the question of the nature and form of the male body stands at the center of Freud's concern, to quote his paraphrase of the child's argument: "Could it be that living beings really exist which did not posses widdlers? If so, it would no longer be so incredible that they could take his own widdler away, and, as it were, make him into a woman!"[9] To this statement Freud appended a long footnote that relates the child's anxiety about castration to the nature of antisemitism.

It is important to follow Freud's unstated train of thought. If, says the child, I can be circumcised and my Jewishness revealed, that is, if I can be made into a Jew, cannot I also be castrated and have my hidden femininity revealed, that is, cannot I be made into a woman? Freud's note attempted to "demonstrate the typical character of the train of thought" of the five-year-old child:

The castration complex is the deepest root of anti-Semitism; for even in the nursery little boys hear that a Jew has something cut off his penis—a piece of his penis, they think—and this gives them a right to despise Jews. And there is no stronger unconscious root for the sense of superiority over women. Weininger (the young philosopher who, highly gifted but sexually deranged, committed suicide after producing his remarkable book, *Geschlecht und Charakter* [*Sex and Character*, 1903]), in a chapter that attracted much attention, treated Jews and women with equal hostility and overwhelmed them with the same insults. Being neurotic, Weininger was completely under the sway of his infantile complexes; and from that standpoint what is common to Jews and women is their relation to the castration complex. (*SE*, 10: 36)

Freud's example of the problematic relationship of the Jew to his circumcised penis is Otto Weininger. Weininger's views on the nature of bisexuality reflect on the model that had been explored in the work of the ethnopsychologists. Qualities of the body are (usually incompletely) transferred to the psyche.

The roots of this view lie deep in the theories of ethnopsychology as formulated by two Jews, the psychologist Moritz Lazarus and his brother-in-law, the philologist Heymann Steinthal, in the 1860s. In the opening issue of their journal for ethnopsychology and linguistics, *Zeitschrift für Völkerpsychologie und Sprachwissenschaft* (note the link of mind and language), they outlined the assumptions about the "knowability" of the mind.[10] Lazarus and Steinthal's object of study was the "psychology of human beings in groups (*Gemeinschaft*)." Unlike in other fields of psychology of the time, where laboratory and clinical work were demanded to define the arena of study, ethnopsychology depended on historical and cultural/ethnological data. Their work was highly medicalized: Lazarus studied physiology with the materialist Johannes Müller and co-founded the Medical-Psychological Society with the Berlin neurologist Wilhelm Griesinger in 1867. While Lazarus and Steinthal wished to separate their psychology from materialistic physiology, they were bound by the scientific rhetoric of the materialistic arguments about inheritance. The great laboratory psychologist, Wilhelm Wundt, remained the greatest proponent of their views of "universal mental creations"[11] well into the twentieth century. And Freud made extensive use of Wundt's explication of these views in his *Psychopathology of Everyday Life* (1901) and *Totem and Taboo* (1913).[12]

Freud, like the ethnopsychologists, needed to separate the idea of the psyche from the idea of the body; he needed to eliminate the image of the fixed, immutable racial composition that determines all thoughts and all actions. Weininger took quite the opposite tack. He saw race, along with gender, as one of two constituent factors of the psyche. For all these thinkers, the psyche was separate from, and yet still part of, the body. For it seemed impossible, even within the needs of such ethnopsychologists to avoid the pitfalls of race, to ever truly separate the mind from the body.

Lazarus and Steinthal constructed the concept of "peoples" (*Völker*), but they stressed that these groups were constituted by the individuals who do not comprise fixed biological "races" (5). "Human beings," as Lazarus observed, "are the creation of history; everything in us, about us, is the result of history; we do not speak a word, we do not think an idea, there is neither feeling nor emotion, which is not in a complicated manner dependent on historical determinants."[13] The standards for defining a people are fluid, and they change from group to group. Thus, the standards for being French are different from those for being German (35). Even though a "people is a purely subjective construction," it reflects itself in "a common consciousness of many with the consciousness of the group" (35–36). This "common consciousness" exists initially because of the "same origin" and the "proximity of the dwellings" of the members of the group (37). And "with the relationship through birth, the similarity of physiognomy, especially the form of the body, is present" (37). For Lazarus and Steinthal this "objective" fact of biological similarity lay the groundwork for the "subjective" nature of the mental construction of a people (38). But the biological underpinnings of this argument are clear: the Irish eat potatoes as a reflex of being in Ireland, which makes them Irish, and they are Irish because they eat potatoes.[14] Could one then not argue that Jews are Jews because they circumcise their male infants, and they circumcise their male infants because they are Jews?

These acquired characteristics are localized not in the body, but within the language of the *Volk*. Lazarus and Steinthal were constructing a definition of group identification that was rooted in a biological (and, therefore, for them, in an observable and demonstrable) relationship, but one that self-consciously built upon this basic identity a sense of group cohesion. This was an answer to the argument about race constructing the mentality of the group. Here the group is constituted based on the biological accidents of birth and dwelling, not on the inborn identity of blood. And yet it is the observable, the biological, that structures their argument.

The relationship between mindset and race reappeared in *Sex and Character*, but with quite a different focus. Weininger's work on the sexual is important in framing Freud's response to his equation of the Jewish male and the Aryan female. But it is also important in seeing how Freud could avoid a claim for the visualization of science. Weininger's "laws of sexual attraction" postulated the existence of a biological (that is, a real) explanation for sexual attraction. This is much the same ground that most of the post-Darwin biologists plowed. Weininger thought that the basis of attraction is the existence in every individual of both male and female qualities of mind. According to his view, just as the Jew is a quality of mind that can be expunged, so is the feminine. Masculinity and femininity were abstractions for Weininger, and thus the possibility for bisexuality arose. Weininger stated this literally in the form of mock formulae, with "M" and "W" representing the male and female mentality and other such pseudomathematical parallels. This model of the "mixed" race was carried over into his representation of the relationship between Jew and Aryan.

In the late nineteenth century, there was a set model for the relationship between models of sexuality and models of race. The model of racial attraction is more directly stated by the nineteenth-century French writer Abel Hermant:

Differences of race are irreducible and between two beings who love each other they cannot fail to produce exceptional and instructive reactions. In the first superficial ebullition of love, indeed, nothing notable may be manifested, but in a fairly short time the two lovers, innately hostile, in striving to approach each other strike against an invisible partition which separates them. Their sensibilities are divergent; everything in each shocks the other; even their anatomical conformation, even the language of their gestures; all is foreign.[15]

Weininger's first law of sexual attraction was an answer to this view. Sexual attraction is based on wholeness and complementarity. One strives to be a complete person by combining the masculine and feminine natures of two individuals, each of whom has both masculine and feminine qualities. Weininger's second law attempted to explain the strength of sexual affinity in any conceivable case. And to that end he added in the "race factor" as well as "the health and absence of deformity in the two individuals."[16] Weininger accepted the premise that Jews look different and that there is a "universally acquired correspondence between mind and body . . . the science of character can be linked with morphology, [and] will be valuable not only to these sciences but to physiognomy."[17]

It is the form of the Jewish body that evoked Freud's interest in his discussion of Weininger, for it is the form of the body that determines the state of the psyche. And the "diseased" body gives rise to the "diseased" mind or, at least, the discordance between the image of the body and that of the mind leads to psychosis, as in the case of the strange autobiography of the "psychotic" Dr. Daniel Schreber (1911). The homology between the body of the Jew and the body of the woman provided (at least for Weininger) the antithetical image, the Aryan male (Weininger as the self-hating convert, the ultimate Aryan). His body is intact, it is not diseased; his soul reflects the natural balance between the masculine and the feminine within the bisexual model.

According to Freud, the intact penis despises the "operated" penis, which is seen as analogous to, but not the same as, the castrated woman. But in the child—the non-Jewish child—it leads to a neurosis, that of antisemitism. Here was Freud's first attempt, so much more detailed in later works such as *Totem and Taboo* and *Moses and Monotheism*, to deal with antisemitism as a disease of the uncircumcised. Cesare Lombroso had stated this quite clearly in a review of Max Nordau's polemic against modernism that was entitled *Degeneration*. Antisemitism is a sort of "disease" that afflicts people like "madness." Richard Wagner is described in Lombroso's works as "not only mad but imbecilic . . . when he wrote 'Judaism in Music' [his polemic against the Jews], he had a sort of delirium of persecution against the Jews."[18] Antisemites are diseased. Antisemitism is a disease, indeed, caused by the presence of the intact penis. As early as Freud's 1907 comments to his Wednesday night discussion circle, antisemitism was seen as a neurotic symptom.[19] Theodor Adorno's work on the authoritarian personality in the 1940s evoked this sense of "anti-Semitism as a 'symptom' which fulfills an 'economic' function within the subject's psychology."[20] Even in contemporary discussions of Jew hatred, psychoanalytic models have been evoked to exemplify the universal underpinnings of this phenomenon.[21] This is not accidental. It is vital to narrate the psychological processing of conflicted emotions through the application of psychological mechanisms such as projection and repression. In a footnote written in 1919 to his 1910 study of Leonardo concerning castration anxiety, Freud again stated that:

Here we may also trace one of the roots of the anti-Semitism which appears with such elemental force and finds such irrational expression among the nations of the West. Circumcision is unconsciously equated with castration. If we venture to carry our conjectures back to the primeval days of the human race we can surmise that originally circumcision must have been a milder substitute, designed to take the place of castration. (*SE,* 11: 95–96)

But Freud also made the point that circumcision is a sign of "primitive peoples" (*SE,* 22: 86). And Freud, like most other commentators of the period, cited parallel cases from Australia (*SE,* 15: 155). In 1893 one of G. Stanley Hall's pupils at Clark University, Arthur H. Daniels, introduced his discussion of the meaning of circumcision with the note that "it is by no means a distinctively Jewish rite."[22] The rite may be "primitive," but its baseline is that it is also assumed to be a primary sign of Jewishness.

The scientific debate about circumcision affects the way the male Jew understands a central part of his anatomy, his penis, but it also forms his understanding of his place in society. For Weininger the debate about the Jewish body became more distant once he reduced the nature of the masculine and feminine to psychological constructs (like the Jew and the Aryan). The real nature of his own circumcised, homosexual body was subsumed to the abstractions lodged in the psyche.

The meaning of the genitalia remained central to Freud. He could, in *Civilization and Its Discontents* (1930), without hesitation paraphrase Havelock Ellis's view that "the genitals themselves, the sight of which is always exciting, are nevertheless hardly ever judged to be beautiful; the quality of beauty seems, instead, to attach to certain secondary sexual characteristics" (*SE,* 21: 83). Now Freud's comments ring with a claim for universality, but he also noted in the case of Dora that "the pride taken by women in the appearance of their genitals is quite a special feature of their vanity; and disorders of the genitals which they think calculated to inspire feelings of repugnance or even disgust have an incredible power of humiliating them, of lowering their self-esteem, and of making them irritable, sensitive, and distrustful" (*SE,* 7: 84). Clearly it is the male who thinks his genitalia are ugly (the traditional antithesis of "beautiful").

But does every male see his penis as unaesthetic? Or do only those males who see their genitalia as "disordered" feel this sense of "repugnance or even disgust"? Perhaps it is the debate about the diseased or disordered nature of the circumcised penis that places these remarks into a meaningful context. Freud's argument in *Civilization and Its Discontents* that the genitalia are ugly was made in a rather odd context. For Freud went on to conclude that: "Happiness, in the reduced sense in which we recognize it as possible, is a problem of the economics of the individual's libido. There is no golden rule which applies to everyone: every man must find out for himself in what particular fashion he can be saved" (*SE*, 21: 83). This quotation, known to every schoolboy in Germany, had been scribbled by Friedrich II on the margin of a report opposing the establishment of Roman Catholic schools in Prussia in 1740. By the fin de siècle this phrase had become standard in the political rhetoric of Jewish emancipation, a fact that would have shocked Frederick the Great, who shared his idol Voltaire's negative attitude toward the Jews.[23] Freud contextualized his understanding of the genitalia in terms of the meaning attributed to his body in the scientific literature of his time.

It is not only in Freud's works that the debate about the nature of the Jewish body appeared within the parameters employed by Otto Weininger. The sexual identity of the Jews became a theme in the early psychoanalytic literature, which is not surprising, considering that most of the first psychoanalysts were Jews who were forced to deal with the meaning of their own bodies within the medical and psychological literature of the day. All the charges about the diseased, pathological, ugly nature of the male Jews' body were leveled at the Jew as sexually diseased, and all these charges were reversed by the Viennese-Jewish literary critic and psychoanalyst Otto Rank. Rank wrote an essay called the "Essence of Judaism" in December 1905.[24] His argument tied a number of the threads from the medical and forensic literature together and reversed their implications. Society, Rank argued, moves toward ever greater sexual repression until it "reaches the neurotic stage of anti-sexuality, a disturbance of consciousness." This diseased state has not yet been reached by the Jews, since they have preserved themselves at a more "primitive," "relatively favorable stage of the repression process" through their closer ties to nature. Echoing Weininger's parallel, Rank equated the now positive, primitive sexuality of the Jew with that of the woman: "like woman, they have remained 'unchanged.'" The "essence of Judaism is its stress on primitive sexuality." And this primitive sexuality is like the well-springs of artistic creativity, which come from a repression of sexuality. Jewish sexuality, unlike that of the artist, provided the impetus for the selection of "specifically Jewish professions, which are simple, sensible attempts at preventing nervous illness." As a result, Jews "became physicians. For, the Jews thoroughly understand the radical cure of neurosis better than any other people. . . . They brought matters to such a point that they could help others, since they have sought to preserve themselves from illness." Here we have the entire repertoire of charges: Jews have perverse, atavistic sexual practices, they are sexually like women, they have a special relationship to mental illness and its cure. Rank's answer to Weininger was much more direct than Freud's. All three remained within the realm of debate outlined by the medical literature of the fin de siècle. Weininger abandoned the Jewish body; Freud reconstituted its meaning, and Rank glorified it.

The Mind of the Jew

If Freud's overt reading of the "highly gifted but sexually deranged" Weininger was in the context of the meaning of the Jewish body, his subliminal reading was in terms of the relationship of madness to the ability to write a book like *Sex and Character*. The relationship between madness and creativity was much discussed at the turn of the century, especially within the reception of Cesare Lombroso's work. But the question of race (which Lombroso addressed) became a central factor in these debates at the fin de siècle. That Jews were active within the spheres of culture and science could not be contradicted. But was their activity to be understood as "creative"? Thus, the seemingly central role of Jews in culture could be disregarded by arguing that their type of art was superficial or perhaps even corrupting. Indeed, it could be argued that the creativity of the Jew was really a sign of his diseased, mad state. And Lombroso cited the key figure who illustrated this relationship more than any other for the fin-de-siècle scientist, Heinrich Heine. Heine's paralysis, whether syphilitic or tubercular, became the exemplary image of the diseased Jew for the turn of the century. His illness was not madness, but, according to Lombroso, a disease of the spinal cord, which "may have given a morbid character" to Heine's writing.[25]

The debate about the nature of the Jews' creativity ran through the medical and popular literature at the turn of the century. It was in Weininger's *Sex and Character* that this view (espoused by German writers such as F. M. Klinger in the early nineteenth century) entered into the discourse of science. According to Weininger, Jews and women have "no genius." He attacked Spinoza and Heinrich Heine as representative Jewish thinkers viewed by his contemporaries as creative geniuses. But they were, for him, incapable of true genius: "The philosopher Spinoza, about whose purely Jewish descent there can be no doubt, is incomparably the greatest Jew of the last nine hundred years, much greater than the poet Heine (who indeed was destitute of any quality of true greatness)" (216). What passes for genius in the Jew and the woman is but "exaggerated egotism" (317). Jewish creativity is inherently superficial.

What characterizes the woman is her language: "The impulse to lie is stronger in woman, because, unlike that of man, her memory is not continuous, whilst her life is discrete, unconnected, discontinuous, swayed by the sensations and perceptions of the moment instead of dominating them" (146). Women's language is lies; Jews' language is speaking so (racially) distinctively that it marks the speaker as a Jew. States Weininger, "Just as the acuteness of Jews has nothing to do with true power of differentiating, so his shyness about singing or even about speaking in clear positive tones has nothing to do with real reserve. It is a kind of inverted pride; having no true sense of his own worth, he fears being made ridiculous by his singing or his speech" (324). Jews and women, for example, have no "true humor," for true humor must be transcendent; Jews "are witty only at [their] own expense and on sexual things" (318). Jews are inherently more preoccupied by the sexual but less potent than Aryans (311). Their obsession is rooted in the fact that sex breaks down boundaries between individuals. Jews, like women, are "devoid of humor and addicted to mockery" (319). "The Jew who does not set out, like the humorist, from the transcendental, and does not move towards it, like the erotic, has no interest in depreciating what is called the actual world, and that never becomes for him the paraphernalia of a juggler or the nightmare of a mad-house" (319).

This is the view reversed by Otto Rank in his essay "The Essence of Judaism" (1905), in which he noted that "where the religion [of the

Jews] is insufficient to do this [to maintain psychic balance], Jews resort to wit; for they do not have their own 'culture'" (171). By using
the word *culture*, Rank was adapting and reversing Weininger's view
of the centeredness of the Christian. "Culture," for Rank, was an advanced state of sexual repression. The Jews exist in a state much more
"primitive" and "natural" in which this level of repression has not yet
taken place. Humor becomes an atavistic sign of the sexuality of the
Jews.

Continuing Weininger's argument, Jews are historically extremely
adaptable, as can be shown by their talent for the superficial areas of
creativity such as journalism. But in their essence they are truly un-
changeable. They lack deep-rooted and original ideas (320). The Jews
are the essential unbelievers, not even believing in themselves (321).
The Jew has no center. He is critical, not a critic. He is not merely a
materialist, rather he doubts all and any truths. He is irreligious; indeed, his religion is not even a real religion. It is a reflection of the
Jewish mind, which always demands multiple choices. It is not the
historical treatment of the Jews that has made them what they are:
"Outward circumstances do not mould a race in one direction, unless
there is in the race the innate tendency to respond" (308). And the
Jewishness of the Jew is immutable. The Jew is a "parasite." He is "a
different creature in every host and yet remains himself" (320). The
Jew is the disease in the body politic.

And it is in one arena that this immutability of mind and spirit,
this moral "madness," most clearly manifests itself, and that is science,
most specifically, medicine. For the Jews there is no transcendental-
ism; everything is as flat and commonplace as possible. Their efforts
to understand everything rob the world of its mystery (314). Evolu-
tionary theory ("the ridiculous notion that men are derived from
monkeys" [314–15]), for example, is mere materialism.

The development of nineteenth-century medicine, from its focus
on bacteriology in the 1880s to its focus on biochemistry at the turn
of the century, meant a real shift of interest from the "organic" to
the "inert" on the part of medical scientists. This argument is to
be found elsewhere in the medical debates of the period. Emil
Dubois-Reymond, for example, excoriated the direction of modern
medicine as "too utilitarian, too materialistic, and . . . in the process
of being destroyed by the very industries to which it gives rise." This

he labeled the "Americanization" of medicine. John S. Billings, founder of the Johns Hopkins University Hospital, defended this "dreadful permeation of European civilization by realism" as merely the natural progress of science.[26] For Weininger, this "Americaniza-tion" was the result of the "Jewification" of modern medicine. Jews are natural chemists, which explains why medicine has become bio-chemistry: "The present turn of medical science is largely due to the influence of the Jews, who in such numbers have embraced the med-ical profession. From the earliest times, until the dominance of the Jews, medicine was closely allied with religion. But now they make it a matter of drugs, a mere administration of chemicals. . . . The chem-ical interpretation of organisms sets these on a level with their own dead ashes" (315). This Weininger interpreted as a "Jewification" of medicine. For the Jews focus on the dead, the inert.

Weininger saw the turn of the century as the age of feminization, of a corruption of society (including medicine) by the Jews: "This is the age which is most Jewish and most feminine. . . . It is a time when art is content with daubs and seeks its inspiration in the sports of animals; . . . a time for originality and yet with the most foolish craving for originality. The choice must be made between Judaism and Christianity, between business and culture, between male and fe-male, between the race and the individual, between unworthiness and worth. . . . Mankind has the choice to make. There are only two poles, and there is no middle way" (329–30). This litany of hate places the Jew in an antithetical relationship to true creativity, and as bear-ing a great risk for madness. And Weininger's position was hardly unique. It reflected the general view of antisemitic racial science about the special nature of the Jew. Thus, "creativity" is linked to Jews; their "madness," and the ultimate source of their madness, is their sexuality.

Now we must imagine Freud confronted with this view. Of all the topics he could have addressed about the nature of the psyche, why was it creativity that so captured him? This choice was indeed as idio-syncratic as his choice of dreams, or jokes, or slips of the tongue as a means of discussing the normal structure of the psyche. And each of these topics can be linked to debates within the racial science of the late nineteenth century.[27]

Freud's view was, on its surface, quite different from the prevailing view of the time. In his writings from the close of the nineteenth century through the onset of World War I, he saw creativity, as he did dreams or slips of the tongue or neurotic symptoms, not as a set of formal processes or disease mechanisms in a subset of the population, but as clues to the normal functioning of the unconscious in everyone. Where Lombroso saw the "mad" and their aesthetic productions as "throwbacks" to an earlier, more primitive state of development or as a sign of the diseased nature of the Jew, Freud saw all creativity as a sign of the universal, underlying forces that make all human beings human. He, too, saw creativity as pathological in that it was the result of deviation from "normal" psychological development. But such pathologies are a potential of all human beings, not merely a predestined subset. He studied the creative to understand the centrality of unconscious processes, especially the role of unconscious motivation in human action.

Freud, in his case studies of Leonardo (1910) and Michelangelo (1914), as well as in his critical readings of the creative works of Wilhelm Jensen (1907) and the autobiography of Dr. Daniel Schreber (1911), looked at the creative work as a sign of the displacement of psychic (read: sexual) energy into a different, seemingly unrelated undertaking.[28] The creative impulse is a form of displacement or repression analogous to the symptoms of the neurotic. The symptoms of the neurotic parallel the experiences or fantasies that underlie them, but they do not directly represent the underlying conflict that gives rise to them. For Freud it was within the sphere of the sexual that these products (whether neurotic symptoms or works of art) always arose. For the creative individual, by Freud's definition, is one who must sublimate his sexual drive into the realm of fantasy. Thus, Weininger, whom Freud saw as "completely under the sway of his infantile complexes," would be creative through his "relation to the castration complex" that underlies his own sexuality. The creative individual, such as Weininger, sublimates his own urges and anxieties into a work of art.

And the reason for this sublimation, as in the case of the artists listed above, is the socially unacceptable direction of the expression of their sexuality (from the homosexuality of Leonardo to the incestuous leanings of Jensen). The active, social repression of these drives, in a few individuals, leads to the total sublimation of sexual curiosity into the creative process and the true work of art (*SE*, 9: 167–76). The "creative" object thus represents the fixed fantasies of the individual. The essential nature of the process of creativity is to mask the inherently objectionable (from the standpoint of society) nature of its origin. Works of art "conceal their personal origin and, by obeying the laws of beauty, bribe other people with a bonus of pleasure."[29] The overarching "laws of beauty," the technique of the aesthetic, are the means by which the creative works. It is the universal mask that hides and manipulates; it is separate from the creative impulse and it shapes how the observer sees the work of art. "Creativity" is seen in terms of the "creator" who produces a product, which is implicitly a commodity, as value is inherently attached to it. That product is cast in a form that is universal, and it manipulates the reader or viewer through its evocation of some universal law (the aesthetic). The creativity of the artist is the placing of a repressed aspect of the artist's psyche into the realm of the aesthetic. As Joseph Breuer commented on the ultimate creative figure for nineteenth-century German culture in the *Studies in Hysteria* (jointly authored with Freud in 1895): "Goethe did not feel he had dealt with an experience till he had discharged it in a creative artistic activity" (*SE*, 2: 207).

But it is the act of seeing—the observer's act of seeing and responding to the creative product of the artist—that defines "creativity" for Freud. To use one of his examples, we, the naive viewer, look at Leonardo's image of the Holy Family and "see" the perfection and beauty of the work, but we are also instructed in its "meaning" by the psychoanalyst. The psychoanalyst is able to see beneath the initial evocation of the aesthetic (which disguises the motivation of the author) and to interpret the work of art and the psyche of the artist. The uninformed viewer's response is aesthetic; with the aid of the interpreter (Freud), we can understand the source of the artist's "creativity" and thus truly understand the "unseen" aspect of the work of art. Analogous to the psychoanalyst's explaining to the patient the typography of the dynamic unconscious, the critic explains to the viewer what he or she is observing. It is here that we learn to distrust the initial act of seeing and to link the act of seeing not to a visceral response, but to the act of knowing. Freud's focus seemed to be solely on the motivation underlying creativity. It is the discovery that the "creative" individual is "subject to the laws which govern both normal and pathological activity with equal cogency" that Freud illustrated (*SE*, 11: 63). But his hidden agenda was to undermine our sense that we can see the world directly.

This agenda is clearest in Freud's popular essay, "Creative Writers and Day-Dreaming," which was presented as a lecture to a lay (that is, nonmedical) audience in Vienna in 1907 (*SE*, 9: 143–53). Freud's overt intention was to present the parallels between creativity and childhood play. In this essay Freud defined creativity and the special status of the creative artist: "We laymen have always been intensely curious to know—like the Cardinal who put a similar question to Ariosto—from what sources that strange being, the creative writer, draws his material, and how he manages to make such an impression on us with it and to arouse in us emotions which, perhaps, we had not thought ourselves capable" (143). Freud placed himself as a layman in opposition to the creative individual who makes a world that seems complete and who uses that world to manipulate our ("lay" or "noncreative") emotions. But it is a very special lay observer, one who has the insight to understand the underlying meaning as well as the immediate effect of the creative. Freud's initial analogy was to childplay. Play is rooted in a child's desire to control at least the immediate world of toys, as opposed to the real world, which is beyond the child's manipulation.[30] In this universe uncontrollable realities are transmuted into manipulable fantasies into which the child escapes: "For many things which, if they were real, could give no enjoyment, can do so in the play of phantasy" (144). But strangely it is humor that was for Freud the ultimate example of how the healthy adult can escape back into this world of playfulness: "By equating his ostensibly serious occupations of to-day with his childhood games, he can throw off the too heavy burden imposed on him by life and win the high yield of pleasure afforded by *humor*" (145, Freud's emphasis).

Fantasizing is like dreaming. It uses everyday impressions that are related to earlier (infantile) experience and "creates a situation relating to the future." The creative individual is thus like the playful child, but also like the neurotic in another central aspect.[31] Like the neurotic, the creative individual is compelled to tell (to represent) their fantasies: "There is a class of human beings upon whom, not a god, indeed, but a stern goddess—Necessity—has allotted the task of telling what they suffer and what things give them happiness. These are the victims of nervous illness, who are obliged to tell their fantasies" (146). In paraphrasing Goethe's Torquato Tasso in this passage ("and when a man falls silent in his torment / A god granted me to tell how I suffer"), Freud elides the artist as figure (Tasso) and the artist as author (Goethe, the ultimate example of the "creative" individual in German culture) with the "mad" person as figure (Tasso) and the healer of the "mad" (Freud). The artificial line that Freud drew between the "creative" individual as neurotic on the one side and himself (and his listeners) on the other is shown to be a false dichotomy. The informed, psychoanalytically instructed observer "sees" below the surface. Freud joined the world of art as artifact and inspiration in his "creative" role as the psychoanalyst, but only in the most hidden and covert way.

In this 1907 essay, the creative individual is not gender neutral. Young women have more erotic fantasies than do young men, who have in turn have more fantasies of ambition. Both must learn to conceal and repress these drives because they are unacceptable to polite society: "The well-brought-up young woman is only allowed a minimum of erotic desire, and the young man has to learn to suppress the excess of self-regard which he brings with him from the spoilt days of his childhood, so that he may find his place in a society which is full of other individuals making equally strong demands" (147). Human sexuality, the wellspring of creativity, is initially and more strongly present in the fantasy world of the female. These trends do merge at some point early in the life cycle. But the female is the gender whose fantasies are the more sexualized in their most primitive (that is, earliest) form.

Thus, in this text Freud provided a set of working hypotheses about creativity. First, that creativity has to do with the representation of internal stories in a highly affective and effective manner; second, that creativity is parallel to the states of childhood and neurosis, in that it is an attempt to create a world over which one can have control (and humor is the prime example of this control); third, that there is a difference, but also a similarity, between the fantasy life (and therefore the creativity) of men and of women. All of these hypotheses are framed by a most ambiguous narrative voice that claims that the creative artist is different from the author of the text that we are reading (this is made evident in the banality of the hypothetical novel that Freud outlines in his essay), yet that parallels his experience with that of both the artist in reality and in the work of art.

Freud, however, was not interested in the problem of creativity for its own sake. He regarded his explanation of the nature of creativity as one of the central proofs for the validity of his science, psychoanalysis. In the programmatic text of 1913, "The Claims of Psycho-Analysis to Scientific Interest," Freud outlined the theory of repression not only as the key to understanding the production of aesthetic objects but also as one of the substantial pieces of evidence of the explanatory power (read: scientific validity) of his views. Freud stresses the power of the aesthetic on the viewer. However, he leaves the door open to further meaningful contributions to the understanding of the aesthetic through the science of psychoanalysis:

> Most of the problems of artistic creation and appreciation await further study, which will throw the light of analytic knowledge on them and assign them their place in the complex structure presented by the compensation for human wishes. Art is a conventionally accepted reality in which, thanks to artistic illusion, symbols and substitutes are able to provoke real emotions. Thus art constitutes a region half-way between a reality which frustrates wishes and the wish-fulfilling world of the imagination—a region in which, as it were, primitive man's strivings for omnipotence are still in force. (*SE*, 23: 187–88)

Freud's reading of the work of art is clearly both within the paradigm of late-nineteenth-century visual and literary art, and, more important, still bound by Lombroso's association of "creative" with the "primitive." But it is not the primitive localized in the inhabitants of the asylum or the prison, the throwback, but the primitive within every human being. Apparently, Freud needed to associate the creative with the universal and with a universal science, psychoanalysis.

A basic difficulty with Freud's argument is clear: if sexual repression is the key to creativity, why aren't all individuals who are sexually repressed creative? After World War I, Freud himself became quite aware of this objection to his theory, as he later noted in his study of "Dostoevsky and Parricide" (1928): "Before the problem of the creative artist analysis must, alas, lay down its arms" (*SE*, 21: 177). Or, as he states in his "Autobiographical Study" (1925): "[Psychoanalysis] . . . can do nothing towards elucidating the nature of the artistic gift, nor can it explain the means by which the artist works—artistic technique" (*SE*, 20: 70). But I would rather ask the question in reverse. Why is it that Freud's early categories of creativity are constructed so as to make all human beings potentially creative? Why does Freud need to universalize creativity? Why does he need to place creativity within those sexual drives and psychic phenomena that are, according to Freud, present in all human beings, not just in the "insane"? Why does the feminine seem to have the closest relationship to the wellspring of the creative? What do "sexuality," "creativity," and "madness" have to do with one another at the turn of the century? Why did Freud maintain that creativity, in its inherent characteristic of repression, is like neurosis?

The meaning of Freud's representation of the creative, not as Lombroso's "throwback" or deviant but as a reflection of universal processes, can be understood in the context of Freud's role as a scientist and a Jew in fin-de-siècle Vienna. We can assume that the question of creativity had a special significance for Freud, especially during the period from 1903 to 1910, the period when Weininger's views were most widely circulated and discussed in Viennese culture. These views were read against the more general debates within psychiatry about the special status of Jewish genius. Freud needed to move the question of the Jew's "madness" and the Jew's "creativity" to another level of debate. For Freud the special definition of these concepts and their relationship becomes part of his proof of the universality of the human psyche. Freud's stress on the sexual etiology of all neurosis led to his view that creativity is analogous to neurosis in its repression of conflicted sexual identity. The subtext that links the creative, the psychopathological, and the sexual is, as we have seen, inherent to the representation of the psyche of the Jew, which existed at precisely the point when Freud's interest turned to the question of the creative.

Freud's response was to separate the question of Jewish madness and Jewish creativity from the universal laws, which he saw as causing psychopathology. These laws are parallel to the laws that determine the creative. Freud began, in the first decade of the twentieth century, to refashion Lombroso's separate categories of the "normal" and the "abnormal." He was forced to do so because, unlike the Italian Jew Lombroso, he first sensed (according to his own active memory) his "difference" from everyone else when he began to study med-

icine and was confronted with the image of his own "racial" difference. For Freud science and race were linked. Weininger saw as the
salient example of this association the nature of "Jewish" medicine—
a purely mechanistic, materialistic medicine, more chemistry than the
art of healing. Jews are not creative, especially in this realm of science,
but rather, destructive.

Freud first struggled to show how everyone who is creative or
dreams or is "mad" responds to the same, universal rules of psychic
organization. Freud's science, the science of psychoanalysis, which
evolved over the closing decade of the nineteenth century while
rooted in a materialistic paradigm, self-consciously attempted to
move medicine toward an understanding of the dynamic processes of
the psyche, the immaterial aspect of the human being. Freud abandoned "chemistry" for "metapsychology." This he was constrained to
do because of his certainty that human sexuality—associated with the
obsessive hypersexuality of the Jews, the very source of their perverse
"madness"—lay at the center of human experience. Freud positioned
himself (more and more successfully as his thought developed after
World War I) in opposition to the positivistic clinical gaze of Charcot
and the materialistic brain mythology of Benedikt. His was not the
medicine sketched by Weininger, and it had, therefore, at least the potential to claim a position as creative. But Freud did not make this
claim unambiguously, as we have seen from his 1907 essay on creativity. For in openly labeling himself as creative, he would be labeling
himself as a Jew. He would be setting himself off from the universal
role of the "layman" (to use his word) as the observer. But he was not
the layman; he was the scientist-physician. And his science must be
universal, not particular, in its claims for creativity. The scientist-
physician lays claim to the universal gaze, unencumbered by national
or racial perspective, especially in the arena of sexology, where the accusation is that Jews, by their very nature, are predisposed to seeing
the sexual everywhere.

Thus, Freud had the creative operate as a reflex of the force present
in all human beings—sexuality. And it is this force that has been used
to label the Jew as different. It now becomes the source of all human
endeavors, including the truly creative. But this is present more in the
feminine fantasy than in the masculine, a view that certainly mirrors
Weininger's dismissal of the sexual contamination of Jewish (not

feminine) creativity. Freud successfully reversed all the poles of the antisemitic discourse on creativity that framed Weininger's view. The link between "madness" and "creativity" is maintained, but these tendencies are now a product of universal rather than of racial psychology. What is striking in all of his discussions of creativity during the period from 1900 to 1919 is that Freud never evoked any Jewish writer or painter—not his contemporary and neighbor, the playwright Arthur Schnitzler, not the best-known German artist of his day, the Impressionist Max Liebermann, not the classic examples of Jewish creativity, Spinoza and Heine[32]—in his discussions of creativity and the nature of the creative. Creativity may be universal, but Freud's examples were not. They self-consciously eliminated the "Jewish" component in European culture.

Freud was still limited by the context of his struggle with the antisemitic implications of "madness" and "creativity" in his age. It is only with the triumph of the Nazis and the degenerate art exhibit that Freud in 1938 finally confronted this question in a German emigré magazine. His answer to the rise of antisemitism was a paraphrase of a lost or invented essay reputedly by a non-Jew, in which the contributions of the Jews to the Diaspora were evaluated: "'Nor can we call them [the Jews] in any sense inferior. Since we have allowed them to co-operate in our cultural tasks, they have acquired merit by valuable contributions in all the spheres of science, art, and technology, and they have richly repaid our tolerance" (*SE*, 23: 292). "Science," such as psychoanalysis, and "art" represent the Jews' "creative" contributions to German culture. But each is creative and each marks the positive presence of the Jew in European society. The ambiguity of creativity in the fin de siècle vanished in the harsh light of the Nazi realization of the view of Jews in German culture represented by Weininger. Against this Freud reacted.

CHAPTER SEVEN

Sibling Incest, Madness, and the Jews

How does one organize the categories that comprise what we call "deviance"? When examining the nosology of the deviant in modern (post-Enlightenment) culture, one is constrained to use categories of analysis that arise in the spheres of law, medicine, and the social sciences. That is, the history of deviance in popular and high culture comes to be the reworking of "scientific" categories of difference that overlay the fantasies of difference, often more complex and more far-reaching than the models themselves. Incest is just such a category of deviance in modern culture. One of the most interesting phenomena in the intense public debate over the past decade about child abuse and incest is the virtual absence of sibling incest as a topic of concern.[1] Ian Hacking, in his book *Rewriting the Soul: Multiple Personality and the Sciences of Memory*, has explored the history and philosophy of memory / false memory and the literature on child abuse in the context of the modern fascination with multiple personality disorder.[2] The object that he is studying simply does not center on sibling incest because the contemporary debate on multiple personalities and abuse does not seem to focus on this problem. However, it was a question that dominated the debates on incest in French culture from 1874 to 1886, which Hacking quite correctly sees as the period in which the concatenation of relationships he is exploring first is made. Sibling incest was a touchstone for the incest and inbreeding discussions of the late nineteenth century and one of the often-cited "social problems" of that time.

Hacking evokes, in the title of his book, "the rewriting of the soul," how singular and one-sided these sciences of the soul were in the discourse of the late nineteenth century. It is the "soul," the concept that links religious imagery to the secularized language of the new science, that gives us a hint as to why Hacking represses the question of sibling incest. For virtually missing in his account of the history of child abuse and multiple personalities is the question of race—and this is also why the question of brother-sister incest vanishes. For the race question is also a question of hygiene, of the breeding of the healthy, as opposed to the ill, races, and it is here that the problem of sibling incest seems to be located.

In his study of the history of child abuse, Hacking does understand liminally that race is a category in the science that he is describing (pace his discussion on pp. 200–201). But he focuses on the debate about memory, from Theodule Ribot and Pierre Janet to Sigmund Freud, as if it were just about the science of memory instead of being only one of the several rooms in the memory palace of nineteenth-century psychology. Hacking's choice of decades, however, should have demanded that he look into the adjacent rooms. For next to the theories of memory, which he provides for the reader in elegant summary, are the theories of organic memory (so ably explicated in Laura Otis's recent book on that topic).[3] There, too, Ribot, Janet, and Freud play dominant roles. And all the discussions of organic memory during the 1870s and 1880s in France led to the discussions of race and racial memory, and discussions of race often lead to the crowning cases of child abuse—the various accusations of ritual murder throughout Europe and North America—in the literature of the late nineteenth century. For memory and child abuse have other relationships with one another within the history of psychology.

Indeed, had Hacking read the Franco-Jewish psychologist Hippolyte Bernheim closely, he would have found this discussion already in his work on hypnotism that so captured Sigmund Freud. Bern-

heim focused on the nature of the child's psyche in the traumatic setting of the trials concerning ritual murder in the latter half of the
nineteenth century. Hacking dismissed Janet's virulently antisemitic
views about Freud as part of a squabble about priorities, rather than
acknowledging it as an inherent bias among the Paris psychologists
(including the neurologist Jean-Martin Charcot) that shaped their basic attitude toward their science and their competition (whether in
Vienna or in Nancy). For the assumption of the medical science of
the day was that Jews harbored illnesses, including madness, because
of their marriage practices.[4] Even child abuse / ritual murder was seen
as a reflection of the Jews' madness. For child abuse cases in the late
nineteenth century usually consisted of a female child victim (Christian) and a male child abuser (Jewish) who reenacted the sexual fantasy of the Jewish rapist/murder and his victims that dominated the
discussion of Jack the Ripper during this period. Child murder and
sibling incest came to be linked in the forensic science of the period
as twin signs of the madness of the Jews, which is a sexual madness,
whether it is focused on the body of the Christian and death or on the
body of the Jew and immoral reproduction.

Antisemites, in the late nineteenth century, saw the Jews as essentially an "ill" people and labeled the origins of that illness as incest/in-
breeding, labeled as "consciousness of kind." The illness that dominated the discourse of antisemitic science was madness, and its origin
was in the "dangerous" marriages of the Jews, that is, their refusal to
marry beyond their inner group. These marriages were regarded as a
criminal activity, even when such "inbreeding" was not consanguineous. In historical terms, writers such as Houston Stewart Chamberlain could comment on the origin of the Jews and its "refreshingly
artless expression in the genealogies of the Bible, according to which
some of these races owe their origin to incest, while others are de-
scended from harlots."[5] Chamberlain's polemic also appeared at the
time under the guise of ethnological description. The Jews were described not only as permitting sibling incest (*Geschwisterehe*), but also
as actually practicing it even after they claimed to have forbidden it.
The pathological result of such open and/or hidden practices is pre-
mature sexual maturity.[6] The various links between deviant forms of
sexuality such as incest (understood as sibling incest) and prostitution
(the ultimate etiology of mental illness in an age of syphilophobia)

placed the Jews and their marriage practices at the center of "biological" concern. And yet there was also a hidden economic rationale in this discussion. For in refusing to marry into general society, the Jews seemed to be signaling that they were a separate economic entity that lived off of the general society, but did not contribute to it. "Inbreeding" was seen as the origin of the economic hegemony of the Jews and as poisonous as their sexual activities.

The claim was that Jews violated the incest taboo by repudiating the European/Christian rule of exogamy, which requires marriage outside of one's perceived inner group, such as the extended or nuclear family. The Jews, in their refusal to marry beyond the inner group, were understood as incestuous or inbred, and their practice of perpetual endogamy, or marriage within specified segments of a society, was harshly condemned by conservatives and liberals alike. If the Jews are an incestuous people, it is because they demand that their children marry one another, and the reason they do so, it was assumed, was so that they could perpetuate their economic power.

A central assumption of the late nineteenth century was that sibling incest was biologically "unnatural."[7] Children of an inner group could not be erotically interested in one another. They were naturally attracted to children beyond the inner group, and this led to the building of political and economic alliances. This "natural" law seemed to be violated by the Jewish Law of the Father, which demanded that one marry within the covenant.

The Jews were seen as advocating consanguineous marriage, which was read by popular culture as well as by canon law as incest. But it was not read as parent-child incest, but rather as an attenuated form of sibling incest. To evoke the late-nineteenth-century Finnish sociologist Edward Westermarck's theory in *The History of Human Marriage,* one can read the conflict in terms of his view of the possibility of psychopathological development when the sexual instinct is caught between the Westermarck effect (aversion to sexual feelings between those raised together) and parental injunctions to marry (that is, the Westermarck trap). Jewish madness results from this nineteenth-century version of the "double bind." Jews are "raised together" as members of an imagined closed society but are then forced to marry within this society. Economic hegemony and sexual perversion are linked within the image of madness.

Theory—as is usually the case—is also the stuff of fiction. One provides material for the other. Within European letters the literary motif of sibling incest is linked in complicated ways to the Jews as an outsider group whose marriage practices are constantly viewed with suspicion. From the end of the eighteenth century, sibling incest was a topic in serious as well as popular literature, from the novels of Jane Austen to the German Storm and Stress poets whom her characters read.[8] In each case it marked a world out of control, even though its inhabitants seem to imagine themselves in control. The world out of control was as much the world of capital (as recent literature on Jane Austen has claimed) as it was the world of the family. Both could be represented by the problem of sibling incest.

And here, too, there are hints of racializing the theme of sibling incest. Byron's use of the motif of the Wandering Jew as the forma-tive theme in his *Manfred* was to no little degree shaped by Manfred's crime—his desire for and seduction of his sister.[9] (Here one could mention Byron's doctor, John William Polidori, and his use of this "Byronic" theme in his tale of vampirism borrowed from Byron. This tale served as the basis for the nineteenth- and twentieth-century as-sociation of Jews and vampirism that culminated in Friedrich Wil-helm Murnau's *Nosferatu* [1922].)[10] But it was Edgar Allan Poe who made the link between Jewishness and sibling incest more or less ex-plicit. While seeming to bear an ancient Irish name, Poe's Roderick Usher, in "The Fall of the House of Usher" (1839), the last offspring of a highly inbred family, is portrayed as degenerate, and, therefore, as Jewish: "A cadaverousness of complex; an eye large, liquid, and lu-minous beyond comparison; lips somewhat thin and very pallid, but of a surpassingly beautiful curve; *a nose of a delicate Hebrew model*, but with a breadth of nostril in similar formations; a finely moulded chin, speaking, in its want of prominence, of a want of moral en-ergy.[11] The physiognomy of the Jew reveals his illness. The Jewish quality of the degeneracy is further underlined by the fact that Poe hints at an incestuous relationship between Roderick and his sister. In complex ways the siblings are Jews, if for no other reason than their incest.

The image of the pathological relationship of the Jews to economy and to child abuse is linked through the accusation of sibling incest. For Jewish marriage practices were understood as incestuous, as inbred, and in eugenic terms, such an inbreeding causes the madness such as that suffered by Jack the Ripper, a sexualized frenzy that turns the individual against the world. The medical literature of the early twentieth century documents the greater rate of inbreeding and the resultant degenerative diseases among Jews.[12] Inbreeding, in both common and Napoleonic law, was defined as a criminal act. It was assumed to be a cause for moral as well as physical degeneration; thus it is not only a crime but a source of crime.

It is the disease of the Jews and therefore also a disease of the city.[13] As Richard Krafft-Ebing noted:

Large cities are hotbeds in which neuroses and low morality are bred, *vide* the history of Babylon, Nineveh, Rome and the mysteries of modern metropolitan life. . . . The episodes of moral decay always coincide with the progression of effeminacy, lewdness and luxuriance of the nations. These phenomena can only be ascribed to the higher and more stringent demands which circumstances make upon the nervous system. Exaggerated tension of the nervous system stimulates sensuality, leads the individual as well as the masses to excesses, and undermines the very foundations of society, and the morality and purity of family life.[14]

The decadence of civilization, of the city, is inexorably linked to the sexual exclusivity and the social/economic mobility of the Jew. In *My Struggle,* Hitler notes this link, thinking back on his fin-de-siècle experience in Vienna:

No, the fact that our big city population is growing more and more prostituted in its love life cannot just be denied out of existence; it simply is so. The most visible results of this mass contamination can, on the one hand, be found in the insane asylums, and on the other, unfortunately, in our—children. They in particular are the sad product of the irresistibly spreading contamination of our sexual life; the vices of the parents are revealed in the sicknesses of the children.[15]

Then Hitler went on to state the doctrine of racial purity: "For since this question primarily regards the offspring, it is one of those concerning which it is said with such terrible justice that the sins of the fathers are avenged down to the tenth generation. But this applies only to the profanation of the blood and the race. *Blood sin and desecration of the race are the original sin in this world and the end of a humanity which surrenders to it*."[16] Incest and racial pollution through crossbreeding were parallel sins for Hitler and for the time. And they represented the "economic problem" of the Jew's presence in modern society.

Certainly the legend of the incestuous nature of the Jews has had a substantial twentieth-century rebirth, if indeed it was ever dead in the first place. Nowhere is this linkage made more evident than in Thomas Mann's parodic novella "The Blood of the Walsungs" (1905).[17] This tale of brother-sister incest ends, at least in his first version, with an emphasis on the sexual exclusivity of the Jew.

What is striking about Mann's text is that it is as much a critique of the Jew as parvenu in the (mocked) world of German high culture as it is a critique of the Jew as incestuous sibling. It takes place in the world of the decadent city, in the hothouse of culture in the corrupting atmosphere of urban, economic life. Urban life, at the turn of the century, came to be read as the world corrupted by the upwardly mobile Jews. Indeed, the link between "class" and "race" in this text is so complete as to make the two interchangeable. But it is not only a critique of the urban "upper classes" but also of the parvenus—those who act as if they were of the upper classes but who are merely mimicking them.

Mann introduces us to the wealthy Aarenhold family, with its Germanic name but Jewish physiognomy, living in the luxury of an unnamed city. The father, a nouveau riche coal speculator from the eastern reaches of the German empire, collects first editions of the classics, but does so "gently rubbing his hands" and speaking in a "slightly plaintive way" (289). The mother, richly jeweled, is "small, ugly, prematurely aged, and shriveled as though by tropic sun" (290). She is badly (if expensively) dressed and coifed. She is the daughter of a "well-to-do tradesman" (and therefore mercantile by character) and reveals herself as Jewish by her speech that was "interlarded with guttural words and phrases from the dialect of her childhood days" (294). If the mother is marked by her Jewish language (*Mauscheln*), the father is marked by disease, dyspepsia, the illness of the rich. "He suffered from a weakness of the solar plexus, that nerve center which lies at the pit of the stomach and may give rise to serious distress" (292). But he revels in his illness since it marks him (much too publicly) as a success. His table talk reveals his trivial nature (to his children and to the reader). For he praises the fact that "every morning that God lets me wake up I have a little thrill because my bed-cover is made of silk." This is the statement of the ill Jew as parvenu.

Their children mimic the Germans of their own age; they are an officer with a dueling scar, a liberated woman at the university with a "hooked nose," and then the precious, nineteen-year-old twins—Siegmund and Sieglinde. They appear with "the same slightly drooping nose, the same full lips lying softly together" (290). They speak (unlike their parents) "well" but also show their Jewish nature as "their gestures were nervous and self-assured" (296). The children are embarrassed by their parents' appearance and demeanor. For their lack of social graces reveals "the way he had earned his money" (293) and "traversed the bounds of good taste" (293). The "blond-haired citizenry of the land" may dress and act in an uncouth manner, but the Jews must "be unassailable and blameless of exterior from head to foot" (300).

Siegmund is the most "Jewish" of the children. His face is marked by a "beard . . . so strong that when he went out in the evening he was obliged to shave a second time" (298). In the antisemitic semiotics at the turn of the century, hirsuteness was a marker of Jewish hypersexuality. Siegmund carefully examines his face in the mirror: "Long he looked at each mark of his race: the slightly drooping nose, the full lips that rested so softly on each other; the high cheek bones, the thick black curling hair" (314). This description, including the shape of the nose, the form of the lips, and the "fact" that Jews have "very heavy body and facial hair" (and are "extremely able in trade and business") were commonplace in the antisemitic ethnography of the age.[18] The economic nature of the Jew is literally written on his/her body.

Sieglinde, too, reveals her Jewishness in her physiognomy, for she "made a little moue which brought out markedly the facial characteristics of her race" (314). The seduction of the siblings at the close of the tale seems to be mutual and has been prefigured by Mann's detailed description of the seduction scene in the opera. For the twins, named after the sibling lovers in Wagner's *Die Valkyre*, undertake one last social occasion on their own before Sieglinde is to be married to the German noble Beckerath. They go to a performance of the opera on their own, and the consummation of the siblings' love on the stage sets the tone for the rest of the evening. Wagner's representation of Sieglinde and Siegmund's sexual consummation is read in the light of the incest of the Jews: it is to perpetuate their species. Thus, the tale of sibling incest among the Walsungs becomes the reproduction of the Jews. In Sieglinde's "womb there grew and waxed the seed of that hated unprized race, chosen of the gods, from which the twins had sprung" (312). The mixed marriage of Jew and German (and the resulting offspring who would be *Mischlinge*) will be circumvented by the incestuous relationship of the two siblings, which will preserve the purity of the race. At the moment following the consummation of Sigmund and Sieglinde's relationship, Sieglinde ponders the fate of her German fiancé.

Sibling incest is, according to August Forel in the standard sexual handbook of the day, "a psycho-pathological form of incest associated with morbid appetites in the families of degenerates."[19] It is also, according to J. G. Frazer, one of the most widespread taboos among "primitive" peoples, as it is the most common of such activities.[20] To ensure that the contemporary audience did not miss the point of the tale, Thomas Mann concluded its unpublished first version with two Yiddishisms, a sign of the damaged and at the same time sexualized discourse of the siblings. Thus, the Jewishness of the parents (remember the mother's guttural language) reappears "naturally" in the children.

Mann's father-in-law, Alfred Pringsheim, so objected to the inclusion of Yiddishisms to represent the hidden *Mauscheln* of the Jews— "We robbed (*beganeft*) the non-Jew (*goy*)"—as a sign of the siblings' ethnic identity that Mann suppressed the planned publication of the story.[21] The novella, which Mann reissued in 1921 to eliminate the Yiddishisms, echoed the sense of the corruption both of "modern life," as typified by the Wagner cult, and of the Jews. The Jews, so the thinking went, through their lack of redemption, are morally weak, and this manifests itself in the most primitive manner, through incest. This theme is found throughout the literature of the period.[22] Indeed, Adolf Hitler, never the most original of thinkers, simply summarized "Jewish religious doctrine" as "prescriptions for keeping the blood of Jewry pure."[23] The view that within the Jews' sexuality is hidden the wellspring of their own degeneration haunts the overtly sexual imagery of antisemitic writings at the end of the nineteenth century. The Jew, the most visible Other in late-nineteenth-century Europe, also bears the sign of the most devastating sexual stigma, the act of incest. In the one novel on this topic by a German-Jewish writer, Kurt Münzer's novel *The Path to Zion* (1907), brother-sister incest among Jews was put into a more historical context, but it remained the central theme of the work. The language that Münzer placed in the mouth of the figures is overly emotional and reveals their own incestuous predisposition.[24] And this in a novel dedicated to "my sister Adele"!

Central to any understanding of Mann's text is the fact that it is a parody of the Siegmund/Sieglinde relationship in Wagner's *Die Walküre* and its meaning for the *Ring* cycle. Wagner took sibling incest to be the highest form of sexual expression in the world of his Germanic myth because of its transgressive nature. Indeed, the archeological and anthropological claims of the period stressed the suspension of the incest prohibition for cultural reasons. Such exceptions were claimed for brother-sister marriage among the royal families in ancient Egypt as well as among the Inca and in traditional Hawaiian society.[25] Sibling incest was a sign of divine transgression, and the Wagner cult accepted it as such. Mann's rather comic image of this scene in the opera, with the badly fitting wigs of the protagonists, seems to undermine the Wagnerian claim. But it is undermined only for those who can distinguish between true art (the platonic Wagnerian opera) and the crude commercialism of the Jewish appropriation of Wagner for their own cultural ends—becoming part of the *Volksgemeinschaft*. Such an appropriation could only take place in the city where the confusion of race and identity (and bastardized high culture) is at home. It is clear that Siegmund and Sieglinde (Aarenhold) are captured by the crude performance they see on the stage, and thus they reveal themselves as truly only parvenus.

The Jewish Wagnerites (one of the great ironies of nineteenth-century European culture was that it was the Jewish audience that legitimized Wagner as their *entre billet* into German avant-garde culture) are seen here as enacting the relationship between the "pure" siblings in a parodic, sexualized, but most important, parvenu manner.[26] The striving for the *Bildung* (culture) and values of the German dominates Mann's tale. And the sense of the unconscious mimicry and therefore the parody of the German and his good taste is also reflected in the tale. Thus, economic and social relationships are compressed in the tale of the two siblings and their incestuous act.

The Jews are represented as mad, just as the upper classes are traditionally seen as mad. This link was not lost on Protestant German culture. Beginning with the Reformation, there was a "critique of the court" that set bourgeois morals against the decadence and corruption of court life.[27] This corruption, in the legend of figures such as Jud Süss Oppenheimer, is linked to the Jews and their incestuous nature. The Jews corrupt the courts; the courts use the Jews as agents of their own corruption; Jews and nobles are interchangeable (when Jewish nobles began to appear with the ennoblement of Jewish converts in Austria during the late nineteenth century, the "proof" of this argument seems to be made). Thus, the madness of the upper classes is paralleled to the madness of the Jews.

I have noted that the theme of Jewish sibling incest in Mann points toward certain turn-of-the-century models of imagining Jewish sexual drive as perverse and as analogous to the economic collapse of "real" society. What happens when this theme resurfaces in another culture and with a quite different focus?[28] Certainly modern French literature, beginning with Jean Cocteau's *Les enfants terribles* (1929), has thematicized incest, including sibling incest, in complex ways. More recently, Michel Tournier's *Les metéores* (1975) (*Gemini* in its English translation) is the tale of two identical twins who sleep together, until one of them decides to claim an identity for himself.[29] Agustin Gomez-Arcos provides an extraordinary tale of two incestuous brothers as a model for understanding the Spanish Civil War in his *L'agneau carnivore* (1975).[30] René Zazzo provides a complex theoretical model for twinning and sibling incest in *Réflets de miroir et autres doubles* (1993).[31]

Recently, in American cultural studies, the theme of sibling incest in William Faulkner's fiction was used by Walter Benn Michaels to exemplify the sexualization of politics in American writing.[32] As Michaels shows, in Anglophone writing the theme can be keyed in complex ways to discourses of race and class. One hidden moment in the cultural history of the trope of Jewish sibling incest in American culture centers on the figure of Barbie. The child's toy was created by the American Jewish designer Ruth Handler, the cofounder, with her husband, Elliot, of Mattel Toys. As the artist Rhonda Lieberman has noted, Barbie, with her blond hair and snub nose, was modeled after a German pornographic doll of the 1950s. She became the fantasy of everything that little Jewish girls were thought to desire to be: "When Barbie was born, in 1959, another Barbie emerged in a parallel universe. . . . Barbie—blonde, Jewish Barbie—brunette or frosted; Barbie—no thighs, Jewish Barbie, thighs; Barbie—mute, Jewish Barbie—whines incessantly about perceived injustices. Jewish Barbie is not evil, merely repressed."[33] It is no wonder that Handler named her after her daughter, Barbara. Barbie was the antithesis of the Western fantasy of the Jewish woman. But what is of interest to us is that when Barbie needed a love interest, Ken was created. Ken was the epitome of the WASP male and was named after the Handlers' son, Kenneth! The sexual attraction between the two dolls was clear. The feminist *Wimmin's Comix #15* (1989) has on its cover a "little girl" (thus the title of the issue, *Little Girls*) holding a Ken doll in one hand and a Barbie in the other. Barbie says to Ken, "Hi! Ken! Ready for our blind date?" Ken replies, "Forget the date, Barbie! Let's get naked." The implication of incest is known only within the Handler family and thus exists only in the fantasy of and about the acculturated Jew.

Martin Amis, in his novel *Success* (1978), presents quite a striking parallel to Mann's tale in his account of the collapse of a British upper-class family.[34] While incest has continued to be a theme in contemporary Anglophone feminist writing—it is present in the works of both Shirley Jackson[35] and Doris Lessing[36]—it is in Amis's novel that *sibling* incest is the theme that links class and race in complicated ways.

Success is the tale of three siblings, Gregory, Ursula, and their adopted brother, Terry. Terry has been adopted by the upper-class Riding family after his father murdered his seven-year-old sister in what is one of the central motifs of child abuse in the tale: "I don't know whether my father killed my mother; but I bloody know he killed my sister, because I was there at the time and watched him as he did so" (25). Terry is adopted into the Riding family because of the curious fact that he and Gregory share a birthday, a fact that Gregory's father commented on when reading the newspaper account of the murder while sitting at River Hall, "the bent metal knocker, the two urns, the retreating steps . . . the long black windows, the vine-matted walls, the grand perpendiculars of the house" (27–28). The estate itself is emblematic of the family and becomes the marker by which the family's decay is indicated. By the time the novel takes place, some decade after the murder, the solid life of the country squire has eroded. The father's madness is more evident, and he starts to spend his more and more limited income on the "improvement" of his estate, the building of follies and mock ruins. His is just a continuation of an eccentric family history (139) that concludes (as in Thomas Mann's *Buddenbrooks*) in the next and final generation.

The class difference is also a physical difference. The physiognomies provide the reader with a catalogue of the markers of "consciousness of kind." Amis gives us the physiognomy of class immediately: Terry is called "Ginger" at school because of his red hair (11), and he sees himself as "the sort of person you walk past in the street every day and never glance at or notice of recognize again" (11). Terry is seen by his stepbrother as having an "ill-bred face" (133). He belongs to the category of the parvenu, just as Gregory is the upper-class degenerate. Gregory has "sickly good looks, delicate and incredibly queer," and dresses as a dandy with "vampiric crimson-lined black opera cape, a waistcoat of his father's, harem trousers" (13). Gregory, unlike the unabashedly heterosexual Terry, is a bisexual.

And sexuality becomes the measure of success in the novel. Indeed, the very term *success* is defined as "fucking" on the first page (7). And Gregory is, at least initially, the sexual success (at least in terms of his own, very unreliable, discourse). He likes "the moneyed chasubles of silence, soft topography of flesh, the trickle of retreating satin" (18) of the women he seduces. This discourse is revealed, in the course of the novel, as a set of elaborate lies about his sexual and financial success. Indeed, by all his own measures, he is a dismal failure.

Ursula, according to Terry's first memories of childhood, had a "sharp, knowing face" (28); Gregory remembers her as "delicious, vague, sleepy eyed" (51). At nineteen (the same age as Siegmund and Sieglinde in Mann's novella), when the novel takes place, she is Terry's "best friend" (36), and he cannot imagine her as a sexual being; she is "pure." He thinks of her as taboo, evoking the Westermarck incest hypothesis: "I'd fall in love with her instantly if she weren't my sister." She seems to him to have the "small body . . . of a well-trained child . . . she looked pre-pubescent—non-pubescent; I felt that if I ever slept with her (these thoughts wriggle up) it would cause some lingering and poignant hurt that would take me my whole life to nurse. (Does she fuck? I wonder suddenly with a nau-

seous lurch. Nah. She probably doesn't know about all that yet)" (56).
"I didn't even want to fuck her" (59). "Ursula-fuck, sister-fuck . . .
foster-fuck? No, I can't do it—I can't even think about it" (60). For
the parvenu Terry, sibling incest is impossible because, it seems, of
the familiarity of the children; but of course it is also because of the
awe in which he holds the upper classes, which are so much better
than he, at least in his imagination.

Terry rejects sibling incest precisely because of his sexual failures
with women outside the family. If he cannot "make it" with the
women of his own class, with the secretaries and shop girls, how can
he hope to possess someone who seems innately superior to him? He
appears as a sexual failure, while Gregory appears as a sexual predator.
And yet it is Gregory, following Terry's rejection of the very thought
of sibling incest, who evokes incest in one of his monologues in an attempt to deconstruct it by historicizing it. He is the incestuous
brother.

Gregory self-consciously quotes the definition of incest from the
O.E.D. and points out that it was only "in 1908, however, [that] leg-
islation was sneaked through (the Punishment of Incest Act) under
which sexual intercourse of a male with his daughter, mother, sister
or granddaughter was made punishable by seven years' imprison-
ment" (65). He provides an economic/biological rationale for the creation of incest as a punishable category: "Clearly, you wouldn't want
your shiftless daughters compacting the familial bastion by marrying
your own sons—when in the next hut or hovel there languished some
strapping ploughboy who would be only too happy to move in and
help you farm, hunt, chop wood" (66). But, of course, such strictures
could not apply to the upper classes, with their economic security.

Gregory's elaborate rationale leads him to acknowledge his incest
with Ursula on an island on the D-Pond, a lake on their estate, when
they were pre-teenagers. It is this account of the idyllic moment of
childhood incest that Gregory couples with Terry's appearance in the
family. For Gregory blames his disillusionment about the perfection
of his childhood on Terry's appearance rather than on the seduction
of his sister. The sexualized word *success* is now keyed to the incest between the siblings (116), an incest that continued "before, during,
and—if less regularly—after my pubescence and then, ultimately,
through hers" (116). Amis allows us to understand the literary import

of the act by having Terry ironically evoke Gregory's "Byronic storm out into the night (marvelous stuff)" (188).

Terry and Gregory live together in a flat, which was initially designed for the oldest son to provide him with a pied-à-terre in London. It is in a section of London near Queensway that once was very posh but that has decayed. Ursula comes to London to study to be a secretary. After the beginning of her descent into schizophrenia and her first suicide attempt, she joins the brothers in their crowded flat. This period marks the onset of Gregory's mental and physical decay and Terry's rebirth as a moneyed member of the new unionized proletariat.

The decay of the "aristocracy" (Gregory and Ursula) into madness is paralleled by an "I'm all right, Jack" rise in the fortunes of the adopted brother, who becomes a union steward. It is at this moment that Terry seduces Ursula (161–62). Terry now has the hold over his "sister" that Gregory had had when they were children: "One thing about incest—there's no point in playing it cool. They cannot get away" (162). Ursula, now the victim of both brothers, finally succeeds in killing herself. The dissolution of the family is completed by Gregory's mental collapse and hospitalization. The novel concludes with the half-mad Gregory and the now-successful Terry returning to the family home, much of which has now been sold to pay the father's debts. Gregory walks down to the D-pond, where he seduced Ursula when they were children, and recognizes his and his family's decay.

Amis's novel is a rather traditional account of the decay of the nobility and the rise of the working class. It is thus clearly an early exploration of themes that Amis fleshes out in his later and more elaborate dystopic novel, *London Fields* (1989). What fascinates me is how the Jew, in the discourse of the novel, comes to mark the decay of upper-class society and the rise of the lower classes. None of the protagonists are figured as Jews, yet their perception of the Jews comes to mark them as incestuous and corrupt.

When Ursula reappears in Gregory's life, he takes her to lunch at a posh restaurant and sees all of the parvenus present: "'Nearer him (don't turn around), Isaac Stamp, banker, entrepreneur and Jew, is clumsily drunkening what I take to be some species of escort girl. He's the lazy fraud who—'" (71). Gregory's sense of his environment (since he is a "success") is that the Jews are haunting its periphery, marking the value of his own world by their attempts to infiltrate it. This paranoia is paralleled at the end of the novel when Gregory returns to his ancestral home and walks to the pond where he had first seduced Ursula: "The D-pond isn't in our land any more. A yid owns it now, but you're still allowed to go there" (223). The "yids" now control the world. They have displaced the aristocracy and the landed gentry and now, in their corruption, own the world. But Gregory sees their corruption as worse than his own. Their economic and sexual strength is a measure of his own decay.

The Jews come to figure in Terry's consciousness after he has seduced Ursula and begins to sense a "leprous and inexorable" fate for him and his adopted siblings. And he remembers his affair with a blind girl: "That's right, totally, congenitally blind. . . . She was small, Jewish and clever; she had dazzling black hair, a large tragic nose, damp-sand complexion and wide lips almost as brown as her skin; she was regretfully agreed by all to be pretty" (170–71). It is illustrative to note the difference between the "pretty" blind Jew with her "large tragic nose" in 1978 and the comment of the Anglo-Jewish artist Moysheh Oyved in 1927: "But my greatest joy was when I saw her giant nose, her awful 'pecker.' In her terribly large Jewish nose I saw the scaffold, the supporting-column, which the Creator of Heaven, Builder of Earth and Decorator of Spring had set down in the very middle of the face of a nation—a nation which is old, falling to pieces, but which is now being rebuilt anew."[37] To Oyved, the Jewish nose is a sign of the decay of the Jew and the potential for Jewish reconstitution; in Amis's novel, Terry finds a Jewish woman beautiful in spite of her nose.

Terry would mock this woman by gesturing at her without realizing it. They sleep together, but she would not let him enter her. In attempting to seduce her, he cries mock tears and, relenting, she permits him to penetrate her: "The point was, you understand, that she knew I was faking, but couldn't say she knew. Because that would have been much too frightening, wouldn't it?" (172) Here is the clue to Terry's sense of his own world. He is "faking" in his role as the adopted son. He does not fit into the Riding family even when he seduces Ursula just like her biological sibling had. Terry remains, in his own self-construction, an outsider, the parvenu, outside the decaying class to which he has been assigned by accident. And yet Amis makes it clear that the working class, represented by the alcoholic, vicious, murderous family from which Terry springs, is in no way better than the Ridings. The murder of Terry's sister by his father is an act of callous and meaningless abuse, which is certainly as violent and vicious as Gregory's seduction of his sister as a child. The figure of the blind Jew springs to mind when Terry has seduced the sister he could not imagine as a sexual partner. Her seduction places him within the same world of exploiters as his father and his stepbrother—but he will be a "success" at it, both finally and sexually. He will become like Isaac Stamp and control the world in which he lives. He is the new Jew.

Contemporary Anglo-Jewish accounts of incest make incest a part of the narrative, but in a rather oblique manner. There is sometimes an odd evocation of sibling identity, even when it is not known. This type of pseudo-Westermarck effect is present in George Lucas's *The Star Wars Trilogy* (1977–83) in the absence of any sexual attraction between Princess Leia Organa (Carrie Fisher) and Luke Skywalker (Mark Hamill):

> *Luke Skywalker*: If I don't make it back, you're the only hope for the Alliance.
> *Princess Leia*: Luke, don't talk that way. You have a power I don't understand and could never have.
> *Luke Skywalker*: You're wrong, Leia. You have that power too. In time you'll learn to use it as I have. The Force runs strong in my family. My father has it. I have it. And . . . my sister has it. Yes. It's you, Leia.
> *Princess Leia*: I know. Somehow, I've always known.

Even though they were not raised as siblings and don't even know they are siblings, the power of the incest taboo seems strong enough to prevent any sexual interest, much to the joy of Leia's admirer, Han Solo (Harrison Ford). Yet it is striking that the leading feminist Anglo-Jewish writer, Elaine Feinstein, in her brilliant novel of the Viennese Jewish experience, *Dreamers* (1994), uses the theme of sibling incest among the Jews of Vienna as the central plot device.[38] The intertwined stories of the poor orphan Clara and the crippled banker's son Anton Shassner lead to a moment of conflict. Clara manages to obtain an education without falling into the social traps set for young, poor women in Vienna during the late nineteenth century. In a turn worthy of a Dickens novel, Feinstein has Shassner befriend Clara, much to his own amazement, without any overt demand for sexual conquest. Yet when she begins, under his tutelage, to remember her childhood, she recalls that she seems to have been prostituted as a child to his best friend. Shassner takes this as a sign that her purity was merely feigned ("I've been waiting so stupidly, and all the while you have been laughing at me.") He viciously rapes her and discovers that she is a virgin (272–73). Taking a gold locket with the portrait of her lost mother, he is able to trace her parentage. He discovers that the beautiful portrait of her mother is that of his own mother's cousin, who had had an affair with his father! "You not need assume she is your sister," his mother tells him, "seeing suddenly that this was the nub of his concern" (313). Here child abuse and sibling incest are coupled. The "nub of his concern" is not sibling incest, but rather, the problem of sexual abuse, including his rape of Clara. Indeed, the question of sibling incest vanishes almost as quickly as it is raised. Are Jews inherently incestuous? Not according to Feinstein, but they can be just as brutal as the society in which they live. For the lust that Anton feels for Clara is that of the upper classes in which he and his non-Jewish friend Anton von Mayerberg, who had abused Clara as a child, lived. They represent the collapse of the nobility, a world without value and creativity, while poor Jews, such as the impoverished Clara and the poor violinist Joseph Kovacs, who becomes a world-renowned star and eventually marries Clara, represent the good and the creative.

Feinstein's account of the Weimar Jewish experience, *Loving Brecht* (1992), was the initial installment in her series of historical novels dealing with German Jewry. In it she places father-daughter incest at the center of her central character's experience.[39] This is a standard fictionalized Freudian rereading of the turn-of-the-century incest taboo. It is the Oedipus complex (which is certainly at the center of Feinstein's text) that presents the central trope of the incest taboo as parent-child rather than as sibling incest.[40] Freud's universalization of incest as something that all human beings do, not just the Jews, is an attempt to project the calumny of brother-sister incest onto the general view that adult-child desire lies at the heart of the civilizing process. His abandonment of the trauma theory, in which the reality of incest was the key to understanding specific hysterical symptoms in specific cases, meant that he was able to categorize incest not as a problem of particular people but of human nature in general.

Feinstein rereads Otto Rank's view (1926) that brother-sister incest derives from the oedipal situation, while reworking into the actual experience of the father's seduction Freud's early theories in
which the fantasy of sibling incest is thought to be based on an actual
incest experience in childhood. Freud's view was that three types of
experiences may be the basis of such fantasies: actual experience of incest in childhood; imaginary fulfillment of the oedipal wish, without
sexual contact having occurred; and a desire to fuse the sexes or to
find a twin or imaginary companion, clearly the basis for Mann's
rereading of the Wagner twin story. Accounts of sibling incest may
also be symbolically transposed from the desired mother to the sister.
Tales of father-daughter incest play a relatively small role for Freud in
his reading of the symbolic nature of sibling incest. For Jewish writers, from Freud to Feinstein, it is necessary to avoid the discussion of
the symbolic nature of sibling incest (since it is part of the discourse
of Jewish difference) and to stress the centrality of the parent-child relationship, whether understood as "real" or "imagined."

Here, too, Philip Roth's representation of a "Jewish" Electra Complex and the pitfalls of potential father-daughter incest in his *American Pastoral* (1997) avoids any specific Jewish references, even though
the novel is about American Jewish acculturation in the 1940s and
1950s.[41] The incestuous moment between father and daughter that
shapes the novel begins with the daughter's seduction of the father
(89), and the kiss she demands becomes the sign of a universal tension
between father and daughter. "Daddy, kiss me the way you k-k-kiss
umumumother," says the seductive, stuttering daughter, and then the
"shoulder straps of her swimsuit had dropped over her arm, and there
was her nipple, the hard red bee bite that was her nipple" (90). This
scene of mutual seduction echoes, and in complex ways answers, the
charges of father-daughter incest leveled against visible American
Jews such as Woody Allen and Roth himself in the recent past.[42]

In Roth's novel, the eleven-year-old child becomes the source of
her father's torment as he remembers her after she disappears, as a
teenager, from the home. She had planted a bomb and killed an innocent passerby during the demonstrations against the Vietnam War:
"The kiss? That kiss? So beastly? How could a kiss make someone
into a criminal?" (92). As in Feinstein's world of representations, the
incestuous force here is universal, not particularistic. Indeed, it is

clearly separate from the Jewish concerns of the novel, the problem of the social acculturation of the Levov family as Americans.

However, in its rereading in the United Kingdom, there is an economic overlay. For Feinstein uses this motif to represent the effect of loss of status among German Jews. The incestuous behavior seems to be precipitated by the father's loss of status when his glove business goes bankrupt, the family is forced to move from its "safe" bourgeois neighborhood, and the great inflation of the early 1920s turns them from members of the middle class to a status even (in his estimation) below that of the proletariat—the disenfranchised bourgeoisie. Here one must note that Amis's account of the fall from the upper classes in *Success* is the result of the family's madness, a madness marked by the father's extravagance as well as by the siblings' incestuous behavior. In all these accounts, the role of race is figured differently, but it is always figured in relationship to the meanings ascribed to the slippage of class—either upward (as in Mann's tale) or downward (as in Amis's novel). The Jew as the marker of class mobility is an image in Karl Marx's "On the Jewish Question" as well as in more contemporary images of antisemitic rhetoric. Its link to the image of sibling incest comes via the older Christian notion concerning Jewish usury, for according to that view, money cannot reproduce, and the taking of interest is an unnatural act—like incest.[43]

Here an early twentieth-century proof text can be found that argues for the idea that the Jew is an economic/incestuous being as well as a model for economic modernity, that "the *homo capitalisticus* . . . is closely related to the *homo Judaeus*."[44] Werner Sombart's *The Jews and Modern Capitalism* (1911) is an antiracialist text that was seen by his antisemitic contemporaries, such as the arch-antisemite Theodor Fritsch, as a defense of the Jews. However, add that his Jewish contemporaries were not all that sanguine about his image of the Jews as the model for modern capitalism. Yet Sombart made an argument that provides the link between Mann's image of the Jew and Amis's class analysis, represented by his character's image of the Jew. What is remarkable is that the bourgeois class analysis that Sombart, Mann, and Amis offer relies on a cryptobiological definition of the Jew and the anxiety about sexual selectivity.

It must be stressed that Sombart (and Mann and Amis) argue for the Jew as the marker of economic change, and yet all find the "Jewish problem" (or the class problem) inscribed on the body. For example, one of the strengths of the Jews as an economic class was "their linguistic ability" (173). The function of language as a marker for the Jews is evident in Mann's tale; in Amis's world, the difference between the ideolect of the upper classes and that of the lower classes gives the novel, structured in inner monologues, its piquancy. Like Mann's notion of the Jewish language, the physiognomy of language and "voice" mark the characters in Amis's novel. But what gave the Jews this linguistic (read: economic) advantage is "their almost caste-like separation from the peoples in whose midst they dwelt. They, the Jews, looked upon themselves as a peculiar people; and as a peculiar people the nations regarded them" (177). Thus, according to Sombart, the Jews created the ghetto through the "flame of pride—from Ezra, who forbade intermarriage as a profanation of Jewish purity" (238). In this way "consciousness of kind" was coded in Sombart's account as at the core of Jewish economic difference.

The Jews remain separate from the peoples among whom they settled; they only appeared to adapt: "By means of the Diaspora they entered into the world. In the Hellenistic cities they adopted the Greek tongue and Greek manners even if only as the outer garb of their Jewishness" (239). The image of internal consistency and external change is at the core of Mann's image; it is always how and why the Jew serves as the marker for economic/incestuous relationships in Amis's world.

Separation is understood as sexual perversion. Sombart quotes the well-known passage by Tacitus (who was certainly no lover of Jews): "They neither eat nor intermarry with strangers; they are a people of strong passions, yet they withhold themselves from other men's wives" (*Historia* V, 1, 5). Here Sombart offered a "positive" reading of Jewish "consciousness of kind." He presented a model of sublimation as the mechanism by which sexuality is turned into profit: by the Law of the Father, the Jews limit their sexual contact even with their own wives (236), and as a result "enormous funds of energy were prevented from finding an outlet in one direction and they turned to others" (237). This repressed sexual power became economic aggression. And thus the "incestuous" Jews intermarried, separated themselves from the strangers among whom they lived, and exploited them through usury: "But it may be observed that even in the earliest collection of laws interest was allowed to be taken from 'strangers'" (242). And this means that the Jew (or his surrogate in the system of representations) can be unscrupulous: "The good Jew must needs draw the conclusion that he is not bound to be so particular in his intercourse with non-Jews" (245). Sombart meant economic intercourse, but it reflects on the transformation of this image that Sombart's repressed Jew becomes the degenerate Jew who is unscrupulous in his sexuality as well as in his economic dealings. And these degenerate, modern Jews move easily from the desert to the "modern city," for "the modern city is nothing else but a great desert, as far removed from the warm earth as the desert is, and like it, forcing its inhabitants to become nomads" (334). The city becomes the place of incest, of the corrupted and corrupting modern.

The image of the city-dwelling, incestuous, inbred Jew in the work of Sombart and Mann comes to form the model for the representation of the modern keyed to the perception of the Jew in Martin Amis's text. For Sombart (and perhaps also for the modern British writer) the

Jewish outlook was the "modern" outlook; the Jew was actuated in his economic activities in the same way as the modern man. Look through the catalogue of "sins" laid at the door of the Jews in the 17th and 18th centuries, and you will find nothing in it that the trader of to-day does not find right and proper, nothing that is not taken as a matter of course in every business. . . . He should have the right to push forward at the expense of others, if he were so able; and the weapons in the struggle were to be cleverness, astuteness, artfulness; in economic competition there should be no other consideration but that of overstepping the law. (153)

And the Jewish representation of the Law according to this antisemitic discourse is one that transgresses natural law as represented by the taboo against sibling incest. It is striking that the move from turn-of-the-century Germany to late-twentieth-century Britain incorporates the Jew as the marker of this violation. It is, of course, *only* in the world of fiction that this occurs, and yet it is clear that the presence of such images in the ironic world of fiction evokes myths that haunt the fringes of British consciousness.

R. B. Kitaj's "Good Bad" Diasporism and the Body in American Jewish Postmodern Art

Kitaj and the Visible/Invisible Body of the Jew

Premise One: R. B. Kitaj stands virtually isolated on the margins of contemporary British art.

Premise Two: R. B. Kitaj stands as a representative figure at its very center.

Or, to quote Kitaj: "All my life I've been a good bad boy."[1]

R. B. Kitaj's paradox of being the inside outsider, the marginal centrist, stood in relief with the great scandal created by his Tate Gallery retrospective in 1994 and the even greater critical and public acknowledgment of his work over the past few years. What I will do in this essay is to examine, in light of Kitaj's sense of being simultaneously peripheral and central to the London art world, his own understanding of himself as a "Diasporist" artist, a term he coined himself (D 9): "The Diasporist lives and paints in two or more societies at once. . . . I don't know if people will liken it to a School of painting or attribute certain characteristics or even Style to it" (D 19). The "two or more societies" into which I shall place Kitaj are simply those of "insider" and "outsider." In doing so, I want to understand how formal or aesthetic categories such as "figurative art," one of the London critic's targets during the Tate retrospective, are shaped by and shape Kitaj's self-consciously Jewish-American "Diasporist" consciousness and how they form his London-based concept of "Diasporism." As Vivianne Barsky has noted, Kitaj's "immersion in Jewish themes offers him the advantage of staking out his own artistic ground."[2] And this is especially the case in the "School of London," a concept that he also coined.

As a fascinating visual parallel to the construction of Diasporism within the aesthetics of Kitaj's oeuvre, I shall evoke a parallel movement among younger American-Jewish artists that seem, in many ways, to undertake artistic gestures similar to Kitaj's Diasporism. Although these artists are a generation younger than Kitaj and are rooted in the American Diaspora experience, much of Kitaj's fascination with the representation of Jewish identity reappears in their work. With these artists there is not so much a question of "influence" (as Kitaj's theoretical work had relatively little impact on American Jewish art circles) as there is a communality of response to specific questions concerning post-Shoah Jewish identity.

Kitaj's Diasporism, like Giles Deleuze and Félix Guattari's "nomadism," is a sense of permanent, creative displacement:

Even Jews must become—Jewish (it certainly takes more than a state). Jews themselves must become-Jewish . . . it is because only a minority is capable of serving as the active medium of becoming, but under such conditions that it ceases to be a definable aggregate in relation to the majority. . . . [Becoming Jewish] therefore implies simultaneous movements, one by which a term (a subject) is withdrawn from the majority, and another by which a term (the medium or agent) rises up from the minority.[3]

This movement to a Jewish consciousness first entails understanding oneself as an actor on a larger stage (for Kitaj the world of modern British art). This is the spirit of Max Weber's "pariah," transposed onto the Romantic artist. Or as Kitaj himself notes more than once, quoting Nietzsche: "I like Nietzsche's definition of art best: art is the desire to be different, the desire to be elsewhere" (R 50). It is this "difference" and this "elsewhere" in art that is both escape and control.

Kitaj is simultaneously insider and outsider and is needing both positions to define each other.

Where Nietzsche's "elsewhere" fits in Kitaj's fantasy is complicated. Julián Rios, in an interview with Kitaj, tells him that: "You are a child of your century, and for a triple reason: as an artist, a Jew and an American."[4] Here he is replying to a claim that Kitaj made in his widely cited *First Diasporist Manifesto* (1989): "I must declare or confess my most complex credential—one of the outstanding facts of my life and Diasporic condition: utterly American, longingly Jewish, School of London, I spin my years away from both my heartlands" (D 41). But Rios misses the key term: *School of London*. For if nothing else, Kitaj is a member of this self-constructed school of London artists, from Francis Bacon to Lucian Freud, and it is in, or perhaps against, this context that I believe his work must be read.[5] Kitaj also writes of his new groundedness in the *First Diasporist Manifesto*: "I've become an Honorary Englishman, a Suspicious Reader" (D 109). This position of the honorary Englishman, of the member of the School of London, is a position on the margin. For Kitaj, the School of London is the world of difference. It is inhabited by the Queer and by the Jew: "my comrades . . . in the School of London, some of whom are Diaspora Jews and some of whom may wander in a sexual Diaspora" (D 47). The idea of Diasporism is closely associated with the pariah status of those constructed both from within and from without as different. And yet these "pariahs" are, of course, the most important British painters of the late twentieth century, if gallery prices are any indication.

The valorization of the periphery is clearly tied to Kitaj's own sense of a marginalized, slippery personal identity. He was born in Cleveland, Ohio, as Ronald Brooks in 1932. His mother and he were abandoned by his Hungarian-Jewish father, who fled to the West Coast. In 1941 she was remarried to an Austrian refugee, Dr. Walter Kitaj, whom Kitaj identifies as his father and as the exemplary Holocaust survivor / refugee.[6] Before her second marriage, his mother dated a man named Joe Singer, and Kitaj notes, "I almost became R. B. Singer" in the mid-1930s.[7] It is "Joe Singer" who, as we shall see, becomes in his art the representative Jew, the ultimate Diasporist.

Names are vital to Kitaj. They shape his sense of self. He was incensed when the Anglo-Jewish novelist Clive Sinclair inscribed a work to "Ron": "I'd rather you didn't call me that, please stick to my surname in future."[8] Kitaj is both Singer and not Singer, Kitaj and not Kitaj. In his self-construction he is both the American Jew and the European Jew. He studied art in post-Shoah Vienna in 1951, a cityscape still marked by the signs of the war through its four-power division. This is the city that Walter Kitaj had fled to survive the Shoah. In London, he becomes both an adult (he marries twice and has children) and an established figure in the art scene. There his membership in the School of London turns him into the artist R. B. Kitaj, the stepson of the refugee and therefore of a survivor, if at one remove, of the Shoah in exile in London.

Kitaj's Diasporism is thus tied to a complicated "good bad" relationship with his own Jewishness. His definition of this Jewishness rings clearly in his writing over the past decade:

I've always been a Diasporist Jew, but as a young man I was not sure what a Jew was. I was unaware that such questions were debated within Jewry, even in the Knesset itself. Jews were Believers, I thought, and I assumed you were whatever you believed in, that if you became a Catholic or an atheist or a Socialist, that's what you were. Art itself was a church, a universalist edifice, an amazing sanctuary from the claims and decrepitude of modern life, where you could abandon self and marry painting. My friend Isaiah Berlin says: "A Jew is a Jew like a table is a table." (D 31)

To Kitaj, Jewishness was marked as "different," and art seemed to be a way of escaping that difference. Jewishness was felt to be "merely a religion" and therefore mutable. Thus, the particular, religious practice, could be replaced by the universal, art. But when he accepts Sir Isaiah Berlin's notion of the immutability of Jewishness, of the inherent, internalized sense of a permanent, Jewish sensibility, Kitaj accepts the idea of his own difference. Here he is very similar to Sigmund Freud, who, though he was never sure of what being Jewish was, knew that he was indelibly Jewish. In 1926, as we discussed earlier, Freud stated in his address to the B'nai B'rith that being Jewish is sharing "many obscure emotional forces, which were the more powerful the less they could be expressed in words, as well as a clear consciousness of inner identity, the safe privacy of a common mental construction."[9] This view works in general with Sir Isaiah Berlin's understanding of his essential Jewish nature.

There is a specific, post-Shoah twist to Kitaj's sense of a Jewish identity. It is what has come to be labeled a "negative symbiosis" between the idea of the rootedness of the American and British Jew and the nomadism of the Diaspora Jew. Each aspect of Kitaj's identity struggles with the others. Being a Jew is tied to the image of the survivor as European wanderer (such as his stepfather). But it is also colored by a specific American problem, so central to the work of his "buddy Philip Roth" (D 79). It is the "guilt" of American Jewry after 1945, who felt that they had survived without ever really having being in danger. Such danger, by the 1980s, comes to be read into the relationship between "real" Jews, that is, those who were born or who lived in Israel, and the Diasporists, who remained beyond the pale, living outside of Israel. Survivors' guilt has become merged with the guilt about "abandoning" Israel.

For Philip Roth, in his 1993 *Operation Shylock: A Confession*, the means of answering this guilt was to reify all the anxieties about Jewish identity created by the politics of the Israeli state and to suggest ironically (?) that the answer is to reestablish the pre-Shoah Jewish communities in Central and Eastern Europe by expelling the Jews of Israel. Thus, both the "Israel problem" (the relationship between Jew and Arab) and the European problem (the absence of Jews) are solved with one blow. Roth's presentation of this new movement, which he labels "Diasporism," is in critical dialogue with Kitaj's Diasporist mentality. But Kitaj's pessimism surfaces when he says to Rios that "When I am in Jerusalem with [the artist] Avigdor [Arikha], I do not feel optimistic about the future of the Jews" (R 55). Surrounded by Israelis, Kitaj is confronted with the complex, often unpleasant daily reality of Jewish experience in the 1980s. No optimism is possible, only the ongoing confrontation with the reality of political experience. These become further, nonreligious markers of Jewish identity for Kitaj, permanent (in Sir Isaiah Berlin's sense) because they seemed tied to the "common mental construction" of post-Shoah Jewry.

It is not incidental that Kitaj's Jewishness is inflected by his reading of Theodor Adorno's admonition "about whether or not 'art' can or should touch upon the Shoah" (D 55). Adorno's comment in his essay *"Kulturkritik und Gesellschaft"* ("Cultural Criticism and Society"), written in 1949, the year he returned in Germany, first appeared in print in 1951. In its closing argument, this essay contained a provocative pronouncement that occupied Jewish writers and artists such as Kitaj dealing with the legacy of the Shoah in their own work:

By being neutralized and processed, traditional culture in its entirety today becomes insignificant. . . . Even the most extreme consciousness of the catastrophe threatens to degenerate into drivel. Cultural criticism exists in confrontation with the final level of the dialectic of culture and barbarism: to write a poem after Auschwitz is barbaric, and that also gnaws at the knowledge which states why it has become impossible to write poems today.[10]

This text comes to be the litmus test for the question of who, and in what context, could represent the Shoah. Adorno's message was aimed at West German (that is, non-Jewish) writers and artists, but how and where could Jewish memory represent the Shoah? For Kitaj the double question that Adorno raised, the ability to "represent" the invisible world of memory and the representation of the Shoah, must be resolved in order for him to become a Diasporist artist.

Yet the catalyst for Kitaj's recognition of this problem was neither Adorno nor the Shoah. R. B. Kitaj "discovered" his Diasporist identity "in the early seventies" in Guernica (D 87, R 157). But it is only in the 1980s that he articulated this sense of Jewish Diasporism in his interviews.[11] It is not Picasso's painting that is central to his understanding of Diasporism, but the rebuilt town in Spain. His visit there in the 1970s, of course, was inspired by Picasso's painting. For Kitaj, Picasso, the most famous painter of the twentieth century, is a Diasporist, and Kitaj, in comparison, is only an "unorthodox Diasporist" (R 109). Kitaj has created his lineage within the definition of Diasporism: "In my time, half of the painters of the great schools of Paris, New York and London were not born in their host countries" (D 25). But why did he choose Picasso and *Guernica*? Because Picasso and his painting reflect the centrality of avant-garde art in representing identifiable if abstracted bodies—bodies dismembered, bodies in pain— as the icon of mass destruction. It is this tortured, mutilated body in the work of the Diasporist painter, which is also the painter's body, that stands at the very center of Kitaj's fantasy of the world and his construction of his image of Picasso.

But is Picasso Kitaj and is Kitaj Picasso? Of course not. It was when Kitaj visited the town of Guernica, with its ugly reconstructed cement buildings of no distinction, that Kitaj crystallized his under standing of his own difference, of the meaning of his own personal Diasporism. He is both Picasso at the center of the modern and Picasso the exile, representing the horrors associated with Germany that would culminate in the Shoah: "Since we artists tend to create our precursors, as Borges said, Diasporist painting now, for me, began in the great art of the West which nourishes all painters, including those of the briefly fluttering congeries of modernist styles, Yiddishkeit and doomed café freedoms which ended in Drancy and the Eastern railheads" (D 47). I would also argue that it was at Guernica, in the light of the most powerful model for figurative art in the twentieth century and his exemplary work, that Kitaj understood Diasporism for the very first time, at least according to his own account. But what are the contours of Kitaj's understanding and representation of the Diasporist body and how can they be measured against the drive for representation in his painting and drawing?

Kitaj claims to be a *bricoleur* of the Jewish experience, "roam[ing] and pick[ing] and choos[ing] in the Yeatsian rag and bone shop for the sake of my art and heart" (R 183). And yet it is less an abstract Jewish mysticism than the mystical, read through the Shoah, that permeates Kitaj multiple senses of his own work: "What holds me in its grip, so that I can't escape its still stinking breath, is the epochal murder of the European Jews. And so, some of my art-life these days concerns the theological 'explanations' of that event" (R 184). He is, as he says of a representational, indeed autobiographical, figure in *Germania (The Tunnel)*, a "man made ill by history" (R 184).[12] Kitaj is virtually always present in his Diasporist paintings, either directly, as in *Germania (The Tunnel)*, or by projecting himself onto the Diasporic figures he represents.

Figurative art is the art of Diasporism. In Kitaj's eyes, at least in the 1950s and 1960s "Jewish painters" (that is, painters who were so identified or so identified themselves) used "universal" forms such as abstraction and minimalism as a means of self-definition. As he notes: "For those whose ideas, painting ideas I mean, were clasped to the advent of a large, metaphysical art, abstraction for instance, the time may not have come ripe to announce the sombre turning in Jewishness clearly in painting. But they knew: Rothko knew, and that other cunning old Russian-American-Diasporist, Barnett Newman, he knew, when he said that the subject matter of the artist is the most

important thing to consider in his work" (D 95). Kitaj states that he
knew both these artists when he was younger. Mark Rothko, with his
Rothko Chapel (1964–67), and Barnett Newman, with his *Stations of
the Cross* (1958–66), are hardly "Jewish" painters, in Kitaj's more limited sense.[13] Rather, both used the universalizing gesture of minimalism to create a "religious" space that seemed transcendental but that
echoed (as much as Matisse's chapel at Vence) an inherently Christian
iconology (following Erwin Panofsky's definition of iconology as
"iconography turned interpretative") of space and form.[14] Kitaj's representative art is thus a gesture (from the School of London) to an
earlier notion of Jewish art—which, in its transgression of the prohibition against the representation of the human figure—becomes a
universal gesture that is not traditionally Jewish. This art is central
and universal rather than peripheral and particular, just as Kitaj needs
his own Diasporist art to be.

Among contemporary American Jewish artists the artist who
comes closest, in many ways, to sharing Kitaj's sensibility is Art
Spiegelman.[15] Spiegelman's visibility in contemporary American visual culture, his use of autobiographical materials, his reliance on his
father's experience as a survivor to define himself and his art all reflect
aspects of Kitaj's construction of his own Jewish identity. Like Kitaj,
Spiegelman relies on figurative art that is iconological in the extreme.

Seeing Jews as mice represents a post-Shoah reading of a major
pre-Shoah trope. The tradition within antisemitic art of representing
the Jew as mouse-like has its most frightening rereading in Franz
Kafka's tale "Josephine the Singer, or the Mouse Folk" (1924), in
which Kafka attempts to recuperate the image of the mouse. Mice are
understood as images of contamination. The proverbial literature of
the Nazi period states it boldly: "Jews have as much value in the
world as mice in corn" or "Jews are as usual in a country as mice in
the granary or moths in clothing."[16] In the rhetoric of nineteenth-
century political antisemitism, the Jews turn out to be "golden rats
and red mice," as the arch-antisemite Wilhelm Marr put it.[17] Mice are
also associated with Jews through the popular etymology of *Mauscheln* (speaking with a Jewish tone) as meaning "mouse-like."[18]
Spiegelman's mice (like his cats and his pigs) have iconological significance in that they rescue the image of the Jewish body while gesturing toward its deformation.

It is clear that Kitaj's Jewishness is closely bound to his art and to its form. Yet he claims to draw on a specific Jewish mystical tradition reaching, according to him, from the Kabbala to Walter Benjamin. In defining his Jewishness, Kitaj stresses "the formal aspects of religion, questions of ritual and observance" as part of recapturing his lost sense of a Jewish identity (R 183). And yet his representational work is not that of a Marc Chagall, the arch-Jewish representational artist whose visual world seems most to parallel the religious, mystical tradition that Kitaj evokes. Chagall does not stand in the cultural lineage of his own Jewish antecedents: "I suspect a depressive connection which formulates its own aesthetic. Typical figures here would be Primo Levi, Soutine, Kafka, Celan, Bomberg, Benjamin, Jean Améry, Rothko, painters X, Y and Z" (D 73). Hidden or effaced is the identity of X, Y, and Z, the missing part of Kitaj's Jewish legacy. Does Chagall lurk here?

Marc Chagall was without a doubt the most popular self-consciously Jewish representational artist of the mid-twentieth century. He was the "Picasso of Jewish art." (And that center/marginal position influenced his reception.) He wrote about himself, in a most teleological manner, that

the soil of Vitebsk, my native town, the thousand years of the Diaspora find themselves mixed with the air and soil of Jerusalem. How could I have imagined that in my work I would not only be led by my own hands, with their paints, but also by the poor hands of my parents, and that behind me would jostle and murmur still others, eyes closed and lips silent, wanting also to take part in my life. It seems to me that your tragic and heroic resistance movements in the ghettos have become mixed with my flowers, my beasts, my fiery colors.[19]

Chagall came to represent, for himself and for Western high culture after the Shoah, the visual tradition of Jewish experience, an experience rooted in the mysticism of Eastern European Jewish life. The representational (if often surreal) iconography of Chagall's paintings came to represent this naive, pure, pre-industrial, mystical world. From public mosaics in the center of Chicago to his evocation in the self-consciously romantic musical *Fiddler on the Roof* (1964) by Jerry Bock (composer), Joseph Stein (author), and Sheldon Harnick (lyricist), Chagall had come, by the time of his death in 1985, to represent "Jewish art" in the post-Shoah Diaspora. It is a visual world that has come to be the stuff of kitsch sold today in Jerusalem's tourist shops. Thus, in his interview with Kitaj, the Anglo-Jewish novelist Clive Sinclair wants to see Kitaj as analogous to (yet different from) Chagall: "Responding to the Holocaust, Chagall famously painted a crucified *Ostjude*. Kitaj, on the contrary, has sought a specific iconography, a Jewish equivalent to the cross. Consequently he produced about eight pictures relating to the Jewish Passion, each of which was marked with a crematorium which could also be seen as a coffin."[20] Chagall's Eastern Jew was, of course, the Jesus of the *White Crucifixion* (1938), covered in a prayer shawl; and most of the contemporary references (German quotes, swastikas) are effaced by Chagall to make the image yet more "universal." It was the most "Christian" of Jewish memorials to the German persecution of the Jews. But even this image has been read as the product of the Chagall of the Eastern ghettos, by 1938 long vanished into the maw of history. Indeed, the ghettos had already begun to vanish when Chagall left Russia in 1922 for Berlin and then Paris. But Chagall had spiritually left his home town of Vitebsk (where he was born in 1887) much earlier when he was transformed from Moses Segal to Marc Chagall. Names matter in this transformation.

Chagall came to represent an antithetical notion of "Jewish art" as Kitaj formulated his notion of the Diaspora. In a recent interview with Richard Morphet, Kitaj was asked about Chagall and especially about Chagall's "series of tall upright paintings of individual 'types'" taken from the Jewish theater.[21] Kitaj's answer explains everything he does not like about Chagall but never engages with the notion of Jewish "types."

Chagall was a painter who never much interested me. My reasons are hard-nosed and wholly unoriginal—the usual suspects: Pont Neuf prettiness and the French cuisined shtetl schmaltz of those long years from some damn good early modernist Yiddishkeit to the Riviera showbiz of his later wholesale trade. . . . Chagall is one of the very few gifted Jewish painters who painted pictures about Jews. Sometimes I think that Matisse painted more Jews than Jews do . . . when I entered my Jewish period, I was, in a way picking up a dying torch, not exactly from Chagall himself but as a new species of Jewish painter for my own era—one who almost stumbled upon Jewishness and became excited and alarmed by it and unable to exclude it from the art equation. Chagall was the exact contemporary of my grandparents, who came from the same Russian-Jewish clay he did. It seems like a sad fairy tale to me with a tragic ending, and I can't pretend that I haven't got that tale and its bright coloured dread somewhere in the back of my art, passed down from grandfathers and grandmothers into my pictures.[22] (CAT 52)

What Kitaj dislikes is Chagall's "centrality," the descent of his Jewish art into kitsch. (Here one is reminded of Spiegelman's use of the mass cultural phenomenon of the comic book and his transformation of it into a high cultural artifact. This is the opposite trajectory of *Schindler's List*, which moved from Thomas Keneally's novel to Steven Spielberg's film.) What he likes about Chagall is that he painted Jews and Jewish bodies. If, in his fantasy, Kitaj is not Picasso, he fears that he may be related to Chagall, at least in terms of his Diasporic fascination with the representation of the Jewish body. Unstated in Kitaj's construction of his Diasporism is an evocation of a distanced past as a nostalgia for the body of the past.

What links Kitaj (he fears) to Chagall is the Jewish body as the subject of Jewish art as painted by another Jewish body, the body of the Jewish artist. For Kitaj, the Diasporist is a nomadic body; the Diasporist body of subject and object is never fixed into a romanticized space. This space is the imagined "center," and the nomadic body is by definition understood as different, as a body on the periphery. The Diasporist can carry only his/her body with him, and he paints — other such bodies. The "good bad" Kitaj, however, fears himself fixed at the center of contemporary British art, the School of London, which is just as central to contemporary British art as Chagall was to Jewish art in the 1980s.

Kitaj must deal with the post-Shoah sensibilities of Britain rather than with the nostalgia of a Russian Diaspora. In being renamed as a child, he became "Kitaj" rather than "Brooks." Now the Diasporist artist is able to position himself between the kitsch Russian-Jewish Diaspora evoked by Chagall (who is of the tradition of his own grandparents) and the lost world of Central European *Bildung* represented by his stepfather, the Viennese chemist Walter Kitaj. The space that Kitaj seeks and finds for the expression of this "good bad" position is in the revitalization of precisely the sort of "Jewish types" that Morphet stressed as Chagall's own contribution to Jewish art. It is not surprising that in Kitaj's major canvas (according to his own estimation) *Cecil Court, London WC2 (The Refugees)* (1983–84), he uses images from the Yiddish theater and from the same Jewish experience that he refuses to acknowledge in Chagall's work.

"Diasporism is my mode. It is the way I do my pictures. If they mirror my life, these pictures betray confounded patterns" (D 29). The "confounded patterns" are indeed the Jewish types that haunt Kitaj's paintings. And these types come, not from the Jewish mystical tradition or from his American roots, but from his exposure to European, especially British, antisemitic visualizations of Jewish difference, of the meanings read into the Jewish body in his London Diaspora.[23] By interpreting a series of paintings, I will show how the visual representation of Kitaj's Diasporism is more an internalization and constructive reworking of European antisemitic representations of the Jew than it is the evocation of Jewish mystical tradition. Kitaj noted that "Jewish Otherness . . . has been identified as a prime cause of anti-Semitism as far back as the Book of Esther" (C 53). In the Western tradition this Otherness concerns itself with the details of the differences of the Jew's body, as I have shown in detail elsewhere.[24] It is the physical difference of the Jew that sets the Jew apart, and yet this physical difference is merely the visible representation of the difference of Jewish character. The effacement of such difference, however, would destroy the essential sense of Jewishness that Isaiah Berlin evoked. Kitaj is caught in his work between an acknowledgment of this difference and its visual restructuring.

How is the Jew's physiognomy read in the European tradition of seeing the Jew as physically different? In the early twentieth century, the pseudonymous French antisemite "Docteur Celticus" produced a handbook on the vocabulary of Jewish physical difference.[25] In his representation, of course, the Jew is male, as we shall see again and again. *His* hand, *his* foot, *his* nose, *his* ears all mark him as different, not theologically, but racially. As the Viennese antisemite Ritter von Schönerer wrote at the turn of the century: "The Jew's belief is nothing / it's his race that makes him swinish!"[26] (This is an antisemitic restatement of Isaiah Berlin's view that a "table is a table, a Jew is a Jew.") Every physical aspect of the Jew points toward his difference. The German-language proverbial literature of the time is full of such references: "He walks like a Jew. He has flat feet like a Jew. God protect us from trichinosis and Jew's noses." But it also points to the diseased nature of the Jew: "There are no Jews without the mange. He is as proud of his work as the Jew of his skin disease. He is as scabby as a Jew."[27] Jewish physical difference is absolute.

Parallel images could be found in the British journal *The Butterfly* during the same period. And in London during the 1940s the antisemitic journal *Truth* insisted "upon a form of biological determinism represent[ing] what Gavin Langmuir terms 'physiocentric anti-Semitism'—a fixation upon the physical characteristics of 'races.'"[28] *Truth* remained a fixture in British culture until 1957, but the image of the physical difference of the Jews remains a trope even today.

The most recent appearance of this image was in the best-selling novel by Martin Amis, *The Information* (1994).[29] In it Amis has his protagonist work part-time for a vanity publisher by the name of Balfour Cohen. Names matter both in Kitaj's and in Amis's London. In this way Amis provides a not-so-subtle juxtaposition of the name of the British prime minister, whose 1917 declaration made the State of Israel a historical possibility, and the essential Jewish name "Cohen" that features prominently in European ethnic jokes. *Nomen est omen.* The physicality of the Jew in the antisemitic imagination is reflected in his hypersexuality and, according to Amis, Cohen is a literary pimp: "'Private' publishing was not organized crime exactly, but it had close links with prostitution. The Tantalus Press was the brothel. Balfour was the madam" (53). And Balfour, in the feminized role as "madam," looked the part:

Had he been around for the Holocaust in which all four of his grandparents were enslaved and then murdered, Balfour would have been dead half a dozen times over. Pink triangle, yellow star: it would have been a complicated badge he wore, in his last days. Racially subhuman (Jewish), sexually perverted (homosexual), mentally unsound (schizophrenic), physically deformed (clubfooted) and politically deviant (Communist). He was also a vanity publisher; he was also entirely uncynical. Furthermore—and as it were disinterestedly—Cohen was a serious collector of anti-Semitic propaganda. Look at him. There never was a gentler face, Richard thought: the bald brown head, the seashell undulations of his temples, the all-forgiving orbits of his hot brown eyes. (53)

With all of Amis's great satirical edge, this is the body of the Jew in the fantasy of British and European culture. Amis's contemporary

Julian Barnes describes in one of his early novels one of his protagonist's Jewish friends:

Toni far outclassed me in rootlessness. His parents were Polish Jews and,
though we didn't actually know it for certain, we were practically sure that
they had escaped from the Warsaw ghetto at the very last minute. This gave
Toni the flash foreign name of Barbarowski, two languages, three cultures,
and a sense (he assured me) of atavistic wrench: in short, real class. He looked
an exile, too: swarthy, bulbous-nosed, thick-lipped, disarmingly short, ener-
getic and hairy; he even had to shave every day.[30]

After the Shoah, Barnes and Amis romanticize all the negative images
associated with the physical difference of the Jew. This is the simple
reversal of Dickens's Fagin (with his "villainous and repulsive face")
or du Maurier's Svengali (whose "Jewish aspect [was] well featured
but sinister"). Faces reveal; names reveal. Thus Barnes's Jew is the
"barbarian," a word hidden in his Polish surname. It is clear that
Barnes and Amis stand very much in a modern British tradition that
sees the Jew as physically different.[31] Kitaj's art is indeed that of an
"allegorist," using Joe Shannon's term, but the elements of the alle-
gories he builds come from the visual and cultural world to which he
gives value—the Western antisemitic fantasy of the Jew.[32]

Kitaj explains his allegorical paintings in extraordinary detail. In
listening to Kitaj or at least in reading his extensive midrashim (interpretations) of his paintings, the viewer is forced to place the painting
into the interpretive framework that its creator desires. But perhaps
it would serve us better to use these midrashim to work against the
interpretations offered and to place Kitaj not only into the realm of a
Jewish mystical tradition where he would have us place him, but also
into a post-Shoah grappling with the materiality of the Jew—the Jew
as found not in the work of Chagall but in that of Julian Barnes and
Martin Amis. What is striking when this is undertaken is how very
much Kitaj's preoccupation with the materiality of the Jewish body
comes to be key to contemporary Jewish artists in the United States
and their dealing, not with an abstract Jewish tradition, but with the
very idea of a radically different physicality and its meaning in the
contemporary world.

Jewish writers in contemporary Britain, such as Clive Sinclair, regularly evoke the physical difference of the Jew. And indeed, as Kitaj

notes, his "buddy Philip Roth and his great book *The Counterlife*, . . . is quite encyclopedic on these questions. . . . Diasporist painting in my own life, begins to assume some of the Jewish attributes or characteristics assigned to that troubled people" (D 79). Roth, another American Jew in the British Diaspora (at least in the 1970s and 1980s), has made the representation of Jewish physical difference and the Jewish internalization of this trope central to his work. Roth's image becomes one of the icons of Jewish identity in Kitaj's *Manifesto*. It is the portrait of the Diasporist, the American Jew in England. Yet in Kitaj's *Manifesto* this image is cropped to focus on the detailed portrait of Roth's face; the full image with is shadowy, outlined body vanishes. Roth's "Jewish" body, with its prominent foot, haunts the *Manifesto* even though it is not present.

Philip Roth's character Nathan Zuckerman is the (semi-autobiographical) protagonist of his great series of novels, *Zuckerman Bound*. To Kitaj, Zuckerman is, according to Sinclair's interview with Kitaj, the origin of Kitaj's exemplary Jewish body, Joe Singer: "Seeing the fun his buddy Roth was having with his fictional alter ego, Nathan Zuckerman, he dreamed up Joe Singer, the exemplary Jew."[33] Rios recognizes the importance of Kitaj's own identification with Singer, for Kitaj had almost become "Singer" in the 1930s: "Joe Singer is your agent, the Jew you send in your place to those dangerous moments of the past in which you couldn't be present. He could also be a father figure of all your Diasporist predecessors" (R 105). In one of Roth's Zuckerman novels, *The Anatomy Lesson* (1983), his arch-Jewish writer Nathan Zuckerman's bad back marks his own internalization of his struggle as a Jew, a man, and a writer: "To sit up in a chair and read he wore an orthopedic collar, a spongy lozenge in a white ribbed sleeve that he fastened around his neck to keep his cervical vertebrae aligned and to prevent him from turning his head unsupported. The support and the restriction of movement were supposed to diminish the hot line of pain that ran from behind his right ear into his neck, then branched downward beneath the scapula like a menorah held bottom side up."[34] This portrait of the artist as a sufferer from back pain, understood as an articulation of the state of Jewish identity, links the body of the Jewish artist with the Jewish artist's representation of the Jewish body. Zuckerman is thus the exemplary literary Jew, just as Singer is to become the exemplary visual Jew.

Kitaj's portrait of Singer, *The Jew Etc.* (1976), provides a self-portrait as the Wandering Jew. Placed in a train compartment, in the contemplative position of Albrecht Dürer's *Melancholia*, what is striking about Singer's physiognomy is the hearing aid that stands prominently at the center of the portrait. Haunting the *First Diasporist Manifesto* (D 59, D 108), Singer's portrait is a self-portrait as afflicted Jewish body. Like the cropped image of Philip Roth, the initial image of Singer is reduced to a profile representing his ear with its hearing aid. In his image of *The Listener (Joe Singer in Hiding)* (C 125) (1980), there is a similar emphasis on the "good ear" of Joe Singer listening "into the void with a large, pricked-up ear."[35] Kitaj's own deafness (and his hearing aid) locates this image within the body of the artist as Diaspora Jew, but it comes to have iconological significance within his work. Only much later in the text does the full portrait of Joe Singer appear, the only image repeated twice in the volume. The hearing aid reappears in the representation of *The Bather (Frankfurter)*, which is one of his attempts to re-do Cézanne's bathers "after Auschwitz."[36] Kitaj's own deafness is present in this image, but so is an older trope in European culture about the Jew's ears as a sign of Jewish physical difference. It can be found in the antisemitic literature of the fin de siècle; but it is also a major subtheme of one of the great works of world literature, Heinrich Mann's *Man of Straw* (1918).[37] In that novel, Mann's self-serving convert, Jadassohn (Judas's son?) "looked so Jewish" (85) because of his "huge, red, prominent ears" (86), which he eventually has cosmetically reduced. This is part of an ongoing tradition of seeing the Jewish body, even the Jewish ears, as different.[38]

Joe Singer's pathological Jewish ears point to Joe Singer's back, which is both Nathan Zuckerman's back as well as Kitaj's "bad back." How deeply embedded the notion of the Jews' physical difference is in Kitaj's manner of representing Jewish difference can be measured in his discussion of Judaism as the determining quality of the Jew. Kitaj stresses, as we have mentioned, the mystical aspects of Judaism as a system of religion and interpretation: "its Covenantal, mythic, Midrashic, ethical, exegetical, schismatic, Zaddick-ridden, arguments" (D 37). This is, however, ironic, the traditional post-Shoah American Jewish understanding of Jewishness and Judaism as absolutely linked concepts. And yet it is not simply an equation of religion and identity. The sense that Jewishness was an inherent aspect of the Jew is what Kitaj learns from Isaiah Berlin. Thus, when he imagines his painting to be within this religious tradition, a strange slippage occurs: "There is a traditional notion that the divine presence itself is in the Diaspora, and, over one shoulder, Sefirot (divine emanations and 'intelligences' according to Kabbala) flash and ignite the canvas *towards which I lean in my orthopedic back-chair*, while from my sub-conscious, from what can be summoned up from mind and nerve, and even after nature, other voices speak more loudly than the divines, in tongues learned in our wide Diaspora" (D 37). It is the artist's bad back that marks his presence within this system. And, as I will show, this is not only Kitaj's bad back, but Zuckerman's; indeed the Jew's bad back is believed to mark his separation from the world in which he dwells. There is an orthopedic chair in Kitaj's studio, but it is the damaged body of the Jewish artist that is central to this image. It is in the physicality of representational art that Kitaj can find his way of working out the anxiety about being a "good bad" Diasporist, that is, at the same time centered and grounded and peripheral and nomadic.

Reading the "Good Bad" Body of the Jew in Kitaj's Work and American Diasporist Art

Let us continue to examine a series of paintings in which Kitaj evokes specific attributes of the Jewish body as the different body, the dangerous body. Let us begin with the subliminal representation of madness in Kitaj's painting as a traditional way of relating the physicality of the represented body to the character of the individual. This is an ancient trope, as I showed in my *Seeing the Insane*, but Kitaj uses it in an interesting way in his Diasporist painting.[39] Martin Amis's "schizophrenic" Jew fits well into this model that associates Jews with madness. And Kitaj's own portrait of *The Jew Etc.*, Joe Singer, uses the standard position of the melancholic for its evocation of the Jew's body. In commenting on *Cecil Court, London WC2 (The Refugees)* (1983–84), Kitaj notes that "One of the first friends to see this painting (a 75-year-old refugee) said the people in it looked *meshuga*. They were largely cast from the beautiful craziness of Yiddish theater, which I knew only at second hand from my maternal grandparents, but fell upon in Kafka" (C 158). The Diasporist figures in this painting are crazy, but they are crazy as the creative Jews in the Diaspora. Madness and creativity, two concepts also long linked in Western thought, come to replace the association of madness and bad character in Kitaj's iconology.

Even as the Jews of Europe followed the guidelines set out for them by the Enlightenment, even as they began to integrate themselves into the body politic during the course of the nineteenth century, the idea of the inherent susceptibility of the Jews to specific forms of mental illness became commonplace.[40] According to this view, Jewish mental illness is the result of the sexual practices of the Jew, here inbreeding, which creates the predisposition to disease, and of the pressures of modern life in the city, which is the direct cause. The dean of fin-de-siècle German psychiatrists, Emil Kraepelin, professor of Psychiatry at Munich and founder of the Institute for Psychiatry there, spoke with authority about the "domestication" of the Jews, their isolation from nature, and their exposure to the stresses of modern life.[41] This domestication is a sign of poor character. The charge that the Jew is mad is echoed in Martin Amis's satiric portrait of the schizophrenic Balfour Cohen. Like Amis's works, the standard handbooks at the beginning of the century, however, paralleled the image of the immediate relationship between the madness of the Jew and his physicality. This image of the mad Jew associated the hidden taint of the Jew's potential mental illness with the visible signs of degeneracy. Georg Burgl's handbook of forensic medicine of 1912 states quite clearly that "the Jewish race has a special predisposition for hysteria." For him this was a result of the degenerative nature of the Jew and was also marked by "physical signs of degeneration such as asymmetry and malocclusion of the skull, malocclusion of the teeth, etc."[42] The visibility of the Jew was identical to the visibility of the degenerate, their signs and symptoms pointing to their susceptibility. Simply stated, these views about the predisposition of Jews to specific forms of mental illness were commonplace. After the Shoah, the extensive literature on survivor neurosis came to be linked, again, to the physicality of the Jew and symbolically to the camp tattoo.

The madness of the Jews in *Cecil Court, London WC2 (The Refugees)* is translated by Kitaj into creativity. Their actor-like bodies

mimic the "creatively mad" in their adaptability. For the trope of
the Jew as the consummate actor is related to the general European
belief that the Jew is the most mutable of people, able to adapt to all
circumstances. This mutability comes to be a sign of the Jew's difference, a madness that literally represents the Jewish body as mad.
The Jew is, in his/her adaptability, the one who is most different because he/she can become most alike. This is Deleuze and Guattari's
notion of the reciprocity/antagonism between a heightened nomadic
(Diasporist) identity and the acceptance of the Jew in contemporary
society.

Kitaj seems to answer this question of simultaneous change and
stasis in one of the portraits in his series of variations on Cézanne's
Bathers, labeled *Psychotic Boy* (1980). Kitaj uses this image to illustrate
his *First Diasporist Manifesto* (D 114). It is the image of a young boy
whose only Jewish difference is the *payess*, the sidelocks that mark his
physiognomy. Like the Jews in Cecil Court, his madness seems not
symbolic or theatrical but inscribed on his body. He is simply the
"psychotic boy," the Jew after Auschwitz. Yet his physiognomy echoes
that of another image of "disorder," the foreground figure in *The Jewish School* (1980), which is again placed in a provocative evocation of
the position of the melancholic hands crossed in a traditional icon of
the madman who cannot work.[43] Here we can trace the figure back to
a "real" antisemitic image, Georg Emanuel Opitz's early nineteenth-
century *The Jews' School*, which Kitaj found in Isaiah Shachar's 1974
monograph on the image of the Jewish swine (C 138).[44] But Kitaj uses
other icons of introspection and melancholy in his portrait of "Joe
Singer" (*The Jew Etc.* [1976]) and his *Passion (1940–45) Reading* (1985)
(D 117) to mark the psychic difference of the Jew after the Shoah.

In *Psychotic Boy*, Kitaj returns to the potential he saw earlier in the
1950s in Aby Warburg's method of image-tracing as the key to symbolic content. Kitaj's familiarity with the Warburg school and its understanding of the function of iconology is reflected in his use of
Shachar's monograph. Introduced to this approach "under the spell
of Diasporists like Aby Warburg, Fritz Saxl, [and] Edgar Wind" (D
59) (he studied with the latter), Kitaj revitalizes the idea of a visual vocabulary of representational art rooted in a specific visual tradition. In
his reading of Opitz's Jews' School, Kitaj transforms the antisemitic
image of the Jewish swine into that of the Jewish creation, the

Golem; but the figure of the Jewish student with his sidelocks remains. The madness of the Jew is tied to the image of the Jew within antisemitic art. But this image is not separate from Kitaj and his sense of the Jewish past and the Shoah.

If Art Spiegelman's *Maus* uses many of the same aesthetic notions of Diasporism as figurative representations in an iconological mode, then other young American Jewish artists play with many of the same images as does Kitaj, with striking results. Brian Weil's 1985 black-and-white photographs (*Untitled*) present the image of young Orthodox Jews as informal portraits of "normal" rather than pathological individuals.[45] Weil, born to a Jewish father and a Catholic mother, spent a year living among the Hasidic communities in the Catskills and Borough Park, Brooklyn. Like Spiegelman's evocation of the traditional antisemitic image of the Jew as mouse, Weil's evocation of the image of the Orthodox Jew as the "authentic" image of the Jew throws the meaning attached to the Jewish body into question. Jews in these contexts are visible and different from everyone else. But are Jewish identity, history, and memory really reducible to these markers of Jewish physical difference?

The irony in Kitaj's use of the image of Orthodoxy as the icon of the Jewish body in the work of Weil becomes the portraiture of an inner difference. Certainly not portraiture as in the freak-show mentality of a Diane Arbus, but rather as a simple portrait, set in the outdoors, of the Jew within. There is no madness present. The Jewish body becomes one version of the American body. Where the ironic mode is introduced, as in Ilene Segalove's rules from a Jewish boy's camp (*Jewish Boys* [1987]), the desire is to highlight what is different about the American Jewish experience of American life, a sense that is echoed in Brian Weil's photographs. Here we have the projected portrait of the "Other" as the portrait of the self—the articulation of visual difference that makes the invisible photographer or printmaker visible as Jewish and as different, while not being different at all.

In *Germania (The Tunnel)* (1985), a self-portrait (D 18) places Kitaj in an image of the Shoah that is framed by a "central tunnel . . . taken from Van Gogh's madhouse gouache" (C 219).[46] It is van Gogh who comes to frame the Holocaust, van Gogh who is himself an exemplar of biographical madness within the Western high art tradition.[47] According to Kitaj, this is his "most difficult painting" (C 219) precisely because of the juxtaposition of three central themes in the form of a representational image: the historical (the Shoah), the art historical (van Gogh), and the thematic (madness). Van Gogh's "two insane passages" not only frame a "historical madness," but they reflect on the very role of the image of the madness (read: inherent difference) of the Jews as one of the rationales for the destruction of European Jewry. Not only is the Shoah "madness"; its roots are in the image of the "mad Jew." According to Kitaj, the madness of Auschwitz is rooted in his reading of Philip Roth's edition of Tadeuz Borowski's short stories about the camp. And yet Borowski, the non-Jew, serves, like van Gogh, to provide an aesthetic, representational veneer that makes the very notion of the madness of the camps comprehensible. Kitaj's work plays with this conflict between art and history, aesthetics and madness, popularity and marginality.

It is the combination of the "good bad" Vincent van Gogh—the figure in art history and the marginal figure who became a brand name—that replaces Picasso or Chagall in Kitaj's pantheon of art. And it is the mad Jew, the artist as husband and father in the tunnel that leads to the ovens who is imagined here. But van Gogh is an important reference to the Jewish body as the mad body. In a recent series of "bad" images, a long work in progress, Kitaj presents a vocabulary of the Jewish artist's body as the Jew's body in a detail unprecedented since Dr. Celticus at the turn of the century. These canvases are signed Ronald. He notes, "I figured if Vincent could sign Vincent, I could sign Ronald" (C 221). These are images of his "own decline in case I forgot something bad" (C 221). Vincent, whose madhouse imagery haunts Kitaj's representation of the madness of the Shoah and his own self-representation as Jew within that tradition, comes to be the analogy to the new Jewish artist, Ronald. Here he is neither Singer nor Kitaj—no pseudonym or label—but rather the Jew within, the Jew without family name, as Jews once lacked, the Jew as the artist of the center and of the periphery. Names do matter. Ronald's images of the "bad" body are also images evocative of the body of the artist as Jew, slowly becoming what the stereotype of the Jew said he must become, slowly unraveling his London body into a Jewish body.

Ronald's Jewish body has a "bad back" (C 196). This back, as we have discussed, has its origins both in autobiographical reality and in a reading of that reality in Philip Roth's *Nathan Zuckerman*. In Roth's *The Anatomy Lesson*, as discussed earlier, his arch-Jewish writer Nathan Zuckerman's bad back marks his own internalization of his struggle as a Jew, a man, and a writer. His back pain is the penance he pays for living—surviving the Shoah, outliving his parents, living as a Jew in America. Like Roth, Kitaj, a.k.a. Ronald, sits *"in my orthopedic backchair,* while from my sub-conscious, from what can be summoned up from mind and nerve, and even after nature, other voices speak more loudly than the divines, in tongues learned in our wide Diaspora" (D 37). The bad back is the sign of the artist as Jew and the Jew as artist. He is an artist with a wide range of disabilities.

Ronald has *"bad eyes"* (C 197). He wears glasses, like the hyperintellectual Jew of the antisemite's fantasy, but his eyes still reveal his character. In the late nineteenth century, the British scientist Francis Galton saw the "cold, scanning gaze of man, woman, and child" as the sign of Jewish difference, of their potential pathology, of their inherent nature: "There was no sign of diffidence in any of their looks, nor of surprise at the unwonted intrusion. I felt, rightly or wrongly, that every one of them was coolly appraising me at market value, without the slightest interest of any other kind."[48] It is in the Jews' gaze that the pathology of their soul, the true meaning of their Jewish superior intelligence, can be found. Following Galton, the anthropologist Hans F. K. Günther, whose anthropology of the Jews was a standard work of Nazi science during the 1930s and 1940s, later attempted to describe the "sensual," "threatening," and "crafty" gaze of the Jew as being the direct result of the physiology of the Jewish face and as reflecting the essence of the Jewish soul.[49]

Ronald has a *"bad foot"* (C 198) *and a "bad knee"* (C 201). I have written extensively about the role that the Jewish foot plays in delineating not only the Jewish body but also the Jewish character.[50] The limping foot is conspicuous in antisemitic discourse of the twentieth century. As we discussed in Chapter 4, in Oskar Panizza's fin de siècle drama, *The Council of Love*, the Devil appears as a Jewish male, his corruption written on every aspect of his body, including on his foot.[51] The crippled leg, as the sign of the degeneracy of the Jew, structures Panizza's image of the seducer of humankind. The trope of the limping Devil and the limping Jew are interchangeable at the turn of the century and are here set within a secularized (and anti-Christian) theological model of the Jewish disavowal of God/Christ and reliance on Mammon.

This lack of good character as represented in the image of the Satanic, limping Jew becomes part of the standard repertoire in seeing the Jew. A century later Martin Amis's Balfour Cohen is "physically deformed (clubfooted)." Another British publisher, this time a real one, can be added to the repertoire. In 1918 Lytton Strachey described the London publisher William Heinemann in a manner not too different from Amis's portrait of Balfour Cohen: "A more absolute jew face couldn't be imagined—bald-headed, goggle-eyed, thick-lipped; a fat short figure, with small legs, and feet moving with the flat assured tread of the seasoned P. and O. traveller. A cigar, of course. And a voice hardly English—German r's; and all the time somehow, an element of the grotesque."[52] But the feet betray his true character. For the legs and feet point to the mercantile and mercenary soul of Strachey's Jew. This is what separates "Heinemann" (or at least his representation) from the self-image of Bloomsbury.

Body parts haunt the visual imagination of other contemporary Jewish artists concerned with constructing a vision of the Diaspora. In Rona Pondick's 1992–93 installation, *Pink and Brown*, at the Israel Museum in Jerusalem, disconnected legs and heads become abstract objects. And yet the disarticulation of the body into its parts highlights the fact that the body is missing. Walking through the installation was like walking through an abattoir or a Boschian nightmare of the death camps. Not stacked bodies, but body parts, made up the terror of the space. And yet these were not victims' bodies. They were the disjointed body parts of the viewers as well as the bodies of memory. Pondick's pink and brown bodies are unsexed bodies; they are the body of the Jewish collective.

An aside on gender is appropriate at this point. Kitaj, a.k.a. Ronald, is not only a Jewish-American-British painter; he is also quite self-consciously a male painter. His awareness of the problems of male Jewish identity after the Shoah is perhaps most clear in his *Self-Portrait as a Woman* (1984). In this portrait he represents himself as his former lover from Vienna in 1951, Hedwig Bacher, who had been marched naked through the streets of Vienna during the Nazi years because she had slept with a Jew. Kitaj's identification with her as victim, as Jew, brings the Jewish male and the female together as victims in the light of history. The battered and bruised body of the non-Jewish woman comes to represent the body of the Jewish male artist, her lover, in the Vienna of Orson Welles's *The Third Man*. The Jewish male body, however, had been long seen in Vienna precisely as the body of the woman.

There is an old Viennese tradition represented by the writing of Adolf Jellinek, a rabbi in Vienna, in his ethnological study of the Jews in the 1860s.[53] Jellinek sees the Jew as inherently feminine, labeling the Jews as the feminine nation among the nations and stressing the Jews' "fantasy" as one of the primary qualities shared with the Woman (90).

The Woman is happy when she pleases a man and the Jew when he is praised by the non-Jew. This unique fantasy combined with the ancient heart and the quick, mutable spirit also influences artistic creativity of the Woman as well as the Jew. Their language is full of a richness of images, in poetry they are more productive in the lyric than in the epic or the dramatic arenas, and only the future will determine if their capabilities in the plastic arts will raise itself above that of an ordinary talent! (95)

Such views frame the ideas of creativity and femininity that are found in Jewish as well as in non-Jewish texts. "In the examination of the various races it is clear that some are more masculine, others more feminine. Among the latter the Jews belong, as one of those tribes which are both more feminine and have come to represent (*repräsentieren*) the feminine among other peoples. A juxtaposition of the Jew and the woman will persuade the reader of the truth of the ethnographic thesis." Jellinek's physiological proof is the Jew's voice: "Even though I disavow any physiological comparison, let me note that bass voices are much rarer than baritone voice among the Jews" (89–90). In 1904, the Elberfeld Jewish physician, Heinrich Singer, commented that "in general it is clear in examining the body of the Jew, that the Jew most approaches the body type of the female."[54] The association of the image of the Jew (read: male Jew) with that of the woman (including the Jewish woman) is one of the most powerful images to be embedded in arguments about race.

Given the extreme importance of Jewish feminism in contemporary American Jewish culture, it is of little wonder that the slipperiness of gender and cross-gender identity among Jews is important to American Jewish women artists. In Hannah Wilke's work, such as her

Venus Parve (1982–84), the figure of the Jewish woman, made "pareve," neutral between the poles of "meat" and "milk," is duplicated and reduplicated as an ironic parallel to the neolithic "Venus of Willendorf" figure. Wilke casts these self-portraits in a variety of materials, including chocolate. Deborah Kass, in her *Double Double Yentl* (1992), uses the image of Barbra Streisand's film *Yentl* (1983) to illustrate the slippery relationship between gender identity and Jewish identity. This image provides a further example of the problems of the infinite duplication of gender identity when linked to the question of the Jewish male/female body. In Streisand's *Yentl*, based on I. B. Singer's story about an Eastern European shtetl, the protagonist must disguise herself as a man in order to undertake the central task of learning. The problem of gender confusion associated with the Jewish body is highlighted in Cary Leibowitz's self-ironic *4 Yarmulkes* (1993), in which the traditional "male" head covering comes to be ornamented with "female" accessories. In all these cases the line between "male" and "female" evoked as an antisemitic trope comes to herald a new sense of the transgressive nature of Jewish identity.

Kitaj's Jewish artist, Ronald, has a *"bad sinus"* (C 200). The Jew's nose makes the Jewish face visible in the Western Diaspora. It is the stuff of which antisemitic jokes are made. The Jewish nose, as the art historian / novelist Carl Einstein noted in 1926, is the physiognomic sign of Jewish difference and was linked to the debased role of the Jews in contemporary capitalism.[55] It is a sign of their character, a character inscribed on their visage. It was even tied to the fantasy of an indelible, identifiable Jewish accent, which was seen as simply a reflection of a different muscular construction. Jews speak differently because the "muscles, which are used for speaking and laughing are used inherently differently from those of Christians and this use can be traced . . . to the great difference in their nose and chin."[56] The Jew's nose marks the inherent difference of the Jew's character.

Of all the icons of Jewish physical identity, none is as powerful as the meaning ascribed to the Jewish nose. In 1993 the contemporary American artist Dennis Kardon began an ongoing series of casts of Jewish noses called—*Jewish Noses*. Unlike Kitaj's sinus image, with its pathological representation of the Jewish nose as diseased, Kardon collects and reproduces healthy, functioning Jewish noses, noses that mark the ethnic difference of the American Jew. Kardon is constrained to do this, as the association of ethnic specific cosmetic surgery still haunts the daily life of American Jews. "Change your nose and you will change your life!"

There is still the cautionary tale of the dangers lurking in the Jewish nose and the anxiety of trying not to look Jewish. Adam Rolston's *Nose Job* (1991) evokes the technical representation of the surgical correction of the Jewish nose that cannot hide the Jew within. Cynthia Madansky's *Rhino* presents six images of Jewish "nose jobs" that trace the notion of shame within the American process of Jewish acculturation. With the rise of a heightened feminist and Jewish consciousness during the late 1980s, the meaning ascribed to being Jewish became the focus of some concern. This is nowhere better illustrated than in the feminist *Wimmen's Comix* #15 entitled *Little Girls* (1989), subtitled "Case Histories in Child Psychology."[57] One of the most striking of these case histories is Aline Kominsky-Crumb's *Nose Job*. Aline Kominsky-Crumb was one of the founders of the feminist comic book movement with her creation in the late 1970s of *Twisted Sisters*, and she is presently the editor of *Weirdo* magazine. *Nose Job* is a cautionary tale about a young woman "growing up with cosmetic surgery all around [her]" who avoids cosmetic surgery in her forties by recalling her earlier temptation as a teenager on Long Island in 1962. There "prominent noses, oily skin & frizzy hair were the norm. . . . (No, we Jews are not a cute race!)" This self-conscious admission of the internalization of the norms of her society even in 1989 underlies the dangers lurking even for those who can articulate the meaning ascribed to the Jew's body. Even as all about her teenagers were having their noses restructured, she holds out. She eventually flees to Greenwich Village where she "felt hideously repulsive." Her "sensitive folks kicked this already beaten dog" by pushing their daughter to have a nose job. After she runs away, her parents agree to postpone the procedure. And she "manages to make it thru High School with [her] nose." The story, at least in the "comix" has a happy ending: "6 months later styles had changed and she looks like the folk singers Joan Baez or Buffy St. Marie." In other words, one could look as "beat" as one wanted, as long as one did not look "Jewish." The Jewish nose came to signify the outsider, but that outsider was never identified as Jewish. The moral of Aline Kominsky-Crumb's tale is that fashions in appearance change and that women should not succumb to the pressures of fashion to homogenize their bodies. But the hidden meaning was: it is all right to look Jewish as long as you are visible as someone else besides a Jew. What is still left in Aline Kominsky-Crumb's memory is the sense that looking Jewish still means looking different, looking marginal, not "looking cute." Even the heightened awareness of feminism does not dismiss the power of the internalization of a culture's sense that one not only looks different, but also ugly. Today Deborah Kass's *Jewish Jackie* (1992) plays with the infinite replication of the Jewish female profile without a nose job!

   Ronald has a "bad heart" (C 202). As with all the physical signs, there is an autobiographical element in this representation. Kitaj has indeed had a heart attack: "After my little heart attack, the doctor told me to walk fast some miles each day to help keep death at bay" (C 51). In the nineteenth century there was a detailed medical literature that claimed that Jews had a much higher incidence of heart illness, which was at the time a vague category. The forensic psychiatrist Cesare Lombroso, in his 1894 study of Jews and antisemitism, argued that Jews in Verona between 1855 and 1864 showed a 9 percent morbidity rate due to heart disease, as opposed to 4 percent among the general population.[58] Lombroso ascribed this to the environment in which Jews were forced to live, their "passionate temperament, the anxiety of wagering and profit, the force that results from poor living conditions." This mix of predisposition and context was typical of debates about Jews and heart disease, but ultimately the Jewish characteristic, Jewish nervousness, is the deciding factor. Thus, it is the madness of the Jews and their inability to adapt that gives them heart attacks. At the end of the century, James Jackson Putnam, the leading American specialist in nervous diseases, claimed that without exception "the psychoneuroses in general are particularly common to the Latin and Hebrew races."[59]

   In his use of representational art, Kitaj represents the body of the artist as Jew as much as the Jew as artist. Through the image of the body the character of the Jew is revealed. *Ronald, the Jewish painter, has "bad thoughts"* (C 199) *and, of course, "bad character"* (C 203). Kitaj's own body—his deafness, his bad back, his bad heart—becomes the Jew's body, Joe Singer's body, the body of the Jew he almost became in his youth and is now becoming in his old age. Dreyfus's uniform ironically appears as a sign of the false claim of the bad character of the Jew. (The image was painted during the centenary of the Drey-fus affair.) Not the Jew he was—the Jew as the "son" of the survivor, the non-victim, the man who escaped from Vienna—but the Jew he is, the man who is becoming marked by the physical signs of Jewish difference. Here is the salient difference between Kitaj and Chagall. For Chagall's images of the "fiddler on the roof" are nostalgic images of a past not only vanished but varnished. Kitaj's images are of a future that is not secured, in which the myths about the body of the Jew and the realities of his own experience of his own body come to merge. Here Kitaj's pessimism toward the aging Jewish body is a specifically American Jewish youthful attitude toward the recupera-tion of the Jewish body, as in John Ellis, Mat Silverstein, and Doug Sadowinock's performance piece *Jew Meat* (San Francisco, 1993). In his art and in the narratives that form part of his art, Kitaj, a.k.a. Ronald, has constructed a series of interlocking counterlives that evolve within his idea of Diasporism. These lives and Kitaj's art are ample proof that the differences we construct in our lives are of equal importance to the differences with which we are born. Kitaj's repre-sentative art constantly reconfigures both the artist and the artist's idea within the very notion of Diasporism.

Early in 1997, R. B. Kitaj unveiled his last London canvas, an im-age reproducing every possible nuance of British antisemitism, and moved to Los Angeles with his son. There he lives close to his chil-dren by his first marriage and his friend David Hockney. He is now part of the London Diaspora in Los Angeles.

CHAPTER NINE

Who Is Jewish?

The Newest Jewish Writing in German and Daniel Goldhagen

Is There a "Jewish" Cultural Renaissance Today?

Recently, a rather pessimistic literature has appeared heralding the death of Diaspora Jewry in Europe. Typical of it is Bernard Wasserstein's study of European Jewry since the Shoah.[1] In a number of books and essays, I have made an equally optimistic counterargument that Jewish culture in Germany is establishing itself (again) as one of the most potent forces in the German cultural sphere.[2] I have stated that German Jewry is at the beginning of a radical explosion in its cultural importance. Wasserstein and analogous critics create a sense of panic with their definition of the Jews. I create a sense of positive development with mine. It is evident, depending on how you define "the Jews" and "Jewish culture," that European Jewry is either vanishing or expanding.[3] The question posed at the outset of this essay then must be: If I claim that there is an expansion of Jewish culture in Germany, then who are the Jews and what is the Jewish culture I am taking about?

"The Jews of Germany are vanishing." Soon, there will be no Jews left at all. They are intermarrying and immigrating. They have a very low birthrate and are not reproducing themselves. This is not only the thesis of Bernard Wasserstein's book. It was also the claim of the Jewish physician Felix Theilhaber, in his *The Decline of the German Jews (Der Untergang der deutschen Juden).*[4] Theilhaber's book was a bestseller, as were the numerous books about the decline of the birthrate in France, England, Germany, and so on. What all these discussions about declining birthrate and vanishing races did, of course, was to 1) label Jews as victims under biological siege and 2) define them in a way that essentially defined the identity of the authors of the works. Certainly the German Jews before World War I were not vanishing; indeed, the only thing that was under debate in Theilhaber's books was the question who is a Jew? And, as an example of early Berlin Zionist rhetoric, this book made sense. The Jews that Theilhaber saw as "vanishing" were the German Jews (by his definition); the Eastern European Jews living in Germany (his bête noire) were thriving, as he himself admits.

Let us begin, however, with the counterargument to the present case as presented by Wasserstein. His is an odd book; it is an example of what happens when one aspect of Jewish history, the history of disaster, becomes the dominant lens through which we see all Jewish history. Wasserstein has written a competent history of all the bad things that happened to Jews in Europe after 1945. But what is missing is any examination of what "bad" is and of whether some good things have been omitted from the narrative. The frame he uses is his claim that the Jews of Europe are vanishing, and he compares them in his conclusion to the tiny community of Jews at Kai-fend, who were assimilated into Chinese culture for over a thousand years. And yet even today the descendants of these Jews still have some sense of themselves as different, perhaps even as Jews, even in light of the difficulty of a claim to such an identity within the ethnic politics of the People's Republic of China.

Better, Wasserstein should have taken the case of the Jews of the Spanish Peninsula, who were expelled in the fifteenth century. There, too, he would have found descendants who had only a vague sense of their difference. In Mexico there are still individuals who light candles in a closet on Friday evenings because it is a family tradition without knowing where this tradition came from. But there is also the world of Sephardic Judaism, ranging from secular, ethnic Jews to ultra-orthodox ones. It is the entire spectrum of Jewish experience that is important, not focusing on one aspect of it to the exclusion of all others. Here one can also draw an analogy to the problems of the Jews of the German-speaking world. For, if one narrowly describes the history of post-Shoah German-speaking Jewry, it seems a history of collapse and dissolution. Certainly the immediate post-War history seems to prefigure this model, if, that is, one defines Jewry only in ritual (halachic) terms.[5] Who is a Jew? is an important question in Germany, and the answer is virtually as complex as that of the Jews of the Spanish Diaspora.

Wasserstein prefaces his account with a tabulation computing the number of Jews in Europe. The commentary to this table—on which all of Wasserstein's arguments rest—is that these numbers are of "varying reliability and in some cases are subject to a wide margin of error and interpretation." Wasserstein and I were just at a meeting in Budapest, and we had dinner with one of the community leaders there. Now, according to Wasserstein's table, there were, as of 1994, 56,000 Jews in Hungary, down from 80,000 in 1967. When I asked the community leader how many Jews there were in Budapest (where most Hungarian Jews now live), he said anywhere from 60,000 to 120,000, depending on how you define who a Jew is. His answer is the crux of such arguments about whether European Jews are vanishing. Wasserstein's book really should read: MY JEWS ARE VANISHING! For it is the definition of what is Jewish that is at the heart of it. Even though Wasserstein is aware of this problem and even though he discusses it in the opening pages of the book, he still falls back on crude biologism. A Jew, according to him, is that person who is biologically/halachically (ritually) Jewish. And sadly, Wasserstein even uses the old biological argument to buttress his thesis. He argues that Anglo-Jewish women marry latter (73) and marry out (74) to account for their "particularly low reproduction rate." He says similar things about French Jewry (243). I would argue that marrying out decreases the number of Jews only if a strict religious definition of Jewish is taken, and even then, according to the Law of Return, the offspring of Jewish women are always Jewish.

The Jews of Europe are not vanishing! And certainly the Jews of the German-speaking world are not. Their numbers were reduced after the Shoah because of emigration to Israel and persecutions in Eastern Europe, but other (perhaps smaller) groups did move to Europe over time. The Jews of North Africa moved to France, and the Russian Jews (no matter how defined) moved into the Federal Republic of Germany. Indeed, there is now a notable Israeli presence (or Diaspora) in Europe, including in the Federal Republic. Russian immigration to Germany (and to elsewhere in Europe) has meant a complex revitalization of Jewish communal and cultural life in even the small urban areas of the German-speaking world. And this world extends from the Federal Republic to Austria to German-speaking Switzerland. Jewish cultural visibility at all levels of society is at its highest point there since the beginning of the century. Jewish culture in Germany is complex, self-contradictory, and difficult. But it is exploding, and I state this not just in terms of romanticizing the Eastern European Jewish past or out of a "necrophilia" (a term used in Wasserstein's book and in general discourse in Germany today) for the victims of the Shoah and their culture.

Wasserstein, by the way, shares the bizarre neoromantic German notion of Yiddish culture in Eastern Europe as consisting of nothing but Klezmer music and bagels. He sees it as "sentimental drama; haunting folk-songs and a dynamic newspaper press" (6). Where is Yiddish literary modernism, such as the work of I. J. Singer; where is the political Yiddish culture of the Bund (which he even discusses); where is the complexity of Eastern European Yiddish life and culture that was in contact with the mainstream of Western European culture before the Holocaust?

The German situation is, in regard to the evocation of a romanticized Jewish past, even more complex. Canadian sociologist Michal Bodemann has argued that Jews in Germany are, or at least they were for decades, virtual Jews, that is, there was such a need to imagine a Jewish presence in both the B.R.D. and the G.D.R. that the culture "created" a new Jewish identity apart from the actual presence of Jews.[6] But the model for this for non-Jewish and Jewish Germans was as much the American and Israeli experience of Jewish life as it was the German Jewish past. But Bodemann, like Swiss historian Erica Burgauer, recognizes that since the mid-1980s something has shifted in the awareness of German culture (especially after reunification) of an active Jewish cultural presence.[7] What Bodemann and

Burgauer seem to draw into question is the "authenticity" of this experience. It is the question of who determines what an authentic Jewish experience is (and who the "authentic" Jews are) that stands at the center of this discussion.

Wasserstein is not alone in creating the Jews he needs. In the summer of 1996 I was sitting on a plane to Budapest next to the leading Jewish bookseller in Germany. Her annual bibliographies form the core of any scholar's hand list of Jewish writers. We were talking about a wide range of writers, many of whom we both knew well. When I turned to the subject of one of them, a well known and widely read woman playwright and novelist, she snapped at me: She's not Jewish, she said—she doesn't even have a Jewish grandparent!

Therein lies the rub. If being Jewish is defined by ritual and by practice, one set of discussions can be generated; if being Jewish is defined by identity and self-understanding as well as by reception, a totally different discussion takes place. Thus, if one author has a Jewish mother and identifies herself as Jewish, there seems to be no problem. If another has a Jewish father and does the same, he is seen as somehow inauthentic. And if this identification has taken place generations earlier, it is somehow even more inauthentic. In religious circles one of the major debates concerns mixed marriages. Children of mixed marriages are regarded as "lost" to their Jewish origins. Given the rejection of children of mixed marriages by the religious establishment, it is little wonder that these children are lost. It is a greater wonder to me that such children do sometimes come to learn about and cherish their Jewish identity. Germany is a place where (at least after 1989) the badge of a Jewish identity has, at least in some circles, an added cachet. One can make an analogy to the "gain from illness" that the sociologists of medicine describe. The positive value of the victim's status after the fact is part of constructing the idea of the Jew in the German-speaking world. And yet it is this victim status that provides a critical edge for the cultural products produced by those who are either self-labeled or externally labeled as Jews that deal with being Jewish in the contemporary world. It is striking (and now scholars other than me recognize this) that there has been an explosion of such cultural manifestations of Jews in Germany, Austria, and Switzerland. Here it is the self-definition of Jews in the public (cultural) sphere through the creation of a Jewish persona of oneself as a writer, filmmaker, artist, photographer. Such individuals are dedicated to the creation of artifacts that deal with what Dan Diner so insightfully called the "negative symbiosis" of being Jewish in Germany.[8]

The Goldhagen Debate: Setting the Stage

The debates about Jewish authenticity in the German-speaking world can be framed by the complex relationship of this world to the very notion of the presence of the Jews. Nowhere was this more clearly differentiated than in the initial German critical response to Daniel Goldhagen's *Hitler's Willing Executioners* before its publication in German in August of 1996.[9] This reception seems to be a litmus test of the new permissiveness that has existed since reunification concerning public expression about the Shoah and the image of the Jews in Germany. The German ability to talk about Jews in contemporary Germany as part of a contested present that relates to the past provides a frame for the images of today's Jews. The fact is that before the publication of the German translation of Goldhagen's book in August 1996, there were more articles in *Die Zeit* (six) than in the *New York Times* (four). This is a mark of this new German fascination with finally "getting it off" in public about the Jews, here defined as American Jewish scholars, and these scholars' "preoccupation" with the Shoah. This is the context in which the most recent Jewish writing in German must be read. In the reception of Goldhagen's book it is not the "Jews" in general who bear the brunt of these attacks, but "American Jews," defined in such a way as to define the absolute location of corruption and evil.

The linguistic taboos in place in the academy about Jews in general have been loosened since German reunification. When one German historian / historian of Germany who is non-Jewish (Hans Mommsen) can call another German historian / historian of Germany who is Jewish (Julius Schoeps) a "well poisoner" (*Brunnenvergifter*) (*FAZ,* June 3, 1996), in the passion of a public debate about Goldhagen's book, one knows that standards have shifted. "Well poisoner" is an ancient libel about Jews and their general danger to the healthy non-Jewish body politic. And indeed, the debates about Daniel Goldhagen in Germany seem to permit the unvarnished use of a language of defamation that has rarely, if ever, been heard in the halls of the German academy since 1945.

I find the new polemical discussion about Daniel Goldhagen's American Jewish identity (rather than about his book) to be much more revealing about the ability of the German academic public sphere to face up to their own long-term sense of intellectual and moral inferiority to their American colleagues than about any inherent desire to confront the issues raised by Goldhagen. As Goethe wrote, "America, you have it better . . . "—at least you do not have ask what your profession—the writing of history—was guilty of during the Holocaust! Claims by German scholars that Goldhagen's book is "unscientific" because it arises out of his biography evoke the anxiety about the claims of objectivity and scientificity that haunted the writing of history in Germany (East and West) after the Shoah. Eberhard Jaeckel, professor of history at Stuttgart, makes the charge that Goldhagen's book uses "the most primitive of stereotypes" and reverts back to the primitive age of German historiography from the 1950s (*Die Zeit*, May 17, 1996). If the debates in the 1950s about the meaning and the origin of the Shoah centered on the question of "collective guilt," they were also about the role that intellectuals and professionals played during the Third Reich. "What did you do in the war, Daddy?" "I wrote history, my son."[10]

Biography seems to play quite an important part in Germany in the discussion of Goldhagen's book, and it is "biography" that defines the role of the Jewish writer in contemporary German-language writing. You write about what you experienced, and you therefore have a claim to a personal identity as a Jew but not to a professional identity as a historian. What is most striking to me is that the discourse about Goldhagen is about the constructed image of American Jews, not about the Jews in general. And this theme reappears in interesting ways in modern Jewish writing in German. Perhaps here we have living proof of Dan Diner's point about the German image of the Americans that "America" became a surrogate term for the "Jews" in the nineteenth and twentieth century.[11] In this debate the "American Jew" becomes the locus of anxiety in complicated ways.

We can begin with the enfant terrible of German right-wing culture, Frank Schirrmacher who, in two pieces in the *FAZ* (April 15, 1996, and April 30, 1996), condemned Goldhagen's book as creating a biologically essential image of the "Germans"—something Goldhagen certainly does not do. This clear misreading is strangely echoed by Eberhard Jaeckel's rather comic assumption (*Die Zeit*, May 17, 1996) that Goldhagen's evocation of an "anthropological" model is a biological one. Because, according to Jaeckel, as everyone knows, "anthropology is a sub-specialty of biology, which studies the inherited and not the acquired qualities of the human being." All anthropology is physical anthropology, because, of course, that is what the anthropology of race was in Germany before 1945. No other kinds of anthropology seem to exist for Eberhard Jaeckel. (Actually, Ingrid Gilcher-Holtey, professor of history at Bielefeld, quietly corrects this amazing gaff in her intelligent and sober discussion of Goldhagen's book as a prime example of the history of images, of *mentalité*, in *Die Zeit*, June 7, 1996.)

But it is necessary for Schirrmacher and Jaeckel to turn Goldhagen—into what? By accusing him of using a biological model for the writing of history, they transform him into "Daddy," those Nazi historians who truly did use a (for them completely "scientific") biological model to explain the glories of the Third Reich and the inherent inferiority of the Jews. The American Jew Daniel Goldhagen becomes the figure all historians of Jaeckel's generation fear—the "objective" Nazi historian, their own teachers and intellectual fathers. Goldhagen imagined as the new Jewish-American Nazi is a fascinating projection of a generation's anxieties. (It is also nothing new. The Jews, then the Israelis, were labeled the "new Nazis" after the massacres in the refugee camps in Lebanon and during the Iraq war.)

If Goldhagen is the new "Nazi," then who are his compatriots? Who is at fault for the popularity of Daniel Goldhagen's book? Frank Schirrmacher attributes the book's popularity to Jewish critics in the United States. Here he joins the owner and editor of *Der Spiegel*, Rudolf Augstein (*Der Spiegel*, April 1996) who wrote about the "mostly Jewish columnists" who were fueling the American debate on the book. His article was titled "The Sociologist as Executioner," inverting the image of victim and murderer, and a picture of Goldhagen was subtitled "Hangman" Goldhagen. Who are these "American Jewish murderers," and why are they conspiring together against the Germans?

I have before me the typescript of the distinguished historian

Hans-Ulrich Wehler's review/critique of Goldhagen's book (which appeared in *Die Zeit* on May 24, 1996). I am a great admirer of Wehler's work. Unlike Schirrmacher, Wehler, professor of history at Bielefeld, is a serious historian of modern German history, whose scholarship is the basis for research throughout the world. Yet precisely because I admire Wehler's mind, I can read his essay as a definition of "American Jews" similar to that of Schirrmacher.

Let me begin by noting that each of us creates the stereotype of the Jews we need. Secular Jews such as myself tend to be dismissive of reactionary religious definitions and of religious Jews contemptuous of cultural notions of Jewishness. Non-Jews create as many different Jews—smart Jews, national Jews, evil Jews, rapacious Jews—as they need. Such stereotypes are an extension of our way of organizing the world, and they reveal our sense of its inherent order. But what sort of American Jews do the most recent critics in Germany need to create? "First, they are conspiratorial and vindictive. Second, they lie." These are trademarks of classic antisemitism. It seems impossible to construct the Jews without evoking such tropes. Let us look at Wehler's presentation of this argument. Seeing Goldhagen as a prototypical vengeful Jew (Shylock with a Harvard degree), he writes:

Should we not attempt to explain the almost complete extermination of the North American Indians from various, different conditions and motives? Or should we capitulate and allow a young Navajo historian to derive everything from the tradition of an "American murderer" beginning with the puritan branding of the red-skinned "children of Satan"—with consequences for My Lai?

This passage is remarkable in its construction of the vindictive American Jew as Indian. It is only because of Wehler's Jewish nature, which is colored by his experience, by the prejudice he feels, that he feels constrained to act out. He is a historian, but only, of course, in name. *Real* historians have objective reasons for selecting their objects. The only possible reason for such a personal and vindictive approach to the "murderers" is personal history. One of the most interesting questions one must ask of historians is how they select their topics. All historians or critics select objects that are meaningful to them. And this includes not only Jewish historians of the Holocaust but also German historians of the Holocaust.

But an even more interesting question for me is why Wehler selects the image of the Native American as the basis for his analogy. For it is not the Sabra and the Palestinians who are evoked in this passage, but the American Jew. It is not that Wehler is creating a "you are as bad as us" scenario. He is too smart for that. But he does imply that the position of the American Jew is as little a part of the "real" American Holocaust, the murder of the Native Americans, as it is of the "real" Shoah. The American Jew was spared the Holocaust, as Philip Roth has shown over and over again, and now desires to gain from the victim status that the "real" victims have. It is not just that Goldhagen has the "blessings of a late birth," but that he was born in the United States, where, unlike the Native American, he cannot claim this victim status.

This trope reappears in odd places in the Goldhagen reception in Germany. Thus, in *Der Spiegel* (June 1996: 59, whose cover story was devoted to Goldhagen), the German Jewish gadfly, Henryk Broder, wrote: "If Daniel Goldhagen had been the child of a Texan cattle breeder and if he had gotten his doctorate writing about the Holocaust as others have writing about the American Civil War, things would be simpler. But he is the son of a Jewish intellectual, who would have most probably have been a German professor had Hitler not intervened." The move from Native American to American cowboy is a slight displacement, but a necessary one. It comes to be a Jewish reading of the Goldhagen "problem" in a German context. Are American Jews real Jews? Or are they inauthentic because they are neither Shoah survivors nor Israelis? Are they really just like cowboys and Indians? Is the survivor's child different, as the Native American historian would be different, not because of his own experience, but because of his identification with the history of his parent, who is a survivor? Why the Wild West analogies anyway?

Here the German construction of the American Jew is shared by Jew and non-Jew alike in Germany. It is Karl May's *Amerika*, with toy pistols and oversized cowboy hats. This Wild West is read differently by Wehler and by Broder, and yet for both, the American Jew becomes the powerful surrogate for the Amis—the intellectual occupying power that dominated (and dominates) German historical consciousness in its every manifestation, from pop culture to academic discourse. And it is the American historian who must, therefore, be seen as corrupt and as unscholarly for German historiography to again lay claim to the objective writing of the history of—the perpetrator. Here is a further violation of the taboo: Goldhagen has the temerity to write as a Jew about the murders, not about the victims, as he "should." He becomes in this discourse the American as corrupt Jew, as Dan Diner has argued, and therefore, the perfect enemy.

American Jews lie, and in that way they fulfill the expectations of the antisemitic trope. Wehler puts Daniel Goldhagen in the same camp as other "false" Jewish American academics such as David Abraham, whose published dissertation on the role of capital in the funding of the Nazis was dismissed as being based on invented documents. Or Liah Greenfeld, whose comparative study of European nationalisms was denounced because it evoked the specter of the uniqueness of German history, the *Sonderweg*. And now Daniel Goldhagen is on Wehler's list. But what is this a list of? Certainly not of bad historical scholarship by graduate students—that list would have to include too many German dissertations. It is not the canon of bad or evil scholarship on the Shoah, for that list would have to begin with David Irving and continue with a very long list of works of French historians before it even got to the trinity of Abraham, Greenfeld, and Goldhagen. What could these three young *American Jews* have in common? They lie, of course, for lying is the special skill of the Jew in this rhetoric. They appear to be smart. They go to Harvard or teach at Princeton. But their intelligence is simply a mask for their mendacity. They are smart Jews within the age-old calumny that claims that Jewish superior intelligence is simply a cleverness designed to trick unsuspecting non-Jews.[12]

Wehler's selection is unconscious. He underlines this by including on his list of good historians of the Shoah Jews such as Alex Bein, George Mosse, Shulamit Volkov, and Leon Poliakov. But there is not one American Jew on his list. German-Jewish émigrés and Israelis are on it, but not one American Jew is to be found on a long list of fine non-Jewish historians. Now, George Mosse is, of course, more American than anyone I can think of. He has shaped the study of Germany in the United States for five decades, and I am in his deepest debt, as are all American historians of Germany. But for Germans, as can be seen in Irene Runge's long interview with him, he remains a German

Jew.[13] In this construction, the canon of lying Jews consists wholly of American Jews.

The German response to Daniel Goldhagen's book is a clear attempt to break with the hegemony that America has had in defining the Germans. The problem with it, for German critics, is not just that the book is controversial, but that it permits a discussion to take place that has been absent for the past four decades. How are the Americans seen? Are they indeed dominated by the Jews, as German right-wing propaganda has said all along? Why does the *New York Times* always seem to have a "German" page in which antisemitic or xenophobic incidents are next to essays on German accomplishments? We know, and we can see how Jewish writers begin to relate to this set of antisemitic tropes well before Goldhagen's work arrived on the scene.

Three Young Jews Writing

Diaspora Jews (such as Wasserstein) find the re-emergence of Jewish culture in Central Europe an imponderable. Contemporary German intellectuals are now able to localize and articulate their anxiety about Jews and Jewishness. These factors can frame the complexity of Jewish writing in contemporary Germany—and not surprisingly a few of its themes. In this section I will examine three first books by some of the youngest authors in German to claim Jewish identity and to articulate it in their writing. They represent, not by accident, three quite different national voices: that of Austria (read: Vienna), Switzerland (read: Zurich), and East Berlin (which although it is now called one of the "new states," Berlin, it is still truly the mirror of West Berlin). All three authors have specific tales to tell, and all use a voice that is authentic to and appropriate for their own fantasy of what it means to sound Jewish. All three are men. A variation on this theme of being read as a Jewish writer in German is to be found if one looks (as I have done in my earlier publications on this theme) at first books by Jewish women writers who are writing on the negative symbiosis of the Jews in contemporary Germany.

Let us begin with the first novel of a new Jewish writer in German Switzerland. Daniel Ganzfried's first novel, *Der Absender* (*The Sender*) appeared in 1995.[14] Ganzfried was born in Israel in 1958 and grew up in Wabern, near Bern. His novel recapitulates the theme of America as the topography (and antithesis) of Jewish identity in the contemporary world. The first strand of the novel is that the protagonist, having grown up in Zurich, now finds himself in New York working for a Holocaust museum that is under development. His job is to listen to audiotapes made by survivors of the Shoah and to use them to document the history of that event. One tape recounts the life of a Hungarian Jew from his carefree childhood to his experience of the Shoah. The protagonist is convinced that he is listening to the life story of his estranged father. The second strand of the novel is the autobiography of this anonymous Hungarian Jew. A third strand of the novel evolves as the protagonist persuades his father to come to New York and then confronts him on the observation deck of the Empire State Building. We never learn whether the *"Absender"* of the title is his father or not.

It is clear that Ganzfried is using "America" as the foil for the false consciousness of modern Jewry. The obsessive yet distanced relationship of his America to the Shoah (as opposed to the real relationship of European Jewry to the Shoah) forms the central theme of the novel's first strand. It is the superficiality and trendiness of American Jews that form the clear antithesis to the world of the Swiss Jews, who are the children of survivors. American Jewish consciousness is represented by the planned Holocaust museum in a city of people who never experienced the Holocaust, except for viewing *Schindler's List*. Indeed, the meeting at the top of the Empire State Building is taken from one of the classic 1990s romantic products of Hollywood, *Sleepless in Seattle*, which concludes with the lovers' meeting on the observation deck of that building. The iconography of Hollywood kitsch is transformed into the unresolved meeting of father and son, survivor and seeker. Authentic Jewish experience is that of the displaced European (whether displaced to America or elsewhere in Europe), not the experience of America.

One can contrast this text with other examples of older Swiss-Jewish writing. There is a tradition of Diaspora writing among Swiss-Jewish writers, perhaps best exemplified by the work of André Kaminski, especially his novel *Kiebitz* (1988).[15] Like the work of Edgar Hilsenrath, Kaminski's comic novels use the world of the Jew in exile as its theme. Born in 1923 (he died in 1991), Kaminski lived in Poland from 1945 to 1968, when he was expelled during the antisemitic purge. Following his expulsion he lived in Israel and in both northern and southern Africa. In the final years of his life, he lived in Zurich and produced a wide range of work using the figure of the Eastern European Jew in the Western European Diaspora as his theme. *Kiebitz* is written as a dialogue in letters between a Swiss-German psychiatrist and Esdur Kiebitz, a Polish Jew living in Switzerland who has lost the power of speech.

What is striking about both Kaminski's novel of 1991 and Ganzfried's novel of 1995 is how they deal with precisely the types of stereotypes that dominate the response to Goldhagen's book. Certainly the central trope of the Goldhagen affair is that Goldhagen claims to be a smart Jew but is, in fact, a lying Jew. Kaminski bemoans the fact that God has damned the Jews with their smarts: "It is Jewish bad luck, he moaned. Yes, we are a chosen people, the luckiest in the history of the world. God always distinguishes us. He makes pianists out of us, chess world masters, Noble Prize winners in physics and medicine. But have you ever heard of a Jewish boxing champion? A Jewish shooting king? Are we ready for war? Naturally not" (99). Or in an exchange with a non-Jew:

"I said something, Ariel."
"What?"
"That you Jews always know more than we do."
"Naturally."
"Why naturally?"
"That is our secret." (231)

"Smart Jews" is a trope from the complex vocabulary of a world that fears and thus stereotypes the Jews. Daniel Ganzfried's comment reverses this theme. He describes the narrative of the anonymous, taped speaker's schooling in Hungary and his teacher's conviction that there are "two kinds of Jews: either the very smart or the very dumb. Sadly, I could figure out what he was talking about, because of the Jews I knew none could have been placed in one or the other group"(79). The naïveté of the schoolboy immediately deflates the claims of the smart (and stupid) Jew. For being called smart, as Ganzfried knows, is not a form of praise but of opprobrium.

Ganzfried plays with the complexity of a Jewish child's dislocation in trying to fit the model of the smart Jew to the experiences of his

world. Ganzfried is aware of the complex history of the meaning of
Jewish difference, specifically the meaning of the circumcised male
body. Again, the anonymous narrator on the tape recounts his baptism as a child by a Christian nanny (88), which he is quite aware does
not change him. His Christian friend, following a sport's hour in
school, has him pull down his gym pants and remarks: "Now look,
not a trace of a Christian." His circumcision remains unregenerated
through the baptism. He remains a Jew, no matter what his religion
(89). Such a biological argument is the kind that Jaeckel uses in his image of Jews and anthropology. It is an affirmation that such models are
to be dealt with only retrospectively and still need to be undermined.

The biological model of the Jew as a race was closely related in the
1930s and 1940s to the parallel image of the Jews as the source of social and societal disease. Thus, Ganzfried's taped narrator, as part of
the discourse of the 1940s, turns this image around. When the Hungarian Jews were forced to wear the yellow star, the narrator says, "I
bore the mark as if it were a deformation from a terrible illness" (147).
The yellow star is the sign of disease—deforms the healthy Jews.
Ganzfried is quite aware that the world of the past, with all its pitfalls,
is parallel to the world of the present. The tape exists as an artifact of
the present, not of the past. And the complex question of memory
and identity raised by the anonymous narrator and his story needs to
be the bridge through which father and son are to be reconciled.
Ganzfried uses images that are taken from the German discourse of
the past but that exist in the German discourse of the present to highlight that continuity and the "negative symbiosis" that Jews experience (even) in the world of Swiss Jewry.

The Viennese parallel to Ganzfried's text is that of Doron Rabinovici, whose volume of short stories, *Papirnik*, appeared in 1994.[16]
Rabinovici stands very much in the tradition of the contemporary Viennese Jewish writing best represented by the work of Robert Schin-
del (to whom the volume is co-dedicated) and Robert Manesse. Born
in Israel in 1961, Rabinovici came to Vienna in 1964 and did doctoral
work in history there. This volume takes place not in America, but
in Vienna, a Vienna virtually masked in these tales but for bits of local color, such as the statue of the antisemitic mayor of Vienna, Karl
Lueger, or the Plague Column in the middle of Vienna that haunts
the text.

The distinction between an authentic place (Zurich or Vienna) and an inauthentic place is important to these young Jewish writers in German. And the inauthentic place, simply put, is America. In the very beginning of the most telling of these tales, "Der richtige Riecher" ("The Right Smeller"), a complex tale about smart Jews and Jewish noses, the Austrian Jewish protagonist, Amos, is confronted by a group of neo-Nazis who taunt him with the line: "If you don't like it go to Israel—or to New York" (61). "New York is more fun," he is later told in English by a Jewish professor from Columbia University, but Amos wants to do his *Matura* (high school leaving certificate) in Israel, not New York. For Israel is the authentic place of Jewish experience. Israel, the Jewish professor from New York says, is indeed the place of purification for American Jews, who can travel to escape the conflicts in Brooklyn, where the Jews hate the Blacks, to Israel where the Jews can hate the Arabs "with still better reasons" (63). This ironic sense of an American Jewish inauthenticity highlights the reality of Vienna as the place where one can prove one is a real Jew.

Central to this story is the trope of the smart Jew. For part of this image is the antithesis between "intelligence" and "strength." If you are smart, the trope has it, you cannot be strong. You must use your mind, not your fists. Who, as Kaminski's character notes, has ever heard of a Jewish boxer? (Many of us have, from Daniel Mendoza to Barney Ross, but that is not the point.) Amos does not make aliyah. He remains in Vienna and is forced to confront the antisemites on a daily basis. "We don't hate the Jews," they say, the Jews hate us (63). This constant overt antisemitism presents quite a different tone than does Ganzfried's portrayal of the Swiss world, which his narrator has left for New York. When a fellow student, Helmut, tells Amos that they should have gassed him in Mauthausen, his response is to talk rationally to him. Amos's mother's reaction is that he should beat him up. But he doesn't want to, he wants to rely on rational means, discussion and argument. He wants to be a smart Jew, not a tough Jew.

His non-Jewish "friend," Peter, tall and handsome, observes to him that not all Jews stink, only Polish Jews (71), and when Amos tells him that his mother is a Polish Jew, Peter's response is "O, I am so sorry." Antisemitic comments are the stuff of daily exchange in this masked city of Vienna. On his walk through the Viennese pedestrian zone, Amos is confronted with the Plague Column, representing the medieval black death, and thinks of the Jews driven from the city because they were accused of having poisoned the wells and caused the plague. The well poisoners, as we saw in the discussion of Goldhagen, today comes again to be the Jews.

Peter continues his quasi-liberal, antisemitic argument by saying that antisemitism is "naturally not to be excused, but when I look at the orthodox: why must they always separate themselves so? They don't have to run around looking like that. Also: why do they only accept those who are circumcised?" (72) Here the line has finally been crossed. As in Ganzfried's text, it is the response to these classic antisemitic tropes that the narrator uses to set his discourse apart from that of the past. At this moment, Amos finally stops his rational responses and punches Peter in the nose: "the classic straight line which had up to then marked his organ of smell was forever changed and bent" (72), and Amos becomes the hero of his family "with a single blow" (73). Peter's classic Aryan profile becomes marked, not with the Jewish nose, but with the physical proof of his antisemitism. In a visible way Amos has branded him an antisemite.

Rabinovici's style is very different from Ganzfried's. Where Ganzfried adopts a pseudorealistic tone, Rabinovici uses the language of the young German-Jewish short story writer, Maxim Biller, who is always on the edge of a surreal moment. Place especially becomes the point of contention. And yet in both the realms of Ganzfried's New York, Hungary, and Zurich and the almost Borges-like image of Rabinovici's Vienna, the question of an authentic place for the expression of a Jewish narrative in German stands at its center. America may be "fun," but the experiences there (and perhaps also in Israel) do not confront the daily topography of the Shoah on its own grounds. This is the authenticity that Ganzfried and Rabinovici claim for themselves, for their characters, and for their readers, Jewish or not.

In Benjamin Stein's first novel, *Das Alphabet des Juda Liva* (*The Alphabet of Juda Liva*), published in 1995, the response to ideas of Jewishness and narrative space are overt.[17] Stein was born in 1970 in East Berlin and now lives in Berlin and Munich. He has won a number of fellowships, including the prized Alfred-Döblin Fellowship of the Academy of the Arts. His novel is seemingly shaped by the discourse of Latin American magic realism. It moves, through the creation of a Jewish narrator, from contemporary Berlin (after reunification) to late-medieval Prague. The novel is framed around the protagonist, who hires a storyteller to come on a weekly basis to provide his wife with an ongoing tale. It is storytelling in a Jewish vein that is at the center of this tale. The language of this novel seems to be shaped by the vocabulary of the Kabbala, indeed so much so that, following the model of many Jewish works of contemporary German fiction, it concludes with a glossary of terms for its evidently non-Jewish audience. Here the authenticity of the fictive topography seems to be guaranteed by the authenticity of the language of the narration.

But the "Jewishness" of this voice is suspect specifically because it makes such demands on the very idea of authenticity. Stein's novel stands in a narrative tradition of the German Democratic Republic, which is being continued here with a massive dose of Jewish mysticism. Beginning with the brilliant and original *Levins Mühle* (1964), written by Johannes Bobrowski, an avowed Lutheran writer in the G.D.R., this tradition continues through the first "Jewish" novel, that is, a novel with a Jewish protagonist, in the G.D.R., *Jakob der Lügner* (*Jacob the Liar*) (1969),written by a Jewish writer, Jurek Becker. In both of these texts we have complex narrative strands that demand the presence of a palpable Jewish voice in the text. What makes the voice Jewish is its claim that it stands in a narrative tradition of a folkloric, Yiddish narrative, such as that of Sholem Aleichem. Indeed, it is the musical *Fiddler on the Roof* in its Felsenstein version at the East Berlin Komische Oper that has acted as midwife to this novel as much as anything else.

Stein's novel, with its magical movements between levels of narrative, uses a self-combusting narrator who moves from contemporary Berlin to medieval Prague through his tale. Stein picks up these G.D.R. traditions of representing a Jewish discourse. But the physicality of the narrator also picks up on the image of the Jewish body and that of the smart Jew. For, like the protagonist of Becker's novel, the narrator (not Jakob) is the smart Jew, insightful about the past and knowledgeable about the present. But Stein's narrator is also physically marked as the Jew of the antisemite's nightmares. He is described by the narrator as "neglectedly bearded and bow-legged" (11) when we are first introduced to him. Again, it is the physicality of the Jew that marks his difference and is used in the novel to delineate Jewish particularity.

Stein's novel uses, in a more complex narrative form, the idea of an internal Jewish narrative form taken from the Kabbala, but it reveals itself to be a German literary response to the world. Here Prague is the antithesis of Germany. The place of non-authenticity is Germany; that of authenticity for Jewish discourse remains Prague. It would seem that the antithesis between modernity and the past, between Berlin and Prague, escapes the "American curse." But it is actually a trope taken from American Jewish writing of the 1980s. Both Philip Roth (in *The Prague Orgy*) and Saul Bellow (in *The Dean's December*) place the search for Jewish authenticity in the present in Prague.[18] Thus, the Prague that Stein's novel represents is not only that of *Der Golem* (both Gustav Meyrink's 1915 novel and Paul Wegener's 1920 film), but it is also the American recapitulation in the 1980s of the notion of Prague as the Jewish place of experience as seen from the world of American Jewish letters. The authenticity of Prague is a place where "real" Diaspora Jews, such as Franz Kafka, lived a life of ambivalence. This is certainly the case in Stein's novel, even with its movement into the Middle Ages as a contrast to the Berlin of post-reunification Germany.

America, you have it better. . . . Certainly these three writers reverse this claim, while at the same time honoring it. America is "fun" for the Jews: they become powerful, win Noble Prizes, and build cultural institutions such as the video archive of the Holocaust. American Jews are smart Jews, but they are not tough Jews. They have it easy. They are superficial and not engaged in the reconstitution of a new Jewish culture, for Jewish culture in America has become mainstream. Since American Jewish culture has never been destroyed, these young writers in Zurich, Vienna, and Berlin/Munich confront the literary tradition of American Jewry as well as the antisemitism present in their own culture. These three first books show a new level of critical engagement among the youngest Jewish writers in German with the complex world of images and texts in which they live. Is there a new Jewish culture developing in the German-speaking world? Evidently so.

Reference Matter

Notes

Chapter 1

1. M. Bulmer, "Race and Ethnicity," in R. G. Burgess, ed., *Key Variables in Sociological Investigation* (London: Routledge, 1986), pp. 54–75, here, p. 54.

2. Sander L. Gilman and Jack Zipes, eds., *The Yale Companion to Jewish Writing and Thought in German Culture, 1096–1996* (New Haven, CT: Yale University Press, 1997).

3. See the chapter "Race, Ethnicity, and Class," in Neil J. Smelser, *Sociology* (Cambridge, MA: Blackwell, 1994), pp. 280–98, here, p. 289.

4. Werner Sollors, "Theory and Ethnic Message," *MELUS: The Journal of the Society for the Study of the Multi-Ethnic Literature of the United States* 8 (1981): 15–17, and his collection *The Invention of Ethnicity* (New York: Oxford University Press, 1989).

5. Vincent J. Cheng, *Joyce, Race, and Empire* (Cambridge, Eng.: Cambridge University Press, 1995). Cheng's talk appeared in *Cultural Critique* 35 (1997): 81–104.

6. Peter Uwe Hohendahl, *Building a National Literature: The Case of Germany, 1830–1870*, trans. Renate Baron Franciscono (Ithaca, NY: Cornell University Press, 1989).

7. Tom Holden, "Viva Elvis II: More Than a Festival, It's the Cultural Revival of a Global Icon," *Virginia Beach Beacon*, May 31, 1996, p. 8.

8. Susan Bickelhaupt and Maureen Dezell, "Keeping up with the Nield-ses," *The Boston Globe*, September 11, 1996, sec. F2.

9. Rahila Khan, *Down the Road, Worlds Away* (London: Virago Upstarts, 1987).

10. Danny Santiago, *Famous All Over Town* (New York: Plume, 1984).

11. John Treadwell Nichols, *The Milagro Beanfield War* (New York: Holt, Rinehart and Winston, 1974).

12. See Jakob Arjouni, *Happy Birthday, Türke! Ein Kayankaya-Roman* (Zurich: Diogenes, 1987).

13. Helen Demidenko, *The Hand That Signed the Paper* (St. Leonards, New South Wales: Allen & Unwin, 1994).

14. Lionel Trilling, *Sincerity and Authenticity* (Cambridge: Harvard University Press, 1972).

15. Friedrich Nietzsche, *Twilight of the Idols*, trans. R. J. Hollingdale (Harmondsworth, Eng.: Penguin, 1972), p. 77.

16. Octavio Paz, "Eroticism and Gastrosophy," *Daedalus* 101 (1972): 67–80, here, 77.

17. James Shapiro, *Shakespeare and the Jews* (New York: Columbia University Press, 1996).

Chapter 2

1. Jonathan Swift, *The Complete Poems of Jonathan Swift*, ed. Pat Rogers (New Haven, CT: Yale University Press, 1983), p. 455. On Swift's better-known text, see Ashraf H. A. Rushdy, "A New Emetics of Interpretation: Swift, His Critics and the Alimentary Canal," *Mosaic: A Journal for the Inter-disciplinary Study of Literature* 24 (1991): 1–32; William Freedman, "Dynamic Identity and the Hazards of Satire in Swift," *Studies in English Literature, 1500–1900* 29 (1989): 473–88; Thomas B. Gilmore Jr., "Freud, Swift, and Narcissism: A Psychological Reading of 'Strephon and Chloe,'" in *Contemporary Studies of Swift's Poetry,* John Irwin Fischer, Donald C. Mell Jr., and David M. Vieth, eds. (Newark: University of Delaware Press, 1981), pp. 159–68; Peter J. Schakel, "Swift's Remedy for Love: The 'Scatological,'" in *Contemporary Studies of Swift's Poetry*, Fischer, Mell Jr., and Vieth, eds., pp. 136–48; Thomas B. Gilmore Jr., "Freud and Swift: A Psychological Reading of 'Strephon and Chloe,'" *Papers on Language and Literature: A Journal for Scholars and Critics of Language and Literature* 14 (1978): 147–51; C. J. Rawson and Maximillian E. Novak, "The Nightmares of Strephon: Nymphs of the City in the Poems of Swift, Baudelaire, Eliot," in *English Literature in the Age of Disguise,* Maximillian E. Novak, ed. (Berkeley and Los Angeles: University of California Press, 1977), pp. 57–99. See also Martin Pops, "The Metamorphosis of Shit," *Salmagundi* 56 (1982): 26–61.

2. I am using the word *marriage* in this essay as shorthand for any explicitly monogamous love relationship, whether straight or gay.

3. Otto Kernberg, *Love Relations: Normality and Pathology* (New Haven, CT: Yale University Press, 1995), p. 45.

4. On this question in the eighteenth century, see Simon Richter, "Medizinischer und ästhetischer Diskurs: Herder and Haller über Reiz," *Lessing Yearbook* 25 (1993): 83–95.

5. Judith P. Butler, *Bodies That Matter: On the Discursive Limits of "Sex"* (New York: Routledge, 1993), p. 1.

6. All of the quotations from Freud's works in this study, unless otherwise noted, are to Sigmund Freud, *Standard Edition of the Complete Psychological Works of Sigmund Freud*, 24 vols., ed. and trans. J. Strachey, A. Freud, A. Strachey, and A. Tyson (London: Hogarth, 1955–74), here, 2: 7. (Hereafter cited as *SE*.)

7. On the discussion of the fetishization of urination in literature, see my *Difference and Pathology: Stereotypes of Sexuality, Race, and Madness* (Ithaca, NY: Cornell University Press, 1985), 115–16.

8. Roy Porter and Lesley Hall, *The Facts of Life: The Creation of Sexual Knowledge in Britain, 1650–1950* (New Haven, CT: Yale University Press, 1995), p. 24.

9. For a cross-cultural view, see T'ien Ju-K'ang, *Male Anxiety and Female Chastity: A Comparative Study of Chinese Ethical Values in Ming-Ch'ing Times* (Leiden: E.J. Brill, 1988).

10. Edward Westermarck, *The History of Human Marriage*, 3 vols.(London: Macmillan, 1921). He sees adultery as a mysterious association between husband and adulterer in some societies (1: 233, 300–316), but he argues that the basis for chastity is inheritance (1: 518–26). See also John R. Gillis, *For Better, For Worse: British Marriages 1600 to the Present* (Oxford: Oxford University Press, 1985), pp. 79–81.

11. There is extensive literature on the literary representation of adultery. The following were of interest for this essay: Michael Neill, "Unproper Beds: Race, Adultery, and the Hideous in *Othello*," in *Critical Essays on Shakespeare's Othello*, Anthony Gerard Barthelemy, ed. (New York: G. K. Hall, 1994), pp. 187–215; Alison Sinclair, *The Deceived Husband: A Kleinian Approach to the Literature of Infidelity* (Oxford: Clarendon, 1993); Dieter Beyerle, "Ehebruch und krankes Kind: Zu einer Motivkombination in französischen Romanen des 19. Jahrhunderts," *Romanistisches Jahrbuch* 41 (1990): 114–38; Naomi Segal, *The Adulteress's Child: Authorship and Desire in the Nineteenth-Century Novel* (Cambridge, Eng.: Cambridge, MA: Polity Press, 1992); Peter von Matt, *Liebesverrat: Die Treulosen in der Literatur* (Munich: Carl Hanser, 1989); Tony Tanner, *Adultery in the Novel: Contract and Transgression* (Baltimore, MD: Johns Hopkins University Press, 1979); Judith Armstrong, *The Novel of Adultery* (New York: Barnes & Noble Books, 1976).

12. Lawrence Osborne, *The Poisoned Embrace: A Brief History of Sexual Pessimism* (London: Bloomsbury, 1993), especially his chapter on the virgin (pp. 18–40). He does not mention disease at all in this context.

13. Porter and Hall, *The Facts of Life*, p. 277.

14. The following literature is of importance in framing this discussion of Shakespeare's understanding of melancholy and syphilis: Greg W. Bentley, *Shakespeare and the New Disease: The Dramatic Function of Syphilis in* Troilus and Cressida, Measure for Measure, *and* Timon of Athens (New York: P. Lang, 1989); Greg W. Bentley, "Melancholy, Madness and Syphilis in *Hamlet*," *Hamlet Studies: An International Journal of Research on* The Tragedies of Hamlet, Prince of Denmarke 6 (1984): 75–80; Gustav Arthur Bieber, *Der Melancholikertypus Shakespeares und sein Ursprung* (Heidelberg: C. Winter, 1913); Sir John Charles Bucknill, *The Mad Folk of Shakespeare: Psychological Essays*, 2nd ed., rev. (London and Cambridge: Macmillan, 1867); Sir John Charles Bucknill, *The Medical Knowledge of Shakespeare* (London: Longman, 1860); Irving I. Edgar, *Shakespeare, Medicine and Psychiatry: An Historical Study in Criticism and Interpretation* ([London]: Vision, 1971); Johannes Fabricius, *Syphilis in Shakespeare's England* (London and Bristol, PA.: Jessica Kingsley, 1994); Lemuel Matthews Griffiths, "Shakespeare and the Practice of Medicine," *Annals of Medical History* 3 (1921): 34–43; David Hoeniger, *Medicine and Shakespeare in the English Renaissance* (Newark: University of Delaware Press; Cranbury, NJ: Associated University Presses, 1992); Nicolas Jacobs, "Saffron and Syphilis: *All's Well That Ends Well*, IV.v.1–3," *Notes and Queries* 22 (1975): 171–72; Aubrey C. Kail, *The Medical Mind of Shakespeare* (Balgowlah, New South Wales: Williams and Wilkins, 1986); A. O. Kellogg, *Shakspeare's Delineations of Insanity, Imbecility, and Suicide* (New York: Hurd and Houghton, 1866); Raymond Klibansky, Erwin Panofsky, and Fritz Saxl, *Saturn and Melancholy: Studies in the History of Natural Philosophy, Religion, and Art* ([London]: Nelson, [1964]); Hans Laehr, *Die Darstellung krankhafter Geisteszustände in Shakespeares Dramen* (Stuttgart: Paul Neff Verlag, 1898); Wolf Lepenies, *Melancholy and Society*, trans. Jeremy Gaines and Doris Jones (Cambridge: Harvard University Press, 1992); Bridget Gellert Lyons, *Voices of Melancholy: Studies in Literary Treatments of Melancholy in Renaissance England* (London: Routledge & Kegan Paul, [1971]); John Moyes, *Medicine & Kindred Arts in the Plays of Shakespeare* (Glasgow: Maclehose, 1896); Francis R. Packard, "References to Syphilis in the Plays of Shakespeare," *Annals of Medical History* 6 (1924): 194–200; Hermann Schelenz, *Shakespeare und sein Wissen auf den Gebieten der Arznei- und Volkskunde* (Vaduz, Liechtenstein: Topos Verlag, 1977); Robert Ritchie Simpson, *Shakespeare and Medicine* (Edinburgh: E. & S. Livingstone, 1959); H. Somerville, *Madness in Shakespearean Tragedy*, preface by Wyndham Lewis (1929; reprint, Folcroft, PA.: Folcroft Press, 1969); Macleod Yearsley, *Doctors in Elizabethan Drama* (London: J. Bale & Danielsson, 1933).

15. On the figure of Jaques, see Alan Rickman, "Jaques in *As You Like It*," in *Players of Shakespeare, II: Further Essays in Shakespearean Performance by Players with the Royal Shakespeare Company*, ed. Russell Jackson and Robert Smallwood, and introduction by Russell Jackson (New York: Cambridge

University Press, 1988), pp. 73–80; J. C. Bulman, "*As You Like It* and the Perils of Pastoral,*"* in *Shakespeare on Television: An Anthology of Essays and Reviews*, J. C. Bulman and H. R. Coursen, eds. (Hanover, NH: University Press of New England, 1988), pp. 174–79; Devon L. Hodges, *Renaissance Fictions of Anatomy* (Amherst: University of Massachusetts Press, 1985); Robert B. Bennett, "The Reform of a Malcontent: Jaques and the Meaning of *As You Like It*,*"* *Shakespeare Studies* 9 (1976): 183–204; Robert Ray, "Addenda to Shakespeare's Bawdy: *As You Like It*, IV. i. 201–18,*"* *American Notes and Queries* 13 (1974): 51–53; M. D. Faber, "On Jaques: Psychoanalytic Remarks,*"* *University Review* 36 (1969–70): 89–96, 179–82.

16. Michael Bath, "Weeping Stags and Melancholy Lovers: The Iconography of *As You Like It*, II. i,*"* *Emblematica* 1 (1986): 13–52; E. Michael Thron, "Jaques: Emblems and Morals,*"* *Shakespeare Quarterly* 30 (1979): 84–89; Winfried Schleiner, "Jaques and the Melancholy Stag,*"* *English Language Notes* 17 (1980): 175–79; Claus Uhlig, "'The Sobbing Deer': *As You Like It*, II.i.21–66, and the Historical Context,*"* *Renaissance Drama*, n.s., 3 (1970): 79–109.

17. Compare Alan Macfarlane, *Marriage and Love in England: Modes of Reproduction 1300–1840* (Oxford: Basil Blackwell, 1986), on adultery and inheritance in Western culture (pp. 239–44); on horns on the male (p. 240).

18. *Lucio*: I grant: as there may between the lists and the velvet. Thou art the list.

    First Gentleman: And thou the velvet; thou art good velvet; thou'rt a three-piled piece, I warrant thee: I had as lief be a list of an English kersey, as be piled, as thou art pilled, for a French velvet. Do I speak feelingly now?

    Lucio: I think thou dost: and indeed, with most painful feeling of thy speech. I will, out of thine own confession, learn to begin thy health; but whilst I live, forget to drink after thee.

    First Gentleman: I think I have done myself wrong, have I not?

    Second Gentlman: Yes, that thou hast; whether thou art tainted or free.

    (Enter Mistress Overdone.)

    Lucio: Behold, behold, where Madam Mitigation comes! I have purchased as many diseases under her roof as come to—

    Second Gentlman: To what, I pray?

    Lucio: Judge.

    Second Gentlman: To three thousand dolours a year.

    First Gentleman: Ay, and more.

    Lucio: A French crown more.

    First Gentleman: Thou art always figuring diseases in me; but thou art full of error; I am sound.

    Lucio: Nay, not, as one would say, healthy: but so sound as things that are hollow, thy bones are hollow; impiety has made a feast of thee. (*Measure for Measure*, II.ii.28–53)

19. Bentley, "Melancholy, Madness and Syphilis in *Hamlet*,*"* 75–80.

20. Bucknill, *The Medical Knowledge of Shakespeare*, p. 108, refers to Jaques's syphilis as "that disease which engrossed so much attention at that time by its novelty and prevalence." More recently, see Fabricius, *Syphilis in Shakespeare's England*, pp. 224–28, on Jaques as syphilitic.

21. David Bevington, introduction to *As You Like It*, by William Shakespeare (Toronto: Bantam, 1980), p. xx.

22. Robert Burton, *The Anatomy of Melancholy*, ed. Holbrook Jackson (New York: Vintage, 1977), 1: 2, 376, citing Botaldus.

23. Geoffrey Eatough, ed. and trans., *Fracastoro's Syphilis* (Liverpool: Francis Cairns, 1984), p. 65.

24. Hieronymus Fracastoro, *Drei Bücher von den Kontagien*, trans. Viktor Fossel (1546; Leipzig: Johann Ambrosius Barth, 1910), p. 69.

25. Eatough, *Fracastoro's Syphilis*, p. 57.

26. See my *Sexuality: An Illustrated History* (New York: John Wiley, 1989), pp. 148–49.

27. Donald F. Bond, ed., *The Tatler* (Oxford: Oxford University Press 1987), vol. III, pp. 317–22.

28. Porter and Hall, *The Facts of Life*, p. 135.

29. Gilman, *Jewish Self-Hatred*, p. 205.

30. On the nature of gender relationships, see Lesley Anne Soule, "Subverting Rosalind: Cocky Ros in the Forest of Arden," *New Theatre Quarterly* 7 (1991): 126–36; Jan Kott, "The Gender of Rosalind," *New Theatre Quarterly* 7 (1991): 113–25; Hsiao-hung Chang, "Transvestite Sub/Versions: Power, Performance, and Seduction in Shakespeare's Comedies" (Ph.D. diss., University of Michigan, 1991); Jean E. Howard, "Crossdressing, the Theatre, and Gender Struggle in Early Modern England," *Shakespeare Quarterly* 39 (1988): 418–40.

31. Alfred Fournier, *Syphilis and Marriage*, trans. Alfred Lingard (London: D. Bogue, 1881); *Syphilis et mariage*, 2nd ed. (Paris: G. Masson, 1890).

32. Gerard Tilles, R. Grossman, and Daniel Wallach, "Marriage: A 19th-Century French Method for the Prevention of Syphilis: Reflections on the Control of AIDS," *International Journal of Dermatology* 32 (1993): 767–70.

33. All references are to call numbers in the Print and Photograph Division of the National Library of Medicine, Bethesda, Maryland.

34. Martin Amis, *The Rachel Papers* (New York: Vintage International, 1992).

35. All quotes are from Martin Amis, *The Information: A Novel* (New York: Harmony Books, 1995). See also Julian Loose, "*The Information* by Martin Amis," *London Review of Books*, May 11, 1995, p. 9; David Nicholson, "*The Information* by Martin Amis," *Book World* 25 (May 1995):3.

36. Porter and Hall, *The Facts of Life*, p. 241.

Chapter 3

1. Yosef Hayim Yerushalmi, *Freud's Moses: Judaism Terminable and Interminable* (New Haven, CT: Yale University Press, 1991), p. 107.

2. Shlomo Avinari, *The Making of Modern Zionism: Intellectual Origins of the Jewish State* (New York: Basic Books, 1981), pp. 101–11; Hans-Peter Söder, "A Tale of Dr. Jekyll and Mr. Hyde: Max Nordau and Degeneracy," in *Disease and Medicine in Modern German Cultures,* Rudolf Käser and Vera Pohland, eds. (Ithaca, New York: Western Societies Papers, 1990), pp. 56–70; Hans-Peter Söder, "Disease and Health as Contexts of Modernity: Max Nordau as a Critic of Fin-de-Siècle Modernism," *German Studies Review* 14 (1991): 473–89; Hans-Peter Söder, "Disease and Health as Contexts of Fin-de-Siècle Modernity: Max Nordau's Theory of Degeneration" (Ph.D. diss., Cornell University, 1991); Steven E. Aschheim, "Max Nordau, Friedrich Nietzsche and Degeneration," *Journal of Contemporary History* 28 (1993): 643–57; Delphine Bechtel, Dominique Bourel, and Jacques Le Rider, eds., *Max Nordau (1849–1923): Critique de la Degenerescence, Mediateur Franco-Allemand, Père Fondateur du Sionisme* (Paris: Cerf, 1996); Birgit R. Erdle, "Der ursprüngliche Schrecken: Zur Liaison von Antisemitismus und Kulturkritik," in *Jüdische Kultur und Weiblichkeit in der Moderne,* Inge Stephan, Sabine Schilling, and Sigrid Weigel, eds. (Cologne: Böhlau, 1994), pp. 11–22.

3. Jens Malte Fischer, "Dekadenz und Entartung: Max Nordau als Kritiker des Fin de Siècle," in *Fin de Siècle,* ed. Roger Bauer (Frankfurt am Main: Klostermann, 1971), p. 107.

4. Wayne A. Meeks and Robert L. Wilken, eds., *Jews and Christians in Antioch in the First Four Centuries of the Common Era* (Missoula, MT: Scholars Press, 1978), pp. 83–104.

5. Raphael Becker, *Die jüdische Nervosität: Ihre Art, Entstehung und Bekämpfung* (Zurich: Speidel & Wurzel, 1918), p. 31.

6. Sander L. Gilman, *Jewish Self-Hatred: Anti-Semitism and the Hidden Language of the Jews* (1986; Baltimore, MD: Johns Hopkins University Press, paperback ed., 1990), p. 177.

7. Ernest Jones, *The Life and Work of Sigmund Freud,* 3 vols. (New York: Basic Books, 1953–57), 1: 101.

8. Theodor Mommsen, *Auch ein Wort über unser Judentum* (Berlin: Weidmann, 1880), pp. 15–16.

9. Heinrich Treitschke, *Deutsche Geschichte im 19. Jahrhunder* (Leipzig: S. Hirzel, 1889), p. 455.

10. *Ein Wort zur Judenfrage* (Berlin: F. Heinicke, 1880), p. 17.

11. A. A. Brill, *Freud's Contribution to Psychiatry* (New York: Norton, 1944), p. 197.

12. Quoted in the translation from Joseph B. Maier, Judith Marcus, and Zoltán Tarr, eds., *German Jewry: Its History and Sociology: Selected Essays by*

Werner Cahnman (New Brunswick, NJ: Transaction, 1989), pp. 162–63. For the broader implications, see Jacques Le Rider, "La 'lutte des races' selon Ludwig Gumplowicz," *Lignes* 12 (1990): 220–316.

13. Erika Weinzierl, "Katholizismus in Österreich," in *Kirche und Synagoge: Handbuch zur Geschichte von Christen und Juden,* 2 vols., Karl Heinrich Rengstorf and Siegfried von Kortzfleisch, eds. (Stuttgart: Ernst Klett, 1970), pp. 483–531, here, p. 525, n. 19.

14. Helen Walker Puner, *Freud: His Life and His Mind* (New York: Dell, 1959), p. 194.

15. Ibid., p. 191.

16. Jones, *The Life and Work of Sigmund Freud,* 2: 17.

17. Cited in the chapter "Difficult to Baptize," in Theodor Reik, *Jewish Wit* (New York: Gamut Press, 1962), p. 92.

18. Max Nordau, *Doktor Kohn: Bürgerliches Trauerspiel aus der Gegenwart* (Berlin: E. Hofmann, 1899); *A Question of Honor,* trans. Mary J. Stafford (Boston and London: John W. Luce, 1907). All quotations are taken from this translation.

19. See my discussion of the Jewish foot in my *The Jew's Body* (New York: Routledge, 1991), pp. 38–59.

20. Jacob Wassermann, *My Life as German and Jew* (London: George Allen & Unwin, 1933), p. 72.

21. Sander L. Gilman, *On Blackness without Blacks: Essays on the Image of the Black in Germany* (Boston: G. K. Hall, 1982), pp. 35–48.

22. Manuscript letter, Max Nordau Archive, Central Zionist Archive, Jerusalem.

23. On the need for later psychoanalysts to deny the relationship between these two pathological states, see the detailed rebuttal by Ernst Harms, *Psychologie und Psychiatrie der Conversion* (Leiden: A. W. Sijthoff, 1939), pp. 11–12. Freud carefully uses the terms *Bekehrung* for religious conversion and *Konversion* for symptom-conversion, even though the term *Konversion* can be and is used for both. See Sigmund Freud, *Gesammelte Werke: Chronologisch geordnet,* 19 vols. (Frankfurt am Main: S. Fischer, 1952–87) for the use of *Konversion* in the sense of the conversion of symptoms (1: 215) and for *Bekehrung* in the sense of religious conversion (14: 396). (Hereafter cited as *GW*.)

24. Cesare Lombroso, "Atavismus und Civilisation," *Politisch-anthropologische Revue* 3 (1905): 152–57, here, 157.

25. *Der Untergang Israels von einem Physiologen* (Zurich: Verlags-Magazin/J. Schabelitz, 1894).

26. Ibid., p. 11.

27. Ibid., p. 15.

28. Ibid., p. 16.

29. Felix A. Theilhaber, *Der Untergang der deutschen Juden: Eine volkswirtschaftliche Studie,* 2nd ed. (Berlin: Jüdischer Verlag, 1921). On the general

background of such arguments, see D.E.C. Eversely, *Social Theories of Fertility and the Malthusian Debate* (Oxford: Clarendon Press, 1959), and E. P. Hutchinson, *The Population Debate: The Development of Conflicting Theories up to 1900* (Boston: Houghton Mifflin, 1967). On Theilhaber, see H. Lehfeldt, "Felix A. Theilhaber—Pioneer Sexologist," *Archives of Sexual Behavior* 15 (1986): 1–12.

30. Theilhaber, *Der Untergang*, p. 93.

31. Arthur Ruppin, *Die Juden der Gegenwart* (Berlin: Jüdischer Verlag, 1904).

32. Arthur Ruppin, *The Jews of the Modern World* (London: Macmillan, 1934), p. 76.

33. Manuscript letter, Max Nordau Archive, Central Zionist Archive, Jerusalem.

34. Max Nordau, *Erinnerungen erzählt von ihm selbst und von der Gefährtin seines Lebens*, trans. S. O. Fangor (Leipzig: Renaissance Verlag, [1928]), p. 186.

35. All references are to Max Nordau, "Psychology of the Anti-Zionist," *American Jewish Chronicle*, May 10, 1918, pp. 7–8

36. *SE*, 20: 274; *GW*, 17: 49–53.

37. Theodor Reik, *Jewish Wit* (New York: Gamut Press, 1962), p. 12.

38. *SE*, 18: 74, and Gustave Le Bon, *The Crowd: A Study of the Popular Mind* (New York: Viking Press, 1960), pp. 72–78. Freud owned the translation of Le Bon by Rudolph Eisler: *Psychologie der Massen* (Leipzig: W. Klinkhardt, 1912). (In the Freud Library, London.)

39. William James, *The Principles of Psychology*, 2 vols. (New York: Henry Holt, 1890), 2: 678.

40. *SE*, 17: 247–48.

41. Heinrich Schnitzler, ed., "Briefe Sigmund Freud an Arthur Schnitzler," *Neue Rundschau* 66 (1955): 95–106, here, 100. The "confession" that Schnitzler was his "double" is made on May 15, 1922 (96). On the background of these two Jewish physicians in the medical establishment of their time, see Bernd Urban, "Schnitzler and Freud as Doubles: Poetic Intuition and Early Research on Hysteria," *Psychoanalytic Review* 65 (1978): 131–65, and Mark Luprecht, *"What People Call Pessimism": Sigmund Freud, Arthur Schnitzler and Nineteenth-Century Controversy at the University of Vienna Medical School* (Riverside, CA: Ariadne Press, 1990).

42. See William Provine, "Geneticists and the Biology of Race Crossing," *Science* 182 (1973): 790–97, as well as his "Geneticists and Race," *American Zoologist* 26 (1986): 857–87.

43. Ernst Lissauer, "Deutschtum und Judentum," *Kunstwart* 25 (1912): 6–12, here, the footnote on 8.

44. Fritz Wittels, *Der Taufjude* (Vienna: Breitenstein, 1904). See my *Jewish Self-Hatred*, pp. 293–94.

45. Ernst Lissauer, "Deutschtum und Judentum," p. 8.

46. Anatole Leroy-Beaulieu, *Israel Among the Nations: A Study of the Jews and Antisemitism*, trans. Frances Hellman (New York: G. P. Putnam's Sons, 1895), p. 209.

47. Wittels, *Der Taufjude*, p. 6.

48. Ibid., p. 7.   49. Ibid., p. 9.

50. Ibid., p. 10.   51. Ibid., p. 40.

52. Harms, *Psychologie und Psychiatrie*, p. 46.

53. *Protokolle der Wiener Psychoanalytischen Vereinigung*, 4 vols., ed. Herman Nunberg and Ernst Federn (Frankfurt am Main: S. Fischer, 1976–81), 2: 66–67; from *Minutes of the Vienna Psychoanalytic Society*, 4 vols., trans. M. Nunberg (New York: International Universities Press, 1962–75), 2: 60–61.

54. Rudolf Kleinpaul, *Sprache ohne Worte*, vol.1 of *Das Leben der Sprache und ihre Weltstellung*, 3 vols. (Leipzig: Wilhelm Friedrich, 1893), pp. 128–29. (In the Freud Library, London.)

55. Felix Goldmann, *Taufjudentum und Antisemitismus* (Frankfurt am Main: J. Kaufmann, 1913).

56. *The Complete Letters of Sigmund Freud to Wilhelm Fliess 1877–1904*, trans. and ed. Jeffrey Moussaieff Masson (Cambridge, MA: Belknap Press, 1985), p. 311.

57. The diagnosis and description of the syndrome of "pseudologica fantastica" is taken from of Alexander Pilcz, *Lehrbuch der speziellen Psychiatrie für Studierende und Ärzte*, 3rd ed. (Leipzig/Vienna: Franz Deuticke, 1912), pp. 272–73. (The 1904 edition is currently in the Freud Library, London.)

58. Emil Kraepelin, *Psychiatrie: Ein Lehrbuch für Studierende und Ärzte*, 3 vols. (Leipzig: Johann Ambrosius Barth, 1909–15), 3: 2043–69. (In the Freud Library, London.)

59. See the discussion of this by Max Sichel, "Über die Geistesstörungen bei den Juden," *Neurologisches Zentralblatt* (1908): 351–67.

60. It is not child abuse of which Freud frees his own father in the letter to Fliess of September 21, 1897, but rather of transmitting the taint of Jewishness. This is intended to universalize the role of the father, rather than being a hidden indicator that Freud himself had been abused. See Larry Wolff, *Postcards from the End of the World: An Investigation into the Mind of Fin-de-Siècle Vienna* (London: Collins, 1989), pp. 197–204.

61. An excellent overview of Freud's attraction to Christianity is provided by Paul C. Vitz, *Sigmund Freud's Christian Unconscious* (New York: Guilford Press, 1988). Vitz's readings and facts are a detailed presentation of the attraction and ambiguity of Christianity for Freud. What is not addressed is why Freud would not have converted to Christianity. Omitted from his argument is that the very concept of "conversion" is medicalized by the turn of the century. This topic seems to have first been addressed in a polemical manner in Charles E. Maylan, *Freuds tragischer Komplex* (Munich: Ernst Reinhardt, 1929). (In the Freud Library, London.)

62. Max Graf, "Reminiscences of Professor Sigmund Freud," *Psychoanalytic Quarterly* 11 (1942): 473.

63. Sigmund Freud, *Brautbriefe: Briefe an Martha Bernays aus den Jahren 1882–1886*, ed. Ernst L. Freud (Frankfurt am Main: S. Fischer, 1988), p. 137.

64. *SE*, 21: 170.   65. *SE*, 21: 64.

66. *SE*, 21: 170   67. *SE*, 21: 171.

68. Compare Jean-François Lyotard, "Jewish Oedipus," *Genre* 10 (1977): 395–411.

69. Theodor Reik, *From Thirty Years with Freud*, trans. Richard Winston (New York: Farrar & Rinehart, 1940), p. 145.

70. *SE*, 4: 136–37. I do not wish to engage here in the debate of whether or not Freud's reading of his professional situation was correct. It is clear that he associates his status as an academic physician and the difficulty of his faculty appointment with his Jewish identity. See Josef and Renée Glicklhorn, *Sigmund Freuds akademische Laufbahn im Lichte der Dokumente* (Vienna: Urban & Schwarzenberg, 1960).

71. Leonid Grossmann, ed., *Die Beichte seines Juden in Briefen an Dostojewski*, trans. René Fülöp-Miller and Friedrich Eckstein (Munich: R. Piper, 1927). (In the Freud Library, London, well chewed by one of the Freud chows.) On the background of this exchange, see David I. Goldstein, *Dostoyevsky and the Jews* (Austin: University of Texas Press, 1981), pp. 88–116.

72. *SE*, 21: 175–98.   73. Grossmann, p. 233.

74. Grossmann, p. 230.   75. Grossmann, pp. 75–76.

76. The original paper was published anonymously in the *Internationale Zeitschrift für ärztliche Psychoanalyse* 2 (1914): 327–53; the translation is taken from Theodor Reik, "On the Effect of Unconscious Death Wishes," trans. Harry Zohn, *Psychoanalytic Review* 65 (1978): 38–67. These quotes are taken primarily from the notes on 49–50.

77. Theodor Reik, *Fragment of a Great Confession: A Psychoanalytic Autobiography* (New York: Farrar, Straus, 1949), p. 230.

78. S. Ehrmann in the "Festsitzung der 'Wien' anlässlich des 70. Geburtstages Br. Univ. Prof. Doktor Sigmund Freud. Wien 1926," *B'nai B'rith Mitteilung für Österreich* 26 (1926): 101–38, here, 102–3.

79. Joseph Wortis, *Fragments of an Analysis with Freud* (New York: Jason Aronson, 1984), p. 144.

Chapter 4

1. See my *The Jew's Body* (New York: Routledge, 1991).

2. See Felix Gilbert, *Bismarckian Society's Image of the Jew* (New York: Leo Baeck Institute, 1978).

3. Cited by Maurice Paléologue, *An Intimate Journal of the Dreyfus Case*, trans. Eric Mosbacher (New York: Criterion, 1957), p. 247.

4. Ibid., 104.

5. On the masculinization of the prostitute, see my *Difference and Pathology: Stereotypes of Sexuality, Race, and Madness* (Ithaca, NY: Cornell University Press, 1985), pp. 95–96; on the bluestocking, see my *Inscribing the Other* (Lincoln: University of Nebraska Press, 1991), p. 21; on the feminization of the male Jew, see my *The Jew's Body*, pp. 60–104.

6. "Im Zorn hat Gott den Juden geschaffen, in der Wut aber die Jüdin (d.h. Die Jüdin ist noch schlechter als der Jude)," from the Nazi compilation of antisemitic proverbs by Ernst Hiemer, *Der Jude im Sprichwort der Völker* (Nuremberg: Der Stürmer, 1942). On this, see Wolfgang Mieder, "Proverbs in Nazi Germany: The Promulgation of Anti-Semitism and Stereotypes through Folklore," *Journal of American Folklore* 95 (1982): 435–64.

7. H. Naudh [H. G. Nordmann], *Die Juden und der deutsche Staat* (Chemnitz, Germany: Schmeitzner, 1883), p. 76.

8. Hans F. K. Günther, *Rassenkunde des jüdischen Volkes* (Munich: Lehmann, 1930).

9. Paul's *Deutsches Wörterbuch* (1921), as cited by Günther, *Rassenkunde*, p. 254.

10. Johann Jakob Schudt, *Jüdische Merkwürdigkeiten* (Frankfurt am Main: S. T. Hocker, 1714–18), 1: 369; cited by Günther, *Rassenkunde*, p. 254.

11. Richard Wagner, "Das Judentum in der Musik" (1850); cited by Günther, *Rassenkunde*, p. 254.

12. Berhard Blechmann, *Ein Beitrag zur Anthropologie der Juden* (Tartu, Estonia: Wilhelm Just, 1882), p. 11.

13. Sander L. Gilman, "Opera, Homosexuality and Models of Disease: Richard Strauss's *Salome* in the Context of Images of Disease in the Fin de Siècle," in *Disease and Representation: Images of Illness from Madness to AIDS* (Ithaca, NY: Cornell University Press, 1988), pp. 155–82.

14. Thus, Fritz Kahn, *Die Juden als Rasse und Kulturvolk* (Berlin: Welt, 1922), p. 154, notes that Salome is a Jewish princess but racially an Edomite!

15. *New York Times*, January 23, 1907, p. 9.

16. See Hyam Maccoby, "The Delectable Daughter," *Midstream* 16 (Nov. 1970): 50–60; Livia Bitton Jackson, *Madonna or Courtesan? The Jewish Woman in Christian Literature* (New York: Seabury Press, 1982); chapter 15 in Stephen Wilson, *Ideology and Experience: Antisemitism in France at the Time of Dreyfus* (Oxford: Oxford University Press, 1983).

17. See his statement before the Munich court on December 1, 1895; reprinted in Kurt Boeser, ed., *Der Fall Oskar Panizza: Ein deutscher Dichter im Gefängnis* (Berlin: Hentrich, 1989), p. 46.

18. See Michael Bauer, *Oskar Panizza: Ein literarisches Porträt* (Munich: Carl Hanser, 1984).

19. Oskar Panizza, *The Council of Love*, trans. O. F. Pucciani (New York: Viking, 1979), p. 79. See in this context the discussion of Panizza in Claude

Quétel, *History of Syphilis*, trans. Judith Braddock and Brian Pike (London: Polity Press, 1990), pp. 45–49.

20. Schudt, *Jüdische Merkwürdigkeiten*, 2: 369. On the later ideological life of this debate, see Wolfgang Fritz Haug, *Die Faschisierung des bürgerlichen Subjekts: Die Ideologie der gesunden Normalität und die Ausrottungspolitiken im deutschen Faschismus* (Berlin: Argument, 1986).

21. Franz Kafka, *The Sons*, trans. Willa and Edwin Muir (New York: Schocken, 1989), p. 3.

22. See the discussion in my *The Jew's Body*, pp. 38–59.

23. See the first-rate study by Anna Foa, "Il Nuovo e il Vecchio: L'Insorgere della Sifilide (1494–1530)," *Quaderni Storici* 55 (1984): 11–34. For a translation of Foa, see Edward Muir and Guido Ruggiero, eds., *Sex and Gender in Historical Perspective*, trans. Carole C. Gallucci (Baltimore, MD: Johns Hopkins University Press, 1990), pp. 24–45. On Jews and syphilis, see also Klaus Theweleit, *Male Fantasies*, 2 vols., trans. Erica Carter and Chris Turner (Minneapolis: University of Minnesota Press, 1987–89), 2: 16.

24. Ignatz Kohn, "Salome," *Ost und West* 2 (1902): 167.

25. On the background of this production and its reception, see Norbert Kohl, *Oscar Wilde: Das literarische Werk zwischen Provokation und Anpassung* (Heidelberg: C. Winter, 1980), pp. 288–95. See also Martine C. Thomas, "La Salomé d'Oscar Wilde: Épanouissement au tournant du 19ième siécle d'une figure des début de l'ère chrétienne" (Ph.D. diss., University of Strasbourg, 1985), and Ewa Kuryluk, *Salome and Judas in the Cave of Sex* (Evanston, IL: Northwestern University Press, 1987).

26. On Sarah Bernhardt's image, see Kerstin Merkel, *Salome: Ikonographie im Wandel* (Frankfurt am Main and New York: P. Lang, 1990), and Simon Koster, *De Legenden van Sarah Bernhardt* (Zutphen, Netherlands: De Walburg Pers, 1974). See also Arthur Gold, *The Divine Sarah: A Life of Sarah Bernhardt* (New York: Knopf, 1991); Elaine Aston, *Sarah Bernhardt: A French Actress on the English Stage* (Oxford and New York: Berg, 1989); Eric Salmon, ed., *Bernhardt and the Theatre of Her Time* (Westport, CT: Greenwood Press, 1984); Sarah Bernhardt, *Memories of My Life: Being My Personal, Professional, and Social Recollections as Woman and Artist* (London: Owen, 1977); William Emboden, *Sarah Bernhardt* (New York: Macmillan, 1975); Maurice Baring, *Sarah Bernhardt* (New York and London: Appleton-Century, 1934); Mme. Pierre Berton, *The Real Sarah Bernhardt, Whom Her Audience Knew, Told to Her Friend*, trans. Basil Woon (New York: Boni and Liveright, 1924).

27. Leroy-Beaulieu, *Israel Among the Nations*, p. 150.

28. Kikeriki [Ottokar Franz Ebersberg], *Sarah's Reisebriefe aus drei Welttheilen (Amerika, Europa, Skobolessia)* (Würzburg: L. Kreßner, n.d.).

29. I am grateful to Jeanette Jakobowski, "Antisemitismus und Antifeminismus von Johann Andreas Eisenmenger bis Houston Stewart Chamberlain" (master's thesis, Free University Berlin, 1991), pp. 309–60, for drawing

my attention to this text. See also *Jüdische Kultur und Weiblichkeit in der Moderne*, ed. Sabine Schilling, Inge Stephan, and Sigrid Weigel (Cologne: Böhlau, 1993).

30. Nadine Sine, "Cases of Mistaken Identity: Salome and Judith at the Turn of the Century," *German Studies Review* 11 (1988): 9–29.

31. See Joanna Richardson, *Sarah Bernhardt and Her World* (London: Weidenfeld and Nicolson, 1977), pp. 104–6, about the rumor that Sarah Bernhardt was a man.

32. Ute Frevert, *Frauen-Geschichte zwischen bürgerlicher Verbesserung und neuer Weiblichkeit* (Frankfurt am Main: Suhrkamp, 1986), p. 77.

33. All references are to Else Croner [-Kretschmer], *Die moderne Jüdin* (Berlin: A. Juncker, 1913). Croner (1878–?) was also the author of *Fontanes Frauengestalten* (Langensalza, Germany: Beyer, 1931) and the editor of *Das Tagebuch eines Fräulein Doktor*, ed. Else Croner (Stuttgart: Deutsche Verlagsgesellschaft, [1908?]). On the general background, see Atina Grossmann, "'Girlkultur' or Thoroughly Rationalized Female: A New Woman in Weimar Germany?" in *Women in Culture and Politics: A Century of Change,* Judith Friedlander et al., eds. (Bloomington: Indiana University Press, 1986), pp. 62–80, as well as her "The New Woman and the Rationalization of Sexuality in Weimar Germany," in Ann Snitow, Christine Stansell, and Sharon Thompson, *Powers of Desire: The Politics of Sexuality* (New York: Monthly Review Press, 1983), pp. 153–71.

34. See Riv-Ellen Prell, "Why Jewish Princesses Don't Sweat: Desire and Consumption in Postwar American Culture," in *People of the Body: Jews and Judaism from an Embodied Perspective*, ed. Howard Eilberg-Schwarz (Albany: State University of New York Press, 1992), p. 329–60.

35. Wilhelm Stapel, *Volk: Untersuchungen über Volkheit und Volkstum* (Hamburg: Hanseatische Verlagsanstalt, 1942), p. 268.

36. Helene Deutsch, *The Therapeutic Process, the Self, and Female Psychology,* ed. Paul Roazon (New Brunswick, NJ: Transaction, 1993), pp. 49–61, all quotations are from pp. 59–60. See also Gertrud Lenzer, "On Masochism: A Contribution to the History of a Phantasy and Its Theory," *Signs* 1 (1975): 277–324. On Deutsch, see Janet Sayers, *Mothering Psychoanalysis: Helene Deutsch, Karen Horney, Anna Freud and Melanie Klein* (London: Hamish Hamilton, 1991), and Paul Roazen, *Helene Deutsch: A Psychoanalyst's Life* (New Brunswick, NJ: Transaction, 1992).

Chapter 5

1. All references to this novel are to Albert Drach, *Das große Protokoll gegen Zwetschkenbaum* (Munich: Carl Hanser, 1989). All translations are mine. See also Karlheinz F. Auckenthaler, "'Ich habe mich erst als Jude zu fuhlen gehabt, als mich der Hitler als einen solchen erklart hat': Albert Drachs

Beziehung zum Judentum im Leben und Werk," *Modern Austrian Literature* 27 (1994): 51–69, and Ernestine Schlant, "Albert Drach's Unsentimentale Reise: Literature of the Holocaust and the Dance of Death," *Modern Austrian Literature* 26 (1993): 35–62.

2. I rely here on the summary of Austrian law prepared for psychiatrists as appended to Eugen Bleuler, *Lehrbuch der Psychiatrie* (Berlin: Julius Springer, 1918), pp. 515–35.

3. For a more detailed discussion of this aspect of Jewish difference, see my *Jewish Self-Hatred: Anti-Semitism and the Hidden Language of the Jews* (Baltimore, MD: Johns Hopkins University Press, 1986).

4. Richard Andree, *Zur Volkskunde der Juden* (Leipzig: Velhagen & Klasing, 1881), p. 117.

5. Otto Fenichel, "Elements of a Psychoanalytic Theory of Anti-Semitism," in *Anti-Semitism: A Social Disease,* ed. Ernst Simmel (New York: International Universities Press, 1946), pp. 11–33, here, p. 21.

6. Arthur de Gobineau, *The Inequality of Human Races,* trans. Adrian Collins (New York: Howard Fertig, 1967), pp. 194–95. See Michael Biddis, *The Father of Racist Ideology: The Social and Political Thought of Count Gobineau* (London: Weidenfeld and Nicolson, 1970).

7. Johann Caspar Lavater, *Physiognomische Fragment zur Beförderung des Menschenkenntnis und Menschenliebe,* 4 vols. (Leipzig: Weidmann, 1775–78), 3: 98, 4: 272–74. This reference is cited (and rebutted) in Paolo Mantegazza, *Physiognomy and Expression* (New York: Walter Scott, 1904), p. 239.

8. Georg Buschan, ed., *Illustrierte Völkerkunde,* 2 vols. (Stuttgart: Stercker und Schröder, 1922–26): 2: 301.

9. See the summary of the literature on the special nature of the language and gesture of the Jew in Hans F. K. Günther, *Rassenkunde des jüdischen Volkes* (Munich: J. F. Lehmann, 1930), pp. 248–59.

10. The authorized German editions of Mantegazza are: *Die Physiologie der Liebe,* trans. Eduard Engel (Jena, Germany: Hermann Costenoble, 1877); *Die Hygiene der Liebe,* trans. R. Teutscher (Jena, Germany: Hermann Costenoble, [1877]); *Anthropologisch-kulturhistorische Studien über die Geschlechtsverhältnisse des Menschen* (Jena, Germany: Hermann Costenoble, [1891]).

11. On Mantegazza, see Giovanni Landucci, *Darwinismo a Firenze: Tra scienza e ideologia (1860–1900)* (Florence: Leo S. Olschki, 1977), pp. 107–28.

12. The relevant passages in the German edition, *Anthropologisch-kulturhistorische* (Jena, Germany: Hermann Costenoble, [1891], are on pp. 132–13. All the quotations are from the English translation, Paolo Mantegazza, *The Sexual Relations of Mankind,* trans. Samuel Putnam (New York: Eugenics, 1938).

13. Spinoza's text, often cited and often commented on in the nineteenth century, labels circumcision as the primary reason for the survival of the Jews as "they have incurred universal hatred by cutting themselves off completely

from all other peoples." It also made them "effeminate" and, thus, unlikely to assume a political role in the future. Benedict Spinoza, *The Political Works*, trans. A. G. Wernham (Oxford: Oxford University Press, 1958), p. 63.

14. Mantegazza, *Sexual Relations*, p. 99.

15. *Herr Moritz Deutschösterreicher: Eine jüdische Erzählung zwischen Assimilation und Exil*, ed. Jürgen Egyptien (Vienna: Droschl, 1988), p. 5.

16. Dr. Maretzki, "Die Gesundheitverhältnisse der Juden," *Statistik der Juden: Eine Sammelschrift* (Berlin: Jüdischer Verlag, 1918), pp. 123–51. On the historiography of hysteria, see Mark S. Micale, "Hysteria and Its Historiography," *History of Science* 27 (1989): 223–61, 319–51. See also the work on the early history of hysteria by Helmut-Johannes Lorentz, "Si mulier obticuerit: Ein Hysterierezept des Pseudo-Apuleius," *Sudhoffs Archiv* 38 (1954): 20–28; Ilza Veith, *Hysteria: The History of a Disease* (Chicago and London: University of Chicago Press, 1965); Umberto de Martini, "L'isterismo: da Ippocrate a Charcot," *Pagine di Storia della Medicina* 12.6 (1968): 42–49; Annemarie Leibbrand and Werner Leibbrand, "Die 'kopernikanische Wendung' des Hysteriebegriffes bei Paracelsus," in *Paracelsus Werk und Wirkung. Festgabe für Kurt Goldammer zum 60. Geburtstag*, ed. Sepp Domandl (Vienna: Verband der Wissenschaftlichen Gesellschaften Österreichs, 1975), pp. 125–33; John R. Wright, "Hysteria and Mechanical Man," *Journal of the History of Ideas* 41 (1980): 233–47; H. Merskey, "Hysteria: The History of an Idea," *Canadian Journal of Psychiatry* 28 (1983): 428–33, as well as his "The Importance of Hysteria," *British Journal of Psychiatry* 149 (1986): 23–28; John Mullan, "Hypochondria and Hysteria: Sensibility and the Physicians," *Eighteenth Century* 25 (1983): 141–73; Monique David-Ménard, *Hysteria from Freud to Lacan: Body and Language in Psychoanalysis*, trans. Catharine Porter (Ithaca, NY: Cornell University Press, 1989); Phillip R. Slavney, *Perspectives on "Hysteria"* (Baltimore, MD: Johns Hopkins University Press, 1990).

17. "A Propos du Proces-verbal," *Bulletins de la societé d'anthropologie de Paris* 7 (1884): 698–701.

18. Whether or not Jews actually had substantially higher incidences of "nervous illness" during this period cannot be reconstructed from the materials and statistics used in such discussions. They are simply too fragmentary and biased. (For example, they do not correct for the urban concentration of Jews in Western and Central Europe.) It would not be surprising to learn that Jews did have a higher incidence of mental illness, given the greater social stresses they were under from the time of civil emancipation through the fin de siècle. But this cannot be substantiated from the materials employed to buttress this discussion in the nineteenth and early twentieth centuries. What is of interest are the rationales employed to provide an etiology for this supposed prevalence of mental illness.

19. J. M. Charcot, *Leçons du Mardi a la Salpêtrière*, 2 vols. (Paris: Progrés Médical, 1889), 2: 11–12. See the translation of the *Poliklinische Vorträge von*

Prof. J. M. Charcot, 2 vols., vol. 1 trans. Sigmund Freud and vol. 2 trans. Max Kahane (Leipzig: Franz Deuticke, 1892–95), 2: 11.

20. Charcot's influence was felt immediately. See Gustav Lagneau, "Sur la race juive et sa pathologie," *Academie de médecine* 3, 26(1891): 287–309.

21. J. M. Charcot, *Leçons du Mardi a la Salpêtrière*, 1: 131; see Freud's translation of the *Poliklinische Vorträge*, 1: 112.

22. Toby Gelfand, "'Mon Cher Docteur Freud': Charcot's Unpublished Correspondence to Freud, 1888–1893," *Bulletin of the History of Medicine* 62 (1988): 563–88, here, 574.

23. Leroy-Beaulieu, *Israel Among the Nations*, p. 168.

24. Cited in E. Morpurgo, *Sulle Condizioni Somatiche e psichiche degli Israeliti in Europa*, Bibliotece dell'idea Sionisa, 2 (Modena, Italy: Tip. Operai, 1903), pp. 66–67.

25. Henry Meige, *Étude sur certains neuropathes voyageurs: Le juif-errant à la Salpêtrière* (Paris: L. Battaille, 1893). On Meige and this text, see Jan Goldstein, "The Wandering Jew and the Problem of Psychiatric Anti-Semitism in Fin-de-Siècle France," *Journal of Contemporary History* 20 (1985): 521–52, and on the background to the figure of the Wandering Jew, see Paul Lawrence Rose, *Revolutionary Antisemitism in Germany from Kant to Wagner* (Princeton, NJ: Princeton University Press, 1990), pp. 23–43.

26. Meige, *Étude sur certains neuropathes voyages*, p. 17.

27. Ibid., p. 25.

28. Ibid., p. 29.

29. T. Maurer, "Medizinalpolizei und Antisemitismus: Die deutsche Politik der Grenzsperre gegen Ostjuden im ersten Weltkrieg," *Jahrbuch für die Geschichte Osteuropas* 33 (1985): 205–30.

30. Meige, *Étude sur certains neuropathes voyages*, p. 29.

31. Georg Burgle, *Die Hysterie und die Strafrechtliche Verantwortlichkeit der Hysterischen: Ein praktisches Handbuch für Ärzte und Juristen* (Stuttgart: Ferdinand Enke, 1912), p. 19.

32. Cesare Lombroso, *L'antisemitismo e la scienze moderne* (Turin: L. Roux, 1894), p. 83.

33. M. J. Gutmann, "Geisteskranken bei Juden," *Zeitschrift für Demographie und Statistik der Juden* N.S. 3 (1926): 103–116.

34. Max Sichel, *Die Geistesstörungen bei den Juden; eine klinisch-historische Studie* (Leipzig, Kaufmann, 1909); "Über die Geistesstörung bei den Juden," *Neurologisches Zentralblatt* 27 (1908): 351–67; "Nervöse Folgezustände von Alkohol und Syphilis bei den Juden," *Zeitschrift für Demographie und Statistik der Juden* 14 (1919): 137–41; "Die psychischen Erkrankungen der Juden in Kriegs- und Friedenszeiten," *Monatsschrift für Psychiatrie und Neurologie* 55 (1923): 207–28.

35. Max Sichel, "Zur Ätiologie der Geistesstörung bei den Juden," *Monatsschrift für Psychiatrie und Neurologie* 43 (1918): 246–64, here, 247.

36. Ibid., p. 249.

37. P. Berthold (Bertha Pappenheim), *Zur Judenfrage in Galizien* (Frankfurt am Main: Knauer, 1900), pp. 18–19.

38. Jacob Jacobson, "Warum wurden die polnischen Juden 'schmutzig'?" *Hygiene und Judentum* (Dresden: Jac. Sternlicht, 1930), pp. 73–74.

39. Josef Czermak, "Ein Beitrag zur Statistik der Psychosen," *Allgemeine Zeitschrift für Psychiatrie* 15 (1858): 265.

40. H. Budul, "Beitrag zur vergleichenden Rassenpsychiatrie," *Monatsschrift für Psychiatrie und Neurologie* 37 (1915): 199–204.

41. Harald Siebert, "Die Psychosen bei der Bevölkerung Kurlands," *Allgemeine Zeitschrift für Psychiatrie* 73 (1917): 493–535, quote from 523.

42. Hermann Oppenheim, *Lehrbuch der Nervenkrankheiten für Ärzte und Studierende*, 2 vols. (Berlin: Karger, 1894–1913).

43. Hermann Oppenheim, "Zur Psychopathologie und Nosologie der russisch-jüdischen Bevölkerung," *Journal für Psychologie und Neurologie* 13 ("Festschrift Forel") (1908): 1–9.

44. Ibid., 4.

45. Ibid., 6.

46. Georg Buschan, "Einfluss der Rasse auf die Häufigkeit und die Formen der Geistes- und Nervenkrankheiten," *Allgemeine medizinische Zentral-Zeitung* 9 (1897): 104–5.

47. Richard Gaupp, *Wege und Ziele psychiatrischer Forschung: Eine akademische Antrittsvorlesung* (Tübingen: H. Laupp, 1907), p. 23.

48. *Lehrbuch der speziellen Psychiatrie für Studierende und Ärzte* (Leipzig: Franz Deuticke, 1904; 1909; 1912; 1926); *Die Anfangsstadien der wichtigsten Geisteskrankheiten,* Bücher der ärztlichen praxis, 1 (Vienna and Berlin: Julius Springer, 1928); *Spezielle gerichtliche Psychiatrie für Juristen und Mediziner* (Leipzig: Franz Deuticke, 1908); *Die periodischen Geistesstörungen: eine klinische Studie* (Jena, Germany: Gustav Fischer, 1901).

49. Alexander Pilcz, *Die periodischen Geistesstörungen. Klinische Studien* (Jena: Gustav Fischer, 1901), and *Lehrbuch der speziellen Psychiatrie für Studierende und Ärzte* (Leipzig: Franz Deuticke, 1904). The quoted material is from the former: on the predisposition of the Jews (p. 18); on sophistry (p. 32). The cases are on pp. 32–33, 37, 37–38, 94.

50. This aspect of the response of Jewish physicians is underrated by Edward Shorter, "Women and Jews in a Private Nervous Clinic in Late-Nineteenth-Century Vienna," *Medical History* 33 (1989): 149–83.

51. Alexander Pilcz, "Geistesstörung bei den Juden," *Wiener klinische Rundschau* 15 (1901): 888–90, 908–10.

52. Alexander Pilcz, "Sur les psychoses chez les juifs," *Annales médico-psychologiques* 15 (1902): 5–20.

53. As, for example, at the Viennese Anthropological Society on January 16, 1906. See the account in the *Monatsschrift für Kriminalpsychologie und*

Strafrechtsreform 2 (1905): 754. This was evidently a topic of wide interest. See Emil Feer's lecture held in Basel on January 31, 1905, and published under the title *Die Macht der Vererbung* (Basel: Helbing & Lichtenhan, 1905). Feer was at that time a lecturer in the medical faculty at Basel. He discussed the predisposition of the Jews for mental illness on p. 23.

54. Alexander Pilcz, *Beitrag zur vergleichenden Rassenpsychiatrie* (Leipzig and Vienna: Franz Deuticke, 1906).

55. Ibid., p. ii.   56. Ibid., p. 18.

57. Ibid., p. 19.   58. Ibid., p. 29.

59. Ibid., p. 31.

60. Alexander Pilcz, "Beitrag zur Lehre von der Heredität," *Arbeiten des Neurologischen Instituts* 15 (1907): 282–309.

61. Alexander Pilcz, "Über vergleichend-rassenpsychiatrische Studien," *Wiener Medizinische Wochenschrift* 77 (March 5, 1927): 311–14. This lecture is typical of the academic activities of such scholars. For an overview of the German academic presentations of racial theory, see Hans-Walter Schmuhl, *Rassenhygiene, Nationalsozialismus, Euthanasie: Von der Verhütung zur Vernichtung lebensunwerten Lebens, 1890–1945* (Göttingen: Vandenhoeck & Ruprecht, 1987), p. 79.

62. Ignaz Zollschan, *Das Rassenproblem unter besonderer Berücksichtigung der theoretischen Grundlagen der jüdischen Rassenfrage* (Vienna: Wilhelm Braumüller, 1911): on the sensitivity of the Jew (pp. 266–67); on syphilis (p. 268); on the struggle for existence (p. 269); on preserving the race (p. 421).

63. Felix A. Theilhaber, "Gesundheitsverhältnisse," *Jüdisches Lexikon*, ed. Georg Herlitz and Bruno Kirschner (Berlin: Jüdischer Verlag, 1927–30) 2: 1120–41, here, 1128–32.

64. Sander L. Gilman, *Difference and Pathology: Stereotypes of Sexuality, Race, and Madness* (Ithaca, NY: Cornell University Press, 1985), pp. 131–51.

65. Jaroslav Hasek, *The Good Solider Svejk and His Fortunes in the World War*, trans. Cecil Parrott (New York: Thomas Crowell, 1974), pp. 24–30.

Chapter 6

1. Jeffrey M. Masson, ed., *The Complete Letters of Sigmund Freud to Wilhelm Fliess 1887–1904* (Cambridge: Harvard University Press, 1985), pp. 463–68.

2. Jacques Le Rider, *Der Fall Otto Weininger: Wurzeln des Antifeminismus und Antisemitismus*, trans. Dieter Hornig (Vienna: Löcker Verlag, 1985), p. 96.

3. See the letter to Sándor Ferenczi of October 6, 1910, in which Freud wrote: "Since Fliess's case, with the overcoming of which you recently saw me occupied, that need has been extinguished. A part of my homosexual cathexis has been withdrawn and made use of to enlarge my own ego. I have

succeeded where the paranoiac fails." Cited in Ernest Jones, *The Life and Work of Sigmund Freud*, 3 vols. (New York: Basic Books, 1955), 2: 83. In this context also see the chapter on Freud and Breuer in Wayne Koestenbaum, *Double Talk: The Erotics of Male Literary Collaboration* (New York: Routledge, 1989), pp. 17–43.

4. On Weininger, see my *Jewish Self-Hatred: Anti-Semitism and the Secret Language of the Jews* (Baltimore, MD: Johns Hopkins University Press, 1986), pp. 244–51; Jacques Le Rider and Norbert Leser, eds., *Otto Weininger: Werk und Wirkung* (Vienna: Österreichischer Bundesverlag, 1984); Peter Heller, "A Quarrel over Bisexuality," in *The Turn of the Century: German Literature and Art, 1890–1915*, Gerald Chapple and Hans H. Schulte, eds. (Bonn: Bouvier, 1978), pp. 87–116; Peter Gay, *Freud: A Life for Our Time* (New York: W. W. Norton, 1988), pp. 154–55; Katherine Arens, "Characterology: Hapsburg Empire to Third Reich," *Literature and Medicine* 9 (1989): 128–55, as well as her *Structures of Knowing : German Psychologies of the Nineteenth Century* (Dordrecht, Netherlands, and Boston: Kluwer Academic, 1989); H. Rodlauer, *Von 'Eros und Psyche' zu 'Geschlecht und Charakter': Unbekannte Weininger-Manuskripte im Archiv der Österreichischen Akademie der Wissenschaften* (Vienna: Verlag der Österreichischen Akademie der Wissenschaften, 1987), pp. 110–39; Franco Nicolino, *Indagini su Freud e sulla Psicoanalisi* (Naples: Liguori Editore, n.d.), pp. 103–10; Chandak Sengoopta, "Science, Sexuality, and Gender in the 'Fin de Siècle': Otto Weininger as Baedeker," *History of Science* 30 (1992): 249–79.

5. See, for example, the discussion in Carl Dallago, *Otto Weininger und sein Werk* (Innsbruck: Brenner-Verlag, 1912), and Emil Lucka, *Otto Weininger: Sein Werk und seine Persönlichkeit* (Berlin: Schuster & Loeffler, 1921), especially pp. 37–80.

6. Charlotte Perkins Gilman, "Review of Dr. Weininger's *Sex and Character*," *The Critic* 12 (1906): 414.

7. Jacques Le Rider, "Wittgenstein et Weininger," *Wittgenstein et la Critique du Monde Moderne* (Brussels: La Lettre Volée, 1990), pp. 43–65.

8. All quotations are from the English translation, Otto Weininger, *Sex and Character* (London: William Heinemann, 1906).

9. Sigmund Freud, *Standard Edition of the Complete Psychological Works of Sigmund Freud*, 24 vols., ed. and trans. J. Strachey, A. Freud, A. Strachey, and A. Tyson (London: Hogarth, 1955–74), 10: 36. (Hereafter cited as *SE*.)

10. Moritz Lazarus and Heymann Steinthal, "Einleitende Gedanken über Völkerpsychologie," *Zeitschrift für Völkerpsychologie und Sprachwissenschaft* 1 (1860): 1–73. See in this context their letters: *Moritz Lazarus and Heymann Steinthal: Die Begründer der Völkerpsychologie in ihren Briefen*, 2 vols., ed. Ingrid Belke (Tübingen: Mohr, 1971–86). On the relationship to the medicine of the late nineteenth century, see Heinz-Peter Schmiedebach, "Die Völkerpsychologie von Moritz Lazarus (1824–1903) und ihre Beziehung zur

naturwissenschaftlichen Psychiatrie," *Trentième Congrès International d'Histoire de la Médecine, 1986* (Düsseldorf: n.p., 1988), pp. 311–21.

11. Wilhelm Wundt, *Elements of Folk Psychology: Outlines of a Psychological History of the Development of Mankind*, trans. Edward Leroy Schaub (London: George Allen & Unwin, 1916), p. 2.

12. On Freud and Wundt, see Christfried Tögel, "Freud und Wundt: Von der Hypnose bis zur Völkerpsychologie," in *Freud und die akademische Psychologie: Beiträge zu einer historischen Kontroverse*, ed. Bernd Nitzsche (Munich: Psychologie Verlagsunion, 1989), pp. 97–106.

13. Moritz Lazarus, "Über das Verhältnis des Einzelnen zur Gesammtheit," *Zeitschrift für Völkerpsychologie und Sprachwissenschaft* 2 (1862): 437.

14. Lazarus and Steinthal, "Einleitende Gedanken," p. 39.

15. Cited by Havelock Ellis, *Sexual Selection in Man*, vol. 4 of *Studies in the Psychology of Sex* (Philadelphia: F. A. Davis, 1920), p. 176.

16. Weininger, *Sex and Character*, p. 38.

17. Ibid., p. 60.

18. Cesare Lombroso, "Nordau's 'Degeneration': Its Value and Its Errors," *Century Magazine* 28 (Oct. 1895): 936–40.

19. Herman Nunberg and Ernst Federn, eds., *Protokolle der Wiener Psychoanalytischen Vereinigung*, 4 vols. (Frankfurt am Main: S. Fischer, 1976–75), 1: 134–37.

20. Theodor Adorno, Else Frenkel-Brunswik, Daniel J. Levinson, and R. Nevitt Sanford, *The Authoritarian Personality* (New York: Harper, 1950), p. 627.

21. See, for example, the following studies from the early 1930s: Erich Kuttner, *Pathologie des Rassenantisemitismus* (Berlin: Philo, 1930); Ewald Bohm, "Antisemitismus im Lichte der Psychoanalyse," *Menorah* 8 (1930): 312–19; F. A. Feller, *Antisemitismus: Versuch einer psychoanalytischen Lösung des Problems* (Berlin: Verlag des Archivs für angewandte Psychologie, 1931). This view has not vanished. See M. Ostow, "A Contribution to the Study of Anti-Semitism," *Israeli Journal of Psychiatry and Related Sciences* 20 (1983): 95–118.

22. Arthur H. Daniels, "The New Life: A Study of Regeneration," *American Journal of Psychology* 6 (1893): 63.

23. See the use of the phrase in the fin-de-siècle text reprinted in my "Hofprediger Stöcker and the Wandering Jew," *Journal of Jewish Studies* 19 (1969):63–69, here, 69. Freud had evoked this quotation in his discussion of quackery in his 1926 defense of lay analysis (*SE,* 20: 236)—another case where there was a clear subtext concerning "Jewish quackery"—a theme in Viennese medicine reaching at least as far back as the 1840s.

24. All references to this hitherto unpublished essay are to the translation by Dennis Klein, Appendix C to his *Jewish Origins of the Psychoanalytic Movement* (New York: Praeger, 1981), pp. 170–72.

25.　Cesare Lombroso, *The Man of Genius* (London: W. Scott; New York: Charles Scribner's Sons, 1896), p. 152.

26.　See the discussion of Du Bois Reymond and Billings in Fielding H. Garrison, *John Shaw Billings: A Memoir* (New York: G. P. Putnam's Sons, 1915), pp. 234–35.

27.　See my discussion in my *Difference and Pathology: Stereotypes of Sexuality, Race, and Madness* (Ithaca, NY: Cornell University Press, 1985), pp. 175–91.

28.　On the question of the history of this tradition, see John E. Gedo, *Portraits of the Artist: Psychoanalysis of Creativity and Its Vicissitudes* (New York: Guilford Press, 1983); Edward Hare, "Creativity and Mental Illness," *British Medical Journal* 295 (1987): 1587–89; John Hope Mason, "The Character of Creativity: Two Traditions," *History of European Ideas* 9 (1988): 697–715.

29.　*SE*, 23: 187. In this context, see C. M. Hanly, "Psychoanalytic Aesthetics: A Defense and an Elaboration," *Psychoanalytic Quarterly* 55 (1986): 1–22, and D. M. Kaplan, "The Psychoanalysis of Art: Some Ends, Some Means," *Journal of the American Psychoanalytic Association* 36 (1988): 259–93.

30.　For a more extensive interpretation, see Sarah Kofman, *The Childhood of Art: An Interpretation of Freud's Aesthetics*, trans. Winifred Woodhull (New York: Columbia University Press, 1988).

31.　See the discussion by Janine Chasseguet-Smirgel, *Creativity and Perversion* (New York: W. W. Norton, 1984), on the relationship between object relations theory and "creativity."

32.　It is the case in which Heine becomes the centerpiece for Freud's discussion of "wit" in his 1905 study of *Jokes and the Relation to the Unconscious*. See my essay "Freud Reads Heine Reads Freud," *Southern Humanities Review* 24 (1990): 201–18.

Chapter 7

1.　There are, of course, exceptions, such as the oddly romantic reworking of the theme of sibling incest in director John Sayles's *Lone Star* (1996), with actors Chris Cooper and Elizabeth Pena as the incestuous lovers. The more traditional view is that of adult-child incest implied in André Techine's *Les voleurs* (1996), with Catherine Deneuve. An older film that touches on this theme in a more oblique manner is director Agnes Varda's *La petit amour* (1987), which provided a projection of mother-son incest in Jane Birkin's role as a forty-year-old divorcée who falls for a fifteen-year-old schoolboy. There is, of course, a popular literature on sibling incest, such as Vernon R. Wiehe, *The Brother/Sister Hurt: Recognizing the Effects of Sibling Abuse* (Brandon, VT: Safer Society Press, 1996). But such works pale in comparison to the much more extensive literature on adult-child incest. In terms of public press, this is still an underrepresented topic. A targeted search in the Nexis "Allnews" catgeory found only 63 hits under "sibling incest," while the search for "child abuse" exceeded the 1,000-hit limit.

2. Ian Hacking, *Rewriting the Soul: Multiple Personality and the Sciences of Memory* (Princeton, NJ: Princeton University Press, 1995).

3. Laura Otis, *Organic Memory: History and the Body in the Late Nineteenth and Early Twentieth Centuries* (Lincoln: University of Nebraska Press, 1994).

4. Christina von Braun, "Blutschande: From the Incest Taboo to the Nuremberg Racial Laws," in *Encountering the Other(s): Studies in Literature, History, and Culture*, ed. Gisela Brinkler-Gabler (Albany: State University of New York Press, 1995), pp. 127–48.

5. Houston Stewart Chamberlain, *Foundations of the Nineteenth Century*, 2 vols., trans. John Lees (London: John Lane / The Bodley Head, 1913), 1: 366.

6. Hans F. K. Günther, *Rassenkunde des jüdischen Volkes* (Munich: J. F. Lehmann, 1930), p. 134.

7. See the general discussion of sibling incest in Robin Fox, *The Red Lamp of Incest* (New York: E. P. Dutton, 1980), pp. 15–51.

8. Glenda Hudson, *Sibling Love and Incest in Jane Austen's Fiction* (New York: St. Martin's Press, 1992); Johanna M. Smith, "'My Only Sister Now': Incest in *Mansfield Park*," *Studies in the Novel* 19 (1987): 1–15; W. Daniel Wilson, "Science, Natural Law, and Unwitting Sibling Incest in Eighteenth-Century Literature," *Studies in Eighteenth-Century Culture* 13 (1984): 249–70.

9. Michael Scrivener, "'Zion Alone Is Forbidden': Historicizing Anti-semitism in Byron's *The Age of Bronze*," *Keats-Shelley Journal* 43 (1994): 75–97, and Alan Richardson, "Astarte: Byron's *Manfred* and Montesquieu's *Lettres persanes*," *Keats-Shelley Journal* 40 (1991): 19–22. See also Alan Richardson, "The Dangers of Sympathy: Sibling Incest in English Romantic Poetry," *Studies in English Literature, 1500–1900* 25 (1985): 737–54. In another context, see J. S. Price, "The Westermarck Trap: A Possible Factor in the Creation of Frankenstein," *Ethology & Sociobiology* 16 (1995): 349–53.

10. Michelle Schwendiman, "Nosferatu, Murnau, and the Jewish Monster: On the Outside Looking In" (master's thesis, Brigham Young University, 1994).

11. Edgar Allan Poe, *Poetry and Tales* (New York: Library of America, 1984), p. 321. (Emphasis added.)

12. Wilhelm Reutlinger, "Über die Häufigkeit der Verwandtenehen bei den Juden in Hohenzollern und über Untersuchungen bei Deszenten aus jüdischen Verwandtenehen," *Archiv für Rassen- und Gesellschaftsbiologie* 14 (1922): 301–5.

13. Robert Gaupp, "Die klinischen Besonderheiten der Seelenstörungen unserer Großstadtbevölkerung," *Münchener Medizinische Wochenschrift* 53 (1906): 1250–1312.

14. Richard von Krafft-Ebing, *Psychopathia Sexualis: A Medico-Forensic Study*, rev. trans. Harry E. Wedeck (New York: Putnam, 1956), p. 27.

15. Adolf Hitler, *Mein Kampf*, trans. Ralph Manheim (Boston: Houghton Mifflin, 1943), p. 248.

16. Ibid., p. 249. (Hitler's emphasis.)

17. All references to the text are to the translation by H. T. Lowe-Porter, as it is still the only one in print. Thomas Mann, "The Blood of the Walsungs," in *Death in Venice and Seven Other Stories* (New York: Vintage, 1989), pp. 289–316. This translates the "official" version of the story without the Yiddish ending. The German text in the complete edition is the same text: Thomas Mann, *Frühe Erzählungen* (Frankfurt am Main: S. Fischer, 1981), pp. 493–524.

18. Thus, all these references are from a single page in Günther, *Rassenkunde des jüdischen Volkes*, p .26.

19. August Forel, *Die sexuelle Frage* (Munich: Ernst Reinhardt, 1906), pp. 172, 179; August Forel, *The Sexual Question*, trans. C. F. Marshall (New York: Medical Art Agency, 1922), p. 166.

20. J. G. Frazer, *Totemism and Exogamy: A Treatise on Certain Early Forms of Superstition and Society*, 4 vols. (1910; London: Dawsons of Pall Mall, 1968), 4: 108.

21. On this story, see "Wagner in verjüngten Proportionen . . . ": Wälsungenblut als epische Wagner-Transkription," *Thomas Mann Jahrbuch* 7 (1994): 169–85; Alan Levenson, "Thomas Mann's Wälsungenblut in the Context of the Intermarriage Debate and the 'Jewish Question,'" in *Insiders and Outsiders: Jewish and Gentile Culture in Germany and Austria*, Dagmar C. G. Lorenz and Gabriele Weinberger, eds. (Detroit, MI: Wayne State University Press, 1994), pp. 135–43; G. R. Kluge, "Wälsungenblut oder Halbblut? Zur Kontroverse um die Schlußsätze von Thomas Manns Novelle," *Neophilologus* 76 (1990): 237–55; John Whiton, "Thomas Mann's 'Wälsungenblut': Implications of the Revised Ending," *Seminar* 25 (1989): 37–48; Sylvia Wallinger, "'Und es war kalt in dem silbernen Kerzensaal, wie in dem der Schneekönigin, wo die Herzen der Kinder erstarren': Gesundete Männlichkeit - gezähmte Weiblichkeit in Thomas Manns *Königliche Hoheit* und 'Wälsungenblut,'" in *Der Widerspenstigen Zähmung: Studien zur bezwungenen Weiblichkeit in der Literatur vom Mittelalter bis zur Gegenwart*, Sylvia Wallinger and Monika Jonas, eds. (Innsbruck: Institut für Germanistik der Universität, 1986), pp. 235–57; Bernd M. Kraske, "Thomas Manns 'Wälsungenblut'—eine antisemitische Novelle?" in *Thomas Mann: Erzählungen und Novellen*, ed. Rudolf Wolff (Bonn: Bouvier, 1984), pp. 42–66; Hans Rudolf Vaget, "*Sang reserve* in Deutschland: Zur Rezeption von Thomas Manns Wälsungenblut," *German Quarterly* 57 (1984): 363–76; Gail Finney, "Self-Reflexive Siblings: Incest as Narcissism in Tieck, Wagner, and Thomas Mann," *German Quarterly* 56 (1983): 243–56; Christine Oertel Sjögren, "The Variant Ending as a Clue to the Interpretation of Thomas Mann's 'Wälsungenblut,'" *Seminar* 14 (1978): 97–104; Peter de Mendelssohn, *Der Zauberer: Das Leben des deutschen Schrift-*

stellers Thomas Mann (Frankfurt: Fischer, 1975), 1: 662–73; Marie Walter, "Concerning the Affair Wälsungenblut," *Book Collector* 13 (1964): 463–72.

22. See the tabulation of literary sources on incest as a literary theme in Max Marcuse, "Inzest," *Zeitschrift für Sexualwissenschaft* 9 (1923): 171–77; Otto Rank, *Das Inzestmotiv in Dichtung und Sage: Grundzüge einer Psychologie des dichterischen Schaffens* (Leipzig: Franz Deuticke, 1926); *The Incest Theme in Literature and Legend: Fundamentals of a Psychology of Literary Creation*, trans. Gregory C. Richter (Baltimore, MD: Johns Hopkins University Press, 1992); R. Victoria Arana, "Sibling Incest Stories," *Dreamworks* 4 (1984–85): 44–51; Pedro Luzes, "Fact and Fantasy in Brother-Sister Incest," *The International Review of Psycho-Analysis* 17 (1990): 97–113; Marc Shell, *The End of Kinship: Measure for Measure, Incest, and the Ideal of Universal Siblinghood* (Baltimore, MD: Johns Hopkins University Press, 1995).

23. Hitler, *Mein Kampf*, p. 306.

24. Kurt Münzer, *Der Weg nach Zion* (Berlin: A. Juncker, 1907), pp. 240–45, 380–87, 600–604. See the discussion, with liberal quotations, in Rank, *Das Inzestmotiv*, pp. 666–67. The theme of brother-sister incest is evoked in the Torah, as, for example, in Abraham's ambiguous representation of his relationship to Sarah. When Abraham (then called Abram) goes to Egypt, he is afraid that because his wife is "a woman beautiful to behold," the Egyptians will kill him because of her (Genesis 12). He tells her that she should say she is his sister. The result of this deception is that the pharaoh takes her into his house and rewards Abraham. Violating Sarah's marital bed, as we have seen in Chapter 1 of this book, results in illness: "great plagues afflicted Pharaoh and his house." The pharaoh is horrified to learn that Sarah is Abraham's wife and orders them all out of Egypt, prefiguring the Exodus. Here sibling incest lends itself to deception and the destruction of the "healthy" heterosexuality of both the pharaoh and Abraham, each acting within the rules of his own world. Through a process of Christianization and then secularization, this charge is made an aspect of the Jew's essence.

25. Keith Hopkins, "Brother-Sister Marriage in Roman Egypt," *Comparative Studies in Society and History* 22 (1980): 303–54; Ray H. Bixler, "Sibling Incest in the Royal Families of Egypt, Peru, and Hawaii," *Journal of Sex Research* 18 (1982): 264–81.

26. Marc A. Weiner, *Richard Wagner and the Anti-Semitic Imagination* (Lincoln: University of Nebraska Press, 1995).

27. Helmuth Kiesel, *"Bei Hof, bei Höll": Untersuchungen zur literarischen Hofkritik von Sebastian Brant bis Friedrich Schiller* (Tübingen: Niemeyer, 1979), and Barbara Gerber, *Jud Süss: Aufstieg und Fall im frühen 18. Jahrhundert: Eein Beitrag zur historischen Antisemitismus- und Rezeptionsforschung* (Hamburg: H. Christians, 1990).

28. On images of the Jew in British culture, see Bryan Cheyette, *Constructions of "The Jew" in English Literature and Society: Racial Representations,*

1875–1945 (Cambridge and New York: Cambridge University Press, 1993); Andrea Freud Loewenstein, *Loathsome Jews and Engulfing Women: Metaphors of Projection in the Works of Wyndham Lewis, Charles Williams, and Graham Greene* (New York: New York University Press, 1993); Anthony Julius, *T. S. Eliot, Anti-Semitism, and Literary Form* (Cambridge, Eng.: Cambridge University Press, 1996).

29. Emma Wilson, "Textuality and (Homo-)sexuality in Tournier's *Les Météores,*" *Romanic Review* 86 (1995): 115–27, and Susan Petit, "Varieties of Sexuality in Michel Tournier's *Les Météores,*" *Literature and Psychology* 37 (1991): 43–61.

30. Elena Gascon-Vera, "Los reflejos del yo: Narcisismo y androginia en Agustin Gomez Arcos, "*Cuadernos de Aldeeu* 7 (1991): 31–52.

31. As indeed does Hillel Schwartz, *The Culture of the Copy: Striking Likenesses, Unreasonable Facsimiles* (New York: Zone Books, 1996).

32. Walter Benn Michaels, *Our America: Nativism, Modernism, and Pluralism* (Durham, NC: Duke University Press, 1995).

33. See Rhonda Lieberman, "Je m'Apelle Barbie," *Artforum* 33 (March 1995): 20–21, here 20, and "Goys and Dolls," *Artforum* 33 (April 1995): 21–22. Lieberman bases her satires on the solid work of M. J. Lord, *Forever Barbie: The Unauthorized Biography of a Real Doll* (New York: William Morrow, 1994).

34. James Diedrick, *Understanding Martin Amis* (Columbia: University of South Carolina Press, 1995).

35. Karen J. Hall, "Sisters in Collusion: Safety and Revolt in Shirley Jackson's *We Have Always Lived in the Castle,*" in *The Significance of Sibling Relationships in Literature*, JoAnna Stephens Mink and Janet Doubler Ward, eds. (Bowling Green, OH: Popular Culture Press, 1993), pp. 110–19.

36. Claire Sprague, "The Politics of Sibling Incest in Doris Lessing's 'Each Other,'" *San Jose Studies* 11 (1985): 42–49.

37. Moysheh Oyved, *Gems and Life* (London: Ernest Benn, 1927), p. 71.

38. Elaine Feinstein, *Dreamers* (London: Macmillan, 1994).

39. Elaine Feinstein, *Loving Brecht* (London: Hutchinson, 1992).

40. On Freud, see a parallel but illuminating representation of "Brothers and Sisters" in William J. McGrath, *Freud's Discovery of Psychoanalysis: The Politics of Hysteria* (Ithaca, NY: Cornell University Press, 1986), pp. 276–312.

41. Philip Roth, *American Pastoral* (Boston: Houghton Mifflin, 1997).

42. See Claire Bloom, *Leaving a Doll's House: A Memoir* (London: Virago, 1996).

43. James William Parkes, *The Jew as Usurer* (Toronto: Committee on Jewish-Gentile Relationships, 1938).

44. Cited from Werner Sombart, *The Jews and Modern Capitalism*, trans. M. Epstein (Glencoe, IL: Free Press, 1951), p. 238. The first edition was *Die Juden und das Wirtschaftsleben* (Leipzig: Duncker & Humblot, 1911). See the

recent biography by Friedrich Lenger, *Werner Sombart, 1863–1941* (Munich: C. H. Beck, 1994), for the context and reception of this work. See also Freddy Raphael, *Judäisme et capitalisme: Essai sur la controverse entre Max Weber et Werner Sombart* (Paris: Presses Universitaires de France, 1982).

Chapter 8

1. R. B. Kitaj, *First Diasporist Manifesto* (London: Thames and Hudson, 1989), here, p. 109. All parenthetic references in text will be to D. In addition to the literature cited below, see H. Platschek, "Nichts paßt und doch stimmt alles," *art* 5 (1988): 32–46; M. R. Deppner, "Jewish School und London Diaspora," *Babylon* (Oct. 1993): 37–57; A. Benjamin, "Kitaj und die Frage nach der jüdischen Identität," *Babylon* (Oct. 1992): 59–71. Kitaj's importance in the German discussion of Jewish identity cannot be underestimated.

2. Vivianne Barsky, "'Home Is Where the Heart Is': Jewish Themes in the Art of R. B. Kitaj," *Studies in Contemporary Jewry* 6 (1990): 149–85, here, 180.

3. Giles Deleuze and Félix Guattari, *A Thousand Plateaus: Capitalism and Schizophrenia*, trans. Brian Massumi (Minneapolis: University of Minnesota Press, 1987), pp. 191–92.

4. Julián Rios, *Kitaj: Pictures and Conversations* (London: Hamish Hamilton, 1994), here, p. 39. All parenthetic references in text will be to R.

5. Michael Peppiatt, "Six New Masters (Why Stodgy Old London Is Now the Art Capital of the World)," *Connoisseur* 217 (1987): 79–85, on Francis Bacon, Leon Kossoff, Michael Andrews, Frank H. Auerbach, R. B. Kitaj, and Lucian Freud. A joint exhibition—*Seven British Painters: Selected Masters of Post-War British Art*—was held at Marlborough Fine Arts in London from June 18 through September 4, 1993. Paintings by Michael Andrews, Frank Auerbach, Francis Bacon, Lucian Freud, David Hockney, R. B. Kitaj, and Leon Kossoff were shown.

6. See the discussion in Barsky, "'Home Is Where the Heart Is,'" pp. 149–50.

7. Marco Livingstone, *R. B. Kitaj* (London: Thames and Hudson, 1985): on background (p. 8); on Joe Singer (p. 33).

8. Clive Sinclair, "The Jews Are My Tahiti: R. B. Kitaj and the Subject of His Paintings," *Judaism* 43 (1994): 388–97, here, 397.

9. Sigmund Freud, *Standard Edition of the Complete Psychological Works of Sigmund Freud*, 24 vols., ed. and trans. J. Strachey, A. Freud, A. Strachey, and A. Tyson (London: Hogarth, 1955–74), here, 20: 274.

10. Theodor Adorno, "Kulturkritik und Gesellschaft," in *Kulturkritik und Gesellschaft I: Prismen. Ohne Leitbild* (Frankfurt am Main: Suhrkamp, 1977), pp. 11–30, here, p. 30.

11. Barsky, "'Home Is Where the Heart Is,'" p. 150.

12. All of the images from Kitaj's work are reproduced in the most recent catalogue: Richard Morphet, comp., *R. B. Kitaj: A Retrospective* (London: Tate Gallery, 1994).

13. Susan J. Barnes, comp., *The Rothko Chapel: An Act of Faith* (Austin: University of Texas Press, 1989); Lawrence Alloway, comp., *Barnett Newmann, The Stations of the Cross, Lema Sabachthani* (New York: Solomon R. Guggenheim Museum, 1966). A counter-reading of Rothko and Kitaj as Jewish artists is Katy Deepwell and Juliet Steyn, "Readings of the Jewish Artist in Late Modernism," *Art Monthly* 113 (1988): 6–9.

14. Marco Livingstone, "Iconology as Theme in the Early Work of R. B. Kitaj," *Burlington Magazine* 122 (1980): 488–97.

15. See the following interviews: "Art Spiegelman: An Exquisite Sense of Balance," *Art Press* 194 (Sept. 1994): 27–32; "A Conversation with Art Spiegelman," *Artweek* 24 (Dec. 1993): 15–16; Michael Silverblatt, "The Cultural Relief of Art Spiegelman: A Conversation with Michael Silverblatt," *Tampa Review* 5 (1992): 31–36. The following bibliographic citations on Art Spiegelman give a sense of the importance of *Maus* in the culture of contemporary American art: "Out of History," *Artweek* 24 (Dec. 1993): 14; "The Maus That Roared," *Art News* 92 (May 1993): 63–64; "High Art Lowdown," *Artforum* 29 (Dec. 1990): 115; "When It's a Matter of Life and Death: Art Spiegelman's Diagrams," *Arts Magazine* 65 (Oct. 1990): 83–87. The following critical essays provide various readings of *Maus*: Michael Rothberg, "'We Were Talking Jewish': Art Spiegelman's *Maus* as 'Holocaust' Production," *Contemporary Literature* 35 (1994): 661–87; Richard Martin, "Art Spiegelman's *Maus*; Or, the Way It Really Happened," in *Historiographic Metafiction in Modern American and Canadian Literature*, Bernd Engler and Kurt Muller, eds. (Paderborn, Germany: Ferdinand Schoningh, 1994), pp. 373–82; Rick Iadonisi, "Bleeding History and Owning His (Father's) Story: *Maus* and Collaborative Autobiography," *CEA Critic: An Official Journal of the College English Association* 57 (1994): 45–56; Joan Gordon, "Surviving the Survivor: Art Spiegelman's *Maus*," *Journal of the Fantastic in the Arts* 5 (1993): 81–89; Stephen E. Tabachnick, "Of *Maus* and Memory: The Structure of Art Spiegelman's Graphic Novel of the Holocaust," *Word & Image: A Journal of Verbal/Visual Enquiry* 9 (1993): 154–62; Robert Storr, "Art Spiegelman's Making of *Maus*," *Tampa Review* 5 (1992): 27–30; Marianne Hirsch, "Family Pictures: *Maus*, Mourning, and Post-Memory," *Discourse* 15 (1992–93): 3–29; Miles Orvell, "Writing Posthistorically': *Krazy Kat, Maus* and the Contemporary Fiction Cartoon," *American Literary History* 4 (1992): 110–28; Kurt Scheel, "Mauschwitz? Art Spiegelmans 'Geschichte eines Überlebenden'," *Merkur* 43 (1989): 435–38.

16. Ernst Hiemer, *Der Jude im Sprichwort der Völker* (Nuremberg: Der Stürmer Buchverlag, 1942), p. 36: "Die Juden un ebenso viel Nutz in der Welt schaffen wie die Mäuß im Weizen (Deutschland); Die Juden sein einem

Land so nutz wie die Mäu· auf dem Getreideboden und die Motten im Kleid."

17. Wilhelm Marr, *Goldene Ratten und rote Mäuse* (Chemnitz, Germany: Antisemitisches Heft 2, 1881). I am grateful to Jay Geller for providing me with a copy of this text.

18. Solomon A. Birnbaum, "Der Mogel," *Zeitschrift für deutsche Philologie* 74 (1955): 249.

19. Charles Sorlier, comp., *Chagall by Chagall*, trans. John Shepley (New York: Harry N. Abrams, 1979), p. 201.

20. Sinclair, *The Jews Are My Tahiti*, here, p. 389.

21. Morphet, *R. B. Kitaj*, here, p. 52. All parenthetic references to this text will be to C.

22. See especially the 1990 exhibition to which Kitaj makes reference in his discussion of Chagall: Avram Kampf, comp., *Chagall to Kitaj: Jewish Experience in 20th-Century Art* (London: Lund Humphries in association with Barbican Art Gallery, 1990).

23. On the visual representation of the Jew's body in the tradition of European anti-Semitism, see Monika Wagner, "[Georg Grosz] *John, der Frauenmörder*," *Im Blickfeld: Jahrbuch der Hamburger Kunsthalle* 1 (1994): 237–46; Peter Dittmar, *Die Darstellung der Juden in der populären Kunst zur Zeit der Emanzipation* (Munich and New York: K. G. Saur, 1992); Maurice Berger, "Painting Jewish Identity," *Art in America* (Jan. 1992): 90–95; Steven Heller and William Eric Perkins, "Dirty Pictures," *Print* 45 (1991): 104–13; Norman L. Kleeblatt, ed., *The Dreyfus Affair: Art, Truth, and Justice* (Berkeley and Los Angeles: University of California Press, 1987); John and Selma Appel, *Jews in American Graphic Satire and Humor* (Cincinnati: [American Jewish Archives?], 1984); Eric M. Zafran, "The Iconography of Antisemitism: A Study of the Representation of the Jews in the Visual Arts of Europe, 1400–1600" (Ph.D. diss., New York University, 1973); *Catalogue of an Exhibition of Anglo-Jewish Art and History: In Commemoration of the Tercentenary of the Resettlement of the Jews in the British Isles: Held at the Victoria and Albert Museum January 6 to February 29, 1956* (London: Victoria and Albert Museum, 1956); Eduard Fuchs, *Die Juden in der Karikatur: Ein Beitrag zur Kulturgeschichte* (Munich: Albert Langen, 1921).

24. Sander L. Gilman, *The Jew's Body* (New York: Routledge, 1991).

25. "Docteur Celticus," *Les 19 Tares corporelles visibles pour reconnaître un Juif* (Paris: Librairie Antisemite, 1903).

26. "Die Religion ist einerlei / In der Rasse liegt die Schweinerei," cited from Hiemer, *Der Jude im Sprichwort der Völker*, p. 10.

27. All references are to Hiemer, *Der Jude im Sprichwort der Völker*: "Er hat e Gang wie ä Judd (Westmark)" (p. 12); "Er hat jüdische Platten (Plattfüße) (Franken)" (p. 14); "Gott schütze uns vor Trichinosen und Judennosen (Süddeutschland)" (p. 13); "Es gibt keinen Juden ohne Räude (Bulgarien)" (p. 38);

"Er wird sich jetzt seiner Arbeit rühmen wie der Jude seiner Krätze (Ostland)" (p. 38); "Er übernimmt das wie der Jude die Räude (Ostland)" (p. 39); "Er ist grindig wie ein Jude (Ungarn)."

28. Claire Hirschfeld, "The Tenacity of Tradition: *Truth* and the Jews 1877–1957," *Patterns of Prejudice* 28 (1994): 67–86, here, 85.

29. See note 34, chapter 2, above.

30. Julian Barnes, *Metroland* (London: Cape, 1980), p. 32.

31. Bryan Cheyette, *Constructions of "The Jew" in English Literature and Society: Racial Representations, 1875–1945* (Cambridge and New York: Cambridge University Press, 1993), and Andrea Freud Loewenstein, *Loathsome Jews and Engulfing Women: Metaphors of Projection in the Works of Wyndham Lewis, Charles Williams, and Graham Greene* (New York: New York University Press, 1993).

32. Joe Shannon, "The Allegorists: Kitaj and the Viewer," in *R. B. Kitaj*, comp. Joe Shannon (Washington, D.C.: Smithsonian Institution Press, 1981), pp. 19–36.

33. Sinclair, *The Jews Are My Tahiti*, p. 389.

34. Philip Roth, *The Anatomy Lesson* (New York: Farrar, Straus and Giroux, 1983), p. 4.

35. Barsky, " 'Home Is Where the Heart Is,' " p. 158.

36. Ibid., p. 162.

37. Heinrich Mann, *Man of Straw*, no trans. (London: Penguin, 1984). First published as *Der Untertan* (Berlin: Kurt Wolff, 1918). On the question of reading Jewish ears, see Itta Schedletzky, "Majestätsbeleidigung und Menschenwürde: Die Fatalität des Antisemitismus in Heinrich Manns Roman *Der Untertan*," *Bulletin des Leo-Baeck-Instituts* 86 (1990): 67–81, here, 74–76.

38. Jüdisches Museum des Stadt Wien, ed., *Die Macht der Bilder: Antisemtische Vorurteile und Mythen* (Vienna: Picus, 1995), p. 173.

39. Sander L. Gilman, *Seeing the Insane: A Cultural History of Psychiatric Illustration* (New York: Wiley Interscience, 1982).

40. See note 18, chapter 5, above. See also the discussion in my *Difference and Pathology: Stereotypes of Sexuality, Race, and Madness* (Ithaca, NY: Cornell University Press, 1985), pp. 150–63.

41. Emil Kraepelin, "Zur Entartungsfrage," *Zentralblatt für Nervenheilkunde und Psychiatrie* 19 (1908): 745–51, here, 748.

42. Georg Burgle, *Die Hysterie und die Strafrechtliche Verantwortlichkeit der Hysterischen: Ein praktisches Handbuch für Ärzte und Juristen* (Stuttgart: Ferdinand Enke, 1912), p. 19.

43. See my *Seeing the Insane*, p. 15.

44. Isaiah Shachar, *The Judensau: A Medieval Anti-Jewish Motif and Its History*, Warburg Institute Surveys, 5 (London: Warburg Institute, 1974). It is important that this is a text written in the Warburg tradition. See Dieter

Wuttke, "Die Emigration der Kulturwissenschaftlichen Bibliothek Warburg und die Anfänge des Universitätsfaches Kunstgeschichte in Grossbritannien," *Artibus et historiae* 5 (1984): 133–46.

45. All references to images from contemporary "Jewish" art are to Norman L. Kleeblatt, comp., *Too Jewish: Challenging Traditional Identities* (New York: Jewish Museum, 1996).

46. See Barsky, "'Home Is Where the Heart Is,'" pp. 174–75, on the role of Anselm Kiefer's art in this image.

47. See my "Vincent van Gogh and the Iconography of Mental Illness," *Forum on Medicine* 2 (1979): 210–17.

48. Francis Galton, "Photographic Composites," *Photographic News* 29 (Apr. 1885): 243–46, here, 243.

49. Hans F. K. Günther, *Rassenkunde des jüdischen Volkes* (Munich: J. F. Lehmann, 1930): on the physiology of the Jewish eye (p. 70); Galton's photographs (pp. 210–11)on the Jewish gaze (p. 217).

50. See my *The Jew's Body*, pp. 38–59.

51. Oskar Panizza, *The Council of Love*, trans. O. F. Pucciani (New York: Viking, 1979), p. 79. See in this context the discussion of Panizza in Claude Quétel, *History of Syphilis*, trans. Judith Braddock and Brian Pike (London: Polity Press, 1990), pp. 45–49.

52. Michael Holroyd, *Lytton Strachey: The New Biography* (New York: Farrar, Straus and Giroux, 1994), p. 436.

53. Adolf Jellinek, *Studien und Skizzen. Erster Teil: Der jüdische Stamm: Ethnographische Studien* (Vienna: Herzfeld and Bauer, 1869).

54. Heinrich Singer, *Allgemeine und spezielle Krankheitslehre der Juden* (Leipzig: Benno Konegen, 1904), p. 9.

55. Carl Einstein, 1919–1928, ed. Marion Schmid, vol. 2 of *Werke*, 4 vols., ed. Rolf-Peter Baacke (Berlin: Medusa, 1981), p. 338.

56. Berhard Blechmann, *Ein Beitrag zur Anthropologie der Juden* (Tartu, Estonia: Wilhelm Just, 1882), p. 11.

57. The self-consciously Jewish dimension of this work can be paralleled to other Jewish works of comic art, such as Sharon Rudahl's extraordinary use of Jewish physiognomies in her illustrated version of Morris Rosenfeld, "Mein rue Platz," *Wimmen's Comix* 8 (1983), and Diane Noomin's "The Agony and the Ecstasy of a *Shayne Madel*: The Epitome of a Perfect Pretty Jewish Girl," *Wimmen's Comix* 3 (1973).

58. Cesare Lombroso, *L'antisemitismo e la scienze moderne* (Turin: L. Roux, 1894), pp. 102–3. On the history of the idea of the heart and its illness, see H. P. Kafka, "Silent Defects," *Journal of the American College of Cardiology* 13 (1989): 1451–52, and on the historical context of heart illness, see Saul Jarcho, ed., *The Concept of Heart Failure from Avicenna to Albertini* (Cambridge: Harvard University Press, 1980).

59. Alfred Lee Loomis and William Gilman Thompson, eds., *A System of Practical Medicine*. 4 vols. (New York and Philadelphia: Lea Brothers, 1897–98), 4: 553.

Chapter 9

1. Bernard Wasserstein, *Vanishing Diaspora: The Jews in Europe Since 1945* (Cambridge: Harvard University Press, 1996).

2. See my *Reemerging Jewish Culture in Germany: Life and Literature Since 1989* (New York: New York University Press, 1994) (with Karen Remmler), and *Jews in Today's German Culture*, Schwartz Lectures (Bloomington: Indiana University Press, 1995).

3. Thomas Nolden, *Junge jüdische Literatur: Konzentriertes Schreiben in der Gegenwart* (Würzburg: Königshausen und Neumann, 1995).

4. Felix A. Theilhaber, *Der Untergang der deutschen Juden: Eine volkswirtschaftliche Studie* (Munich: Ernst Reinhardt, 1911).

5. Michael Brenner, *Nach dem Holocaust: Juden in Deutschland 1945–1950* (Munich: C. H. Beck, 1995).

6. Y. Michal Bodemann, *Gedächtnistheater: Die jüdische Gemeinschaft und ihre deutsche Erfindung* (Hamburg: Rotbuch Verlag, 1996), and Y. Michal Bodemann, ed., *Jews, Germans, Memory: Reconstructions of Jewish Life in Germany* (Ann Arbor: University of Michigan Press, 1996).

7. Erica Burgauer, *Zwischen Erinnerung und Verdrängung—Juden in Deutschland nach 1945* (Reinbek bei Hamburg: Rowohlts Enzyklopadie, 1993).

8. The term is from Dan Diner, "Negative Symbiose: Deutsche und Juden nach Auschwitz," *Babylon* 1 (1986): 9–20. On its applicability in the present context, see Jack Zipes, "Die kulturellen Operationen von Deutschen und Juden im Spiegel der neueren deutschen Literatur," *Babylon* 8 (1990): 34–44; Klaus Briegleb, "Negative Symbiose," in *Gegenwartsliteratur seit 1968*, Klaus Briegleb and Sigrid Weigel, eds. (Munich: Carl Hanser, 1992), pp. 117–52; Hans Schütz, *Juden in der deutschen Literatur* (Munich: Piper, 1992), pp. 309–29.

9. Daniel Goldhagen, *Hitler's Willing Executioners: Ordinary Germans and the Holocaust* (New York: Knopf, 1996).

10. To frame any discussion of the meaning of the Jews in the cultural life of the new Germany, such projections and attitudes on the part of German intellectuals must be taken seriously. However, let me begin by stating my own views about the various theses represented by Goldhagen's book; then, I hope, my "hidden agenda" will become evident. Like Goldhagen, I believe that mass education can inculcate negative images or stereotypes into various cultural groups and that individuals in such groups can respond to these images. However, I believe that the response can be either affirmative or criti-

cal. Thus, the universal presence of negative images can potentially create as much resistance as it does advocacy—but it rarely does. Unlike Goldhagen, I believe that there is a complicated history of antisemitism (for me a blanket term for "Jew Hatred") in the Christian West, which is different from simple ubiquitous xenophobia. I see this as stemming from the very origins of Christianity and its constant need to distance itself from Judaism and the Jews. What Goldhagen views as eliminationist antisemitism is present in the early Church. Yet given the specificity of the self-conscious construction of a *Staatsnation* (in the sense of Friedrich Meinecke) in the place of a *Kulturnation* and the movement from the status and power of religious antisemitism to the new status of scientific racism at the close of the nineteenth century, the function of antisemitism in Germany is different from that in France or Austria. The *Sonderweg* debate, whether Germany and "the Germans," however defined, were different in their specificity at the end of the nineteenth and beginning of the twentieth century, whether in their understanding of colonialism or the "Jewish Question," is not resolved. Indeed, comparative studies are beginning to pinpoint specifically the function of such stereotypes in understanding German culture in contrast with other self-consciously constructed national and local cultures in Central Europe. This is not to say that nineteenth- and early-twentieth-century German culture in its construction of "Germanness," the "Germans," and the "Jews" was better or worse than other national cultures, only that it fulfilled a different function. All of this means that, in my reading, the presence of what Goldhagen labels "eliminationist" (rather than exclusionist) antisemitism in Germany was necessary, but not sufficient, for the Shoah to take place.

11. Dan Diner, *America in the Eyes of the Germans: An Essay on Anti-Americanism* (Princeton, NJ: Markus Wiener, 1996).

12. Sander L. Gilman, *Smart Jews: The Construction of the Idea of Jewish Superior Intelligence at the Other End of the Bell Curve*, The Inaugural Abraham Lincoln Lectures (Lincoln: University of Nebraska Press, 1996).

13. George Mosse, *"Ich bleibe Emigrant": Gespräche mit George L. Mosse / Irene Runge, Uwe Stelbrink* (Berlin: Dietz, 1991).

14. Daniel Ganzfried, *Der Absender* (Zurich: Rotpunkt, 1995).

15. André Kaminski, *Die Gärten des Mulay Abdallah: Neun wahre Geschichten aus Afrika* (Frankfurt am Main: Suhrkamp, 1983); *Herzflattern: Neun wilde Geschichten* (Frankfurt am Main: Suhrkamp, 1984); *Nächstes Jahr in Jerusalem* (Frankfurt am Main: Insel Verlag, 1986); *Schalom allerseits: Tagebuch einer Deutschlandreise* (Frankfurt am Main: Insel, 1987); *Kiebitz* (Frankfurt am Main: Insel, 1988); *Flimmergeschichten* (Frankfurt am Main: Insel, 1990); *Der Sieg über die Schwerkraft und andere Eräzhlungen* (Frankfurt am Main: Insel-Verlag, 1990).

16. Doron Rabinovici, *Papirnik* (Frankfurt am Main: Suhrkamp, 1994). The stories are Papirnik - ein Prolog—Die Bank—Noemi—Sechsneunsechs-

sechsneunneun—Der richtige Riecher—Ich schreibe Dir—Über die Säure des Regens—Die Exekution—Der Schauer und die Seherin—Lola—ein Epilog.

17. Benjamin Stein, *Das Alphabet des Juda Liva* (Zurich: Ammann, 1995).

18. Saul Bellow, *The Dean's December* (New York: Harper & Row, 1981), and Philip Roth, *The Prague Orgy* (London: Cape, 1985); also, as the epilogue to *Zuckerman Bound* (New York: Farrar, Straus and Giroux, 1985), comprising *The Ghost Writer—Zuckerman Unbound—The Anatomy Lesson*—Epilogue: *The Prague Orgy*. See also Sepp L. Tiefenthaler, "American-Jewish Fiction: The Germanic Reception," in *Handbook of American-Jewish Literature: An Analytical Guide to Topics, Themes, and Sources*, Lewis Fried, Gene Brown, Louis Harap, eds. (Westport, CT: Greenwood Press, 1988), pp. 471–504.

Index

In this index an "f" after a number indicates a separate reference on the next page, and an "ff" indicates separate references on the next two pages. A continuous discussion over two or more pages is indicated by a span of page numbers, e.g., "57–59." *Passim* is used for a cluster of references in close but not consecutive sequence.

Library of Congress Cataloging-in-Publication Data

Gilman, Sander L.
  Love + marriage = death : And other essays on representing difference /
Sander L. Gilman.
      p.   cm. — (Stanford studies in Jewish history and culture)
    Includes bibliographical references and index.
    ISBN 0-8047-3261-2 (cloth) — ISBN 0-8047-3262-0 (pbk.)
    1. Jews—Austria—Intellectual life.   2. Ethnicity.   3. Jews in literature.
4. Holocaust, Jewish (1939–1945)—Germany—Influence.   5. Austria—
Intellectual life—20th century.   I. Title.   II. Series.
DS135.A9G55   1998
305.8924—dc21   98-23979
                                                                      CIP

Original printing 1998
Last figure below indicates year of this printing:
07   06   05   04   03   02   01   00   99   98